Multiple Sclerosis: My Story
By Antony A Kelly

Dedicated to all my friends and family that have
helped me along this journey (you know who you are)
and to all my fellow sufferers

Book cover photograph by:
James Maddox (jamesmaddox.co.uk)
Location:
Ashton-under-Lyne Library

IGNORANCE

It was one of those rare occasions during the summer that the sun is actually hot enough to enjoy a pub lunch outdoors. Richard Christou (a fellow sufferer) and I decided to enjoy the warmth of the sun and a couple of pints of bitter. We chose a pub that boasted great views of the surrounding countryside. I volunteered to carry the meals to the table whilst Ricky trailed behind carrying the two pints of bitter. It was a time when I was in really good form and Ricky was a little unsteady on his feet.

As I took my place at the nearest table I turned to face Ricky, his legs were heavy with the burdens of Multiple Sclerosis. Although he struggled to walk in a straight line and prevent his left leg from trailing behind, he was determined to reach the table without my aid.

The table behind me was taken by two girls who were also enjoying the afternoon sun, when I overheard one of them say, "Look at him he's pissed already"!

I swung round and immediately jumped to my friends defence by sarcastically replying,

"I'll say he's pissed, there's no cure for MS".

Chapter 1
The Sand Syndrome

It was mid August 1989; I had a night out with my girlfriend Jennifer and my brother Darren and his girlfriend Kathi. It wasn't a particularly special night, just the usual visit to the local pubs then off to the nightclub up the road. I woke up on Sunday morning with the usual Arab's sandal in your mouth feeling, so I decided to go downstairs for a drink. Slowly rising to my feet I felt disorientated and I must admit I still felt a bit pissed. The saliva drained from my mouth to create a mental picture of a dried up riverbed. I got to the top of the stairs and I felt dizzy. I tentatively started descending the staircase one by one just like a child and anticipation of something abnormal was rife.

Halfway down the stairs an intense vertigo attack hit me as hard and fast as Mike Tyson's uppercut. I leaned against the wall trying desperately not to fall. Tunnel vision brought an unwelcomed fear; everything was blurred and I couldn't remember why I'd ended up on the living room sofa. I was face down; completely limp and I couldn't lift my head.

The sensation I experienced was like being buried up to the neck in sand. As a child me and my brothers would bury one another on the beach then try to muster up the strength to break free; this is exactly how I felt. The energy drained from my body like that of a rechargeable battery at the end of its charge span. My surroundings seemed to be rotating at the speed of the earth, gravity had eluded me. Dismay ravished my mind, every inch of my body felt as if some entity had laid itself upon it and I had now become its prisoner. Nausea battled with vertigo for control of this now captive body and with evil against evil the results for me would be a living nightmare.

Without heating, the wind and rain lashing against the patio windows produced an atmosphere of exaggerated cold thus causing my half-naked body to shiver uncontrollably. With my parents on holiday and Darren and Kathi still in bed the isolation increased the symptoms to such a degree that I couldn't even raise a murmur. It was to be the longest hour of my life.

Temporary relief came with the sound of the bedroom door opening and minutes later the flushing sound increasing in decibels as the opening of the toilet door directed the noise down the staircase. Anticipating help my mind instinctively increased alertness but my mumbling went unheard.

Desperation took me to a lower level; all the fight had been sapped as I tried to comprehend just what was happening to me. At the age of twenty-five I'd never wanted to see my mother as much. As the fear intensified a mothers comfort would have eased my suffering. I'd have to wait a further half an hour before once more the familiar sound of the bedroom door brought a renewed hope of this time being found.

I heard the bedroom door open again followed by footsteps on the stairs, which signalled the end of the isolation but unfortunately not the end of the torment. Not being able to turn my head in the direction of the living room door the voice of Kathi comforted me like a cool cloth on a fevered brow. With immense tenderness her soft voice enquired,

"Ant, what's the matter?"

How could I possibly explain something I couldn't even comprehend myself? All I could do was to explain how I felt. Kathi knelt down beside me and when our eyes met her expression changed from inquisitive to that of total disbelief. With great urgency and panic she summoned my brother from his bed to help her with this unexpected crisis. Darren immediately tried to sit me up but my head had the characteristics of a new born baby. I was a dead weight to him, as strong as he was, it took some manoeuvring.

Whilst Darren struggled to support my head with cushions from the sofa I could hear Kathi explaining to Jennifer that she should make her way to the house as soon as possible because she was phoning the emergency doctor.

With the emergency doctor and Jennifer on the way all that Darren and Kathi could do was to make sure that I was comfortable but even simply bringing a bowl in case of emergencies saw the pair of them running around like headless chickens. The desperation we all felt eased with the knowledge that a doctor would walk through the door at any time, but the fear remained. They brought me a blanket and I was soon sweating; I think this was fuelled by a massive adrenaline rush.

I heard a knock at the door. Who was it, Jennifer or the doctor? I needed to hear the comforting voice of the woman I loved. I felt a strange disappointment when I heard the doctor's voice but it was to be short lived for moments later Jennifer walked through the door. Her concerned expression echoed in the eyes of a now bewildered doctor. Jennifer was so dismayed by my inability to hold my head upright that she started to cry.

Jennifer, Darren and Kathi just stood staring at the doctor waiting for her to administer a miracle cure; I was asked the usual questions to illuminate all possible scenarios such as food poisoning. The doctor requested a glass of water then asked me to try to swallow a tablet she'd produced from her handbag. It had hardly passed my gullet before returning. Placing my hand upon the doctor's thigh I looked her straight in the eyes and pleaded with her to help me. Never had I been so ill or scared before.

Her persona was that of a professional, yet faced with a unique situation she strained to withhold her caring feminine side. She thought that I'd got an ear infection and that's why I'd been dizzy. As the authorising signature was placed on the dotted line of the prescription slip there seemed to be a defined hesitance in her actions. Slowly she rose to her feet and without displacing her glance she suggested that I make an appointment to see her the following week.

This was the first time I'd been this ill. I was really fit because of my job and I played football twice a week. This was to be the first of many similar attacks that I now respectfully refer to as the *Sand Syndrome*.

Chapter 2
Window Cleaning

I grew up in a typical working class background just outside Manchester through the 60's and 70's when money was scarce and life was hard. In the school holidays I would work for my father in his window-cleaning business and had decided at an early age exactly what I wanted to do. Being born in October presented me with the opportunity to leave school at Easter without taking any exams; I walked out of those school gates for the last time on the 10th April 1981.

Unsurprisingly my first official day at work wasn't by any means different to working the round previously; the only mental alteration was that there was no pending homework to do and I could now bin that dowdy grey and blue uniform. I started my working life like many others - at the bottom of the ladder (forgive the pun). Being restricted to the part-time hours my father worked, it would be six long months before I could apply for a provisional driving licence. That small green piece of paper would be highly significant to my earning potential. I could already drive thanks to my father's tuition on spare ground; all I could do was to patiently wait for my seventeenth birthday. Receiving that letter from the D.V.L.A. was for me like winning the lottery.

The winter of 81 was one of the worst on record, grid-locking the country with heavy snowfall for many weeks. Window-cleaning became increasingly hazardous and earning a living by these means lost its appeal for a while. Customers' generosity increased in the 'cups of tea' department but shear dread waited by the door with the numerous layers of clothes needed to keep away the chill. A welcoming layer of ice in our bucket greeted us with a masochistic smile.

The adverse weather conditions postponed my driving test until the 22nd February 1982. I passed at the first attempt thanks largely to my father and Mr. Michael Brakes my aptly named driving instructor.

With the arrival of my licence came the unpaid employment of chauffeur to my parents, which I relished. Armed with the pink pass slip and the L-plates peeled from the bodywork, driving without a chaperone brought an exciting apprehension. I could now pursue the vision that had been suppressed only by age restrictions; relying on others will always take you up next doors path. Relishing a new challenge I worked my arse off doing any job I got asked to do. Word of mouth was by far my greatest advertisement and within a few short months I was finding it difficult to cope with the workload alone.

During the summer I'd collect my two brothers from school and employ them for the remainder of the day. I had so much work that I employed my mate Geoff Kerfoot and set about expanding the business. At the tender age of eighteen I was made a partner in my dad's business and the day to day running of a thriving business fell to me; that schoolboy ambition had started to unfold.

Darren and Shaun were about to leave school so I had to find enough work for five of us. Me and Geoff worked our nuts off to get enough work for us all but we did it.

With the arrival of Darren and Shaun it created a scenario where (with four family members) there were too many Chiefs and not enough Indians. The constant barrage of commands from two snotty-nosed school-leavers was just too much for Geoff; a bloke that was now being held back from his true potential. It was particularly difficult for me to let Geoff go but I knew I couldn't help him to fulfil his personal ambitions; I had a long way to go before I could possibly do that. With the four of us now working and living together friction began to creep into our everyday lives and with our fiery tempers full-scale arguments were common.

To be successful in a family business takes considerable discipline and each member must possess collective ambitions, anything short of that is a recipe for disaster. The inevitable breakdown of simple communication resulted in my father losing patience with my two brothers and an ultimatum saw them walk away to try to make their own living. I then took a significant look at my own life and the direction it had taken. I was less than content with the degree of success I'd achieved at this point. Although I'd instigated (with the assistance of Geoff), the round doubling in size, it was in completely the wrong direction. Success for me would be in the form of a huge industrial round; the transformation would be lengthy and immensely sacrificial but I was more than willing to have a go at it.

My father reverted back to working alone, which I think he relished due to him being preoccupied with his hobby; coaching athletics. Re-employing my two brothers and continuing with around seventy percent of the round would be both frustrating and challenging, for my brothers kept me on my toes.

A welcoming distraction from all the modifications and subsequent bickering came in the form of a Goddess, a young, beautiful blonde called Jennifer.

She walked into my life casually by gate crashing my twenty-first birthday party. Unfortunately I was far too inebriated to appreciate this timid beauty. She captivated me the moment she looked at me - whilst hiding her glance behind her long fringe. My twenty-first birthday actually fell on the following weekend and an invitation was offered for Jennifer and a friend to accompany the lads to a nightclub; which was accepted with school girl innocence. The moment she walked into the pub I was mesmerised, those delicate pink dungarees were completely unflattering to her perfectly formed figure. Trying to be aloof I ignored her glances and tried to concentrate on the game of pool, I'd never missed so many shots! Once at the club we began to chat, well I talked and she listened still glancing from behind her long blonde fringe.

Work was driving me to total frustration. My brothers were supposed to be my employees but just as if we were still kids they tended to close rank; you can have a dog wagging a tail but you can't have a tail wagging a dog. The vision started to slowly slip away, so just as I'd done with my father I gave my brothers their own round whilst I worked alone trying to build a larger industrial round.

My early twenties were very difficult, having to travel around in two hundred quid cars that broke down every other week. It was as if I'd started from scratch but this time I had some really good contracts, it was only a matter of perseverance and a strong will that would finally reap rewards. Jennifer kept me sane in all the dark days and our conversation turned to maybe getting engaged and eventually living together. I now possessed the added inspiration to create a future for us both. As the round expanded it became increasingly more difficult to maintain demand, a day or two of bad weather and I'd be chasing my tail.

That prompted me to employ one of our neighbours Ian (Tiggy) Turner, a school leaver who as a child always had a money making scam. With two of us now working the round I began to look for more industrial work because Ian was settling into a routine that warranted me taking on extra responsibility.

Each morning at around nine-thirty all the window-cleaners would congregate outside Joe's burger bar in Ashton. In the winter months a coffee and a bacon butty came absolutely nowhere near the warmth radiated from the sweet, pure white smile worn by Karen Duff (the real reason half of us went there).

On several occasions the conversation would turn to who's selling a particular round; discussion would be ripe as to the feasibility and true value. For the vendor this was all the advertising needed, for there would be no shortage of potential buyers and in some cases this inflated the asking price. On one such occasion in December 1988 one of the old boys - John - announced that he would be retiring the following April, this caused a major stir for the round in question boasted some outstanding contracts and competition for this round would be fierce. Conversation quickly turned to who could afford to buy the round; the same two names were mentioned and I had to beat them to it.

Later that morning I found out where John lived with the intention of visiting him that afternoon. When I arrived at John's flat the expression of surprise increased my confidence; bold as brass I walked into his living room and announced that I wanted to buy his round. His wife immediately warmed to me purely because like most people she saw pound signs. To be truthful at this point I was completely out of my depth, I didn't have the money but a hundred-pound deposit (non-refundable) just before Christmas was enough to persuade an amicable deal to be struck. We agreed a price and date for the hand over, all that was left for me to do now was to find the money from somewhere.

As I walked down the path toward my car apprehension crept into play as I had to think of a way of finding the money in three short months. The beginning of April 1989 would be the target set by John and now a solution had to be found.

As March approached I made an appointment to see the small business adviser at the bank. The outcome was quite simple: first and foremost I'd not been a customer at this particular bank long enough for them to assess the risk element of such a loan and secondly, the banks were apprehensive about lending money on good will alone. The result of that meeting left me with a major dilemma, how would I now be able to save face? Still I continued with the charade.

Some two weeks later I had a casual conversation with my mother's cousin Ronnie. He possesses a remarkable 'legal' brain; he was in the middle of helping my brother Darren to fight for substantial damages due to a motorbike accident. The court case was drawing to a close and I'd approached Darren to loan me the money for the round. Once I'd found out that end of the court case would be after April it became apparent that my deadline would not be met.

When I explained to Ronnie that my intention was to pay the amount borrowed plus twenty per-cent interest within a forty-week period, his ears soon pricked up. That man then changed my life by offering to lend me the money, his curiosity and the reward on offer played its part in what would become an amicable business agreement. I was now on my way; nothing could stop me now!

Chapter 3

What was wrong with me?

After I had the vertigo attack on the Sunday it took ten days to get in to see the doctor. At this point the problem thankfully hadn't reoccurred. The doctor thought that I'd suffered at the hands of a virus. I was given a prescription for ear drops, which I had to use four times a day. It was funny sitting in the van trying to get the drops into my ear without it trickling down my neck. They irritated me and I wanted to scratch the inside of my ear but I couldn't. I stopped using them after a couple of days because the inside of my ear was burning.

A matter of days later I developed a permanent buzzing noise in my left ear which I was told was something called Tinnitus. The effects would last between two to three days and the longest spell was fifty-four days and nights. Simply trying to concentrate and perform day to day functioning was extremely difficult. I was always tired because I couldn't sleep properly at night. When people spoke to me, their voices would sometimes be mumbled and I would constantly have to ask them to repeat what they'd just said. It was really frustrating, not only for me but for my family and Jennifer.

Once the Tinnitus had been present for more than a couple of days the left side of my face would become numb, the sensation was like the after effects of a dentist's anaesthetic. Anxiety saw me at the doctor's surgery once more in the hope of ending this ordeal. It was suggested that a simple syringing of the ear may be the answer to the problem; a visit to the practice nurse led to yet another consultation with the doctor for the problem lay elsewhere. With the initial diagnosis being an ear infection I was given drops again, this time the doctor assured me that these drops wouldn't burn my eardrum. They did. I tried again with a different brand but after three attempts I was getting frustrated. I'd become desperate by this time because I couldn't concentrate at work and I was struggling with fatigue.

I found myself consulting with another doctor for the doctor I'd seen previously was on holiday. He gave me tablets this time, only they didn't work. The Tinnitus was driving me insane.

I had a casual chat with my friend's mother and I was complaining that I felt like a sheep in a sheep dip where diagnosis was concerned. She suggested that I see a relatively new doctor in the practice because she said he listened to her without hurrying her along. In one last-ditch attempt to find the truth, an appointment was made to see the man with a huge preceding reputation, Dr. Travis.

Sitting in the waiting room glancing around desperately trying not to make eye contact, I couldn't help finding myself wondering why each person was there and the circumstances surrounding it. The buzzer sounded and it seemed to wake everyone from their personal daydreams. The flashing light signalled to the surgery that Dr. Travis was ready to see his next patient and from behind the desk the distinctive voice of Sue announced,

"Antony Kelly for Dr. Travis."

The moment of truth had arrived and with a little trepidation I glanced across at the familiar reassuring smile Sue gave out in abundance, before making my way down the corridor to the doctor's office. I gave a hesitant knock at the door,

"Come in"

I entered and was asked to take a seat without his concentration being broken from updating the computer files of the previous patient. I sat down with the same dread as a naughty schoolboy summoned to the headmaster's office. When his attention was turned to me, he sat there and just listened. I told him about how it had started and how it was affecting me. He only interrupted when he wanted to ask about what happened when I had the attacks.

He made a call to reception to connect him to the local ear, nose and throat specialist. After replacing of the handset this man (with an ever replenishing queue), casually chatted about my job and my hobbies; it was as casual as sitting in my own living room chatting to a friend over a cup of tea. I was amazed at his non urgent manner; his reputation was richly deserved. The phone rang and it cut short exchanging pleasantries. He explained the circumstances and then after a couple of minutes with a broad caring smile and an unselfish gloat he said,

"Dr. Curtis's secretary will be in touch with you, we'll get to the bottom of this."

With a renewed spring in my step, I floated out of that surgery with a quiet confidence that maybe, just maybe, the end of this nightmare could be in sight.

Dr. Curtis came to the house on the 24th October 1989. I was both apprehensive and relieved at the same time. I couldn't wait to get some answers and I was hoping they were going to walk through the door.

My father ushered an immaculately dressed gentleman with a Middle Eastern appearance into the living room and my immediate reaction was that this is a guy who knows what it's all about. I explained in depth what had happened and how I'd felt throughout the attacks. He asked me to keep my head still and follow his finger. He checked my reflexes and asked me to walk towards him heel to toe with my eyes closed.

After about forty minutes he told me that he wanted me to go up to the hospital for some tests but in the meantime he'd give me something for the vertigo. He gave me Tegratol, Stematil and the Distachlor. This was the start of me having to take a cocktail of drugs everyday. These tablets made me feel sick all the time and I didn't feel like eating.

I attended the ear, nose and throat clinic on the 14th November 1989. I had to be optimistic because my business was growing quicker than weeds. I was at the hospital for a hearing test but then after that had finished my head was restrained in a head vice and I had to look at a bar with small bulbs that illuminated in a random sequence. I had to follow the lights with one eye and then the other. This was to test my reactions. He told Dr. Travis afterwards that he thought I was suffering from a left side viral Labyrinthitis (a virus), but I would have to have an x-ray to determine whether the small bones in the inner ear were damaged. I was advised to stay on the Stematil until the results of the x-rays were known.

The Christmas rush had helped to take my mind off waiting for the results but when they eventually came through the post on the 27th December they were disappointingly normal. That statement may sound strange but there was a genuine underlying deep-rooted problem that no one seemed to have found. Life became somewhat normal over the festive period and the whole of January but the mystery remained a mystery.

It was now early February 1990 and I'd bought yet another round and I'd employed another school leaver Jimmy Ashton, a quiet lad but willing to work hard. He soon fitted into our routine and things were running along smoothly. The Tinnitus had returned and the whole saga of not being able to sleep started to repeat itself.

I was about to start work on this new round early one morning when I felt that familiar dryness in my mouth again. I tried to ignore it and carry on as normal. I bent over to clean my chamois when I was overcome with the most violent attack to date. With twice the force as before I collapsed into the gutter and was violently sick. I was laying half on the pavement and half on the road with absolutely no strength to move. The rain soaked ground was cold and I began to shiver. I was vomiting so much that a yellow greenish bile was all I could bring up. Ian and Jimmy tried to comprehend what was happening and help at the same time but it was such a bizarre sight that all they could do was to help me to my feet and into the passenger seat.

Jimmy placed a comforting hand on my shoulder and told me not to worry about work and Ian volunteered to drive me home. It had been about ten minutes since I collapsed on the floor but now it was time to go home and try to sleep.

At around eight thirty in the morning mid week in any town sees a large number of people battling to get to work and this always creating long queues at roundabouts. I was wishing for this day to be an exception but it wasn't to be. We joined the queue, Ian impatiently inching forward doing his utmost to get me back home. I had the window wound down and I had my head out of it despite the cold. I was trying not to make eye contact with anyone because I felt embarrassed. Staring at the blurring tarmac slowly coming into focus meant unwelcome attention from other road users. It's not every day you see someone hanging out of their window in the middle of a bitterly cold winter.

I tried to sit back in the seat and in doing so I glanced at the woman driver next to us. She was busy doing her hair in the mirror and being a typical woman, pretending not to notice male attention. Curiosity got the better of her and as she returned an inquisitive look, she was met with my blood-drained complexion and an expression of despondency. Then she was forced to share one of the most embarrassing moments of my life; right on queue I spewed up all down the door. I'll never forget her look of disdain. Her stare was transferred to the now moving traffic ahead and I skulked away like a scalded cat.

When I got back home my mother's characteristic smile was wiped clean as once again she could do nothing but watch her son's frantic piercing eyes cry out for help. She put me to bed as she'd been forced to do before, only this time her eyes were heavier with heartache than ever before. Her anxiety and our unresolved answers brought about desperate measures; she phoned Dr. Curtis's secretary and the distress in her voice crept upstairs; a slight relief came with a new house call. The Sand Syndrome had hit harder than ever before and with Jennifer at my bedside I felt that I could stick a two fingered gesture up to this strange illness.

15th February 1990 saw Dr. Curtis back at the house. As with his prior visit my father ushered the doctor through to the lounge and with a puzzled expression he asked,

"Haven't I been here before?"

"Yes last October."

"Could you remind me of my findings?"

Once I'd finished briefly explaining the results of the tests his team had undertaken with no noticeable abnormalities; he said profoundly,

"There's something more to this than meets the eye, I'd like one of my colleges to come and visit you."

With that he asked to use the phone and made an appointment only hesitating to verify the arrangement with me.

"Dr. Ward will visit you at 10 o'clock next Tuesday morning."

"Dr. Ward that's a proper name for a doctor isn't it."

With a smile Dr. Curtis left the house and I never saw him again. A week can be a long time when you're so charged up with emotion and I also had the added pressure of a large loan to repay and two wages to find each week. I needed to resolve this mysterious illness and get on with living the dream.

The following Monday saw yet another ill timed attack right in the middle of yet another hectic morning and stole another day from me. Tuesday morning and I was still in bed with the irritation of knowing the script would have been completely different had the doctor seen the attack for himself. As it were I had to be content to just get another stage further to finding the cause of these attacks. There was a knock at the door and I held my breath as I strained to hear an unfamiliar voice. It was the doctor and I heard my mother telling him that I was in bed convalescing from an attack the day before.

Hope came walking through the door in the form of a smile that was changed instantly by a cry for help. The interrogation seemed scripted, as I knew the answers before being asked the questions; all the time my mother peered over his shoulder hoping he was going to finish her child's suffering.

"May I use your phone Mrs. Kelly?" He asked.

"Hello its Dr. Ward, I need a bed for a patient I'm sending in." There was a short pause before he returned an authoritative,

"What do you mean there's no beds, I don't care where you put him as long as he's in today I'm sending him right now."

The man had arrived. He was a problem solver and wouldn't except negativity. There was a puzzle to be cracked and as he instructed my mother to pack a few things, I had a mental picture of the man at the foot of the stairs rolling up his sleeves. I seemed to melt into the mattress with a wave of relief at the very thought of going into hospital for the truth to surface.

Chapter 4

Searching for the truth

Walking through the hospital corridors with my mother and her best friend Joan as substitute crutches, would under normal circumstances have given me a complex but as we made our way towards ward sixteen, people passed without glancing at me. The ward was only a short walk from the car park but it felt like a marathon. As we got to the ward all the nurses were busy so we just stood there patiently waiting to be seen to.

Within moments a nurse with a stressed smile show me to my temporary home for the next couple of days. All that was left to do now was to pass the time until a doctor arrived. An understudy of Dr. Ward came to my bedside and performed a thorough investigation and a welcomed interrogation; he tried to hide his bewildered expression by completing the examination in a scripted fashion.

It was extremely difficult to sleep in that sterile paper thin sheeted bed with the noisy ramblings and flatulence surrounding me like an ambush. I was regimentally awoken before it seemed I'd had the luxury of sleeping to a breakfast that had been chosen by someone three days earlier. I was anticipating some good news so all that was left to do was to wait for the doctor to make his rounds. It was late morning before Dr. Ward approached the end of my bed, a half smile told me the story before any words left his lips. Deep within my heart I just knew that there was more to this illness than met the eye. Dr. Ward explained in great detail the tests he and Dr. Curtis's team had carried out over the last couple of months. I was really disappointed and still no further forward. I sat there feeling sorry for myself but Dr. Ward revived my fading faith by telling me that he'd asked a reputable neurologist to look into my case. On Wednesday afternoons Dr. Vaughan had a clinic at the hospital and he'd agreed to come to see me before he made his way home.

The hands on the clock above the ward entrance appeared to stand still. I tried to pass the time by sketching but all I ended up doing was doodling. All the nurses on the ward busied themselves making sure the ward was spotless in readiness for Dr. Vaughan's visit later that day. I was astounded to be told by one of the nurses that this particular doctor happened to be one of the neurological consultants for the Royal family! True or not, that man's notoriety preceded him to such a degree that I found it quite amusing that the ward had now turned into his domain. As I sat on the bed contemplating my future; I didn't know what would happen now. The questions overlapped each other. What's wrong with me? How will it affect me? How long will it last? Will it affect me for the rest of my life? Is it life threatening? But most of all - WHY ME?

One of the most frustrating things for me to deal with was the simple *control* factor that this mysterious illness had stolen; as if this wasn't enough to deal with, I also had the extra burden of trying to control my business from the constraints of a hospital bed. As six o'clock drew nearer I sat on my bed with total focus on the ward entrance waiting for somebody I'd never laid eyes on before to make an appearance.

The big hand on the clock eased its way past twelve and all that I could think about was to prepare for the questions that he would ask. Memories of each attack replayed themselves for analysis but looking around the ward at bedridden men made me feel fortunate. Quarter past six and all of a sudden the nurses spilled from behind the desk onto the ward as seconds later a well presented man was ushered in my direction. With his arm outstretched in a gesture to shake my hand the man with a strong Scottish accent announced to me with a broad smile,

"Hello, I'm Dr. Vaughan, what seems to be the problem?"

He sat on the bed next to me and patiently allowed me to tell my story. It wasn't until I'd finished telling him how I'd ended up in hospital that he started to ask questions. My responses to his questions made his smile broaden and his examination followed the same routine as his colleagues had the day before except for one; a piece of cotton wool was manipulated into a point and then pushed into the corner of my eye to test its reaction. My eye started to water and he apologised.

I became aware that it was almost visiting time but still that didn't deter the doctor's determination to at least give me some sort of explanation. The longer the man took, the greater my confidence grew. That moment is as fresh in my mind today as the day that it took place. The man who came to my bedside that day was like an angel wrapping me with his wings. The voices of visitors tried to overlap the soft Scottish accent but still this man blanked out the surroundings and continued to ask and answer questions until he eventually came out with a statement that left me absolutely gobsmacked!

"I think you're suffering from migraine of the spine." He said with total conviction.

I didn't know what to think about that but this doctor was very experienced and I trusted him implicitly. Dr. Vaughan told me that he wanted me to go to North Manchester General Hospital for a week of extensive tests to try and get to the bottom of it. The arrangements were to be finalised by his secretary and he finally left the ward at twenty-five past seven.

Jennifer, Darren, Kathi and my mother rushed over to my bed with many different questions all being asked at the same time. I had their undivided attention as I told them just what had been said but I was confronted by four confused blank expressions. I think I could interpret what they were thinking 'what the hell's he talking about?' Like most people I associated migraine with headaches.

The couple of weeks in-between my hospital stays were to be the worst attacks to date. They returned every 3 or 4 days. The time span of attacks was lasting from between four hours, to a disturbing ten hours. The dizziness was so fierce that once it had taken hold it would literally knock me off my feet. As in the beginning it would start with my mouth going dry followed by a gradual increase in disorientation until I was rendered unable to stand. The dryness to disability would normally take around thirty minutes. Trying to sleep it off was impossible because the moment my eyes closed the more violent the vertigo became. Double vision would occur every other second, which was caused by my eyes involuntarily rotating. This caused violent bouts of vomiting until I felt as if I'd been kicked in the guts by a donkey. The day of an attack was from that moment, a complete write-off. The following day I'd be so physically drained that I would have to crawl up the stairs like a toddler and without even the strength to stand long enough while I emptied my bladder.

While all this was going on, the worry of trying to run my business was taken care of by Darren in a fashion that allowed me to concentrate on trying to regain some form of normality. With the attacks at their peak the only time I could venture out was when I was accompanied. Many an evening Jennifer and Darren would walk around the block one on each arm supporting me like a drunk. It was a real relief to be outdoors and I disregarded the embarrassment I felt from bewildering stares from the neighbours. My morale hit an all time low because as I'd be getting over an attack, I'd be struck down with another. It seemed relentless at the time and I became really depressed and irritable.

The date had been set for my admission to North Manchester General hospital and waiting became a little less stressful. Four days before my admission I had an attack that lasted eight hours with vomiting lasting one and a half hours. As a result, the following morning my torso felt more strained than on previous occasions. I woke up to the sound of squabbling Starlings and the room bright from the winter sun. I felt compelled to rise from my pit and try to fight this bastard. My mother's anguish met me at the breakfast table along with her now heavy eyes. To try and ease my mother's frustration I told her that I felt better and that I was going for a walk around my favourite haunt - Daisy Nook Country Park. Fearing for my safety she tried to dissuade me but I can be a stubborn sod and off I went.

My first few steps were tentative and slow but I reached my first goal; the main road. I took advantage of the low wall by the old folk's home at the foot of Downshaw Road. Sitting with almost an immediate arse chill I thought the whole world had gone mad, cars were sounding their horns as they tried to drive around the bus which had stopped to pick up passengers. The fumes from the cars were choking the first fresh breaths for what seemed days and I wanted to get to the country park and taste the freshness of a spring morning.

A cold wind breathed sensation back into my limbs and I was joined by the sweet sound of a Blackbird's call. I closed my eyes trying to disregard the noise of the heavy daytime traffic but it was no use, I had to venture further into the park to find the silence I wanted to hear. My legs felt as though I was trudging through thick wet mud but time was on my side and my lackadaisical demeanour ceased to be a problem; after all I wasn't in bed feeling sorry for myself. All the burning and stiffness in my legs was rewarded with nothing simpler than a three hundred and sixty degree atmospheric stereo of delightful bird song.

Each bench that I reached became yet another successful stage and some three hours later I had completed the two-mile hike I had set out to do. The euphoric sense of achievement is hard to put into words; I'm a really determined and self-motivated person and this was something I had to do to make me feel more in control of my own body. When I eventually got back home my mum was waiting at the gate. She told me that she almost came to look for me and that she'd been going to the gate to look down the road for me every ten to fifteen minutes. She threw her arms around me as if I was a child again. God knows what was going through her head; I'm not a parent so I've no idea.

On Friday the 2nd March 1990, I was admitted to North Manchester General Hospital for what hopefully would be the end to my personal nightmare. I hesitantly knocked on the door of the nurses' office and announced myself to three nurses busy updating patients' charts. I was shown to a bed at the bottom of the Victorian ward with its high ceilings and typically dry hospital heat. I'd no sooner started to place my toiletries in my bedside cabinet when that familiar dryness in the roof of my mouth signalled yet another pending attack. This was the only attack I'd ever welcomed. Now the doctors could witness for themselves the true extent of the debilitation brought on by this mystery illness. The timing of this attack couldn't have been orchestrated better if I'd tried to instigate it myself. I looked up the ward towards the nurses' office hoping that one of them would glance in my direction but with the early afternoon paperwork to do, their concentration was elsewhere. I made my way up the ward exchanging polite smiles with fellow patients. I'd attracted the attention of one of the senior nurses', who met me at the door with a smile,

"I'm in here for investigation into the reason for these attacks I've been getting and I'm going to have one right now."

Without her expression changing she completely took over the situation with an unfazed semblance, escorting me back to my bed before sending for the doctor. With the doctor due to arrive, I was given an injection to prevent the vomiting normally brought on by an attack. Lying there I didn't know how violent or how long the attack was going to last but I smiled because of the circumstances I now found myself in; a doctor was about to document exactly what happens during an attack.

I was in the foetus position and facing away from the ward entrance, the first I knew of the doctor's presence was seeing an open white coat with a black skirt and black tights underneath. My eyes made their way up towards her face but before I'd made eye contact I was instructed to strip down to my underpants. Our eyes locked together and I was looking at an attractive woman. Embarrassment overwhelmed me as I realised that I was wearing my turquoise 'posing-pouch' underpants. I'm not the most endowed of men but that day my manhood resembled a short stack of buttons. The embarrassment didn't last too long for the doctor's examination combined with the vertigo preceded any male ego trip. Following each section of an hour-long procedure, she frantically wrote on a chart pinned to a clipboard. Her puzzled looks reconfirmed that whatever was causing these all consuming symptoms was abnormal and I began to doubt whether or not she would be able to give me a diagnosis.

Visiting that night was quite upbeat because an attack had been documented at its peak. Jennifer and the rest of the family tried to bring a sense of humour to the ward with them that night but the fear remained. Seeing me in that familiar situation didn't ease with time. The feeling of helplessness still remained etched in their encouraging half smiles. As Jennifer and I exchanged loving, lingering glances, everyone's conversations fell upon deaf ears. As visiting time came to a close and the nurses signalled for visitors to vacate the ward, Jennifer lingered at my bedside so we could steal just a few moments together. It was a particularly difficult period for us to come to terms with but one that none of us had any form of control over. We didn't understand it! After each visit I'd patiently wait an hour or so just to make sure Jennifer had arrived home before phoning her so we could talk privately. All I seemed to do was to try to avoid causing her unnecessary concern. She was going through the same hell alongside me.

That first night in such a huge ward was exactly like going back to the Victorian age except with the addition of mod cons such as; TV's and walkmans. At 'lights out' a library silence descended upon the ward and the nurses would pull the curtains around each bed in a vain attempt to give the patients a sense of privacy. The vertigo had started to wear off but the fatigue had set in which made me feel like I'd been glued to the bed. The light of the portable television screen illuminated the curtain of the next bed and as I lay listening to the lowered volume I could make out that I lay next to a closet 'Prisoner Cellblock H' fan. As the night wore on - a man in a bed opposite (who remained unconscious throughout my stay there) was crying out in his sleep,

"Land ahoy Captain! Abandon ship!"

It was simply too noisy to sleep. I was forced to attend the breakfast table with minimum fuss but the nurses wanted all their patients to try to help themselves. I spent the morning lying on my bed making small talk with the bloke to my left, briefly explaining the reason for me being there. With the encouragement of the nurses; I began using the toilets at the top of the ward - trying to exercise as much as possible. I was still a little unsteady on my feet as I exchanged glances with a man who's facial cast seemed to weigh as much as the wheelchair he was sitting in. On my way back from the toilets the man in the wheelchair had moved towards the end of his bed as though waiting for me, I smiled politely once more.

"I saw you yesterday, what are you in for?" He asked inquisitively.

I sat on the edge of his bed and told him the story from the very beginning. With time on our side I had the chance to be quite graphic. As soon as I'd finished he pointed out two other patients on the opposite side of the ward.

"See him over there?"

"Yes."

"And him with the beard?"

"Yes." I replied once again.

"Well they've got MS and so have I." he said trying to gauge a reaction from me.

I'd known someone with MS and so I was familiar with the debilitating effects it had on him. The man introduced himself as Stuart and proceeded to tell me without any moralistic conscience that as far as he was concerned he was convinced that I was also suffering from MS. I didn't really know how to react to his statement. I just sat and stared at him before defensively remarking,

"Well we'll see what the doctor's say."

I returned to my bed and I was absolutely floored. How could anyone be so recklessly callous with such a mind-blowing subject? I just couldn't understand why he felt he had to make such a profound observation with blatant disrespect for the doctors' involved with my case. The man to my left commented that I looked as if I'd seen a ghost, then I told him what Stuart had said. His reply, like mine was,

"He's not a doctor what does he know?"

All I could do was to watch the other two blokes with MS and absorb the varying disabilities of the three men in my ward with this strange illness. I couldn't stop thinking about that wheelchair; it scared the hell out of me. That night when my visitors arrived I didn't dare tell them what Stuart had said for they all knew John (the man I'd known with MS) and the difficulties he endured. To place such fear at this stage would've had a disastrous effect on the family, especially Jennifer. I simply couldn't afford to take fellow patients' views on board no matter how much he personally knew about *his* illness.

All night Stuart's words were playing over and over in my mind - like a tape recording. The noisy mumblings, flatulence and the 'sailor still warning his captain of the imminent danger ahead' meant that sleeping at night was nigh impossible.

I really wanted to get into the mind of Stuart following his revelations and try to understand this man's anger. I got the feeling that it ran a little deeper than him directing anger at being confined to his wheelchair. Nothing much happened on a Sunday so I sat on Stuart's bed; it was now my turn to ask the questions and I was as direct as he was the day before. I started the conversation with not the usual "why are you in here?" but "what treatment are you receiving?" As our conversation unfolded he told me that he'd been in the ward since the previous October (a total of 5 months) and had not set foot outside since. He explained that our ward had now become his prison and his wheelchair was now a ball and chain around his ankles. The anger and frustration at the situation he now found himself in was understandable self-pity but channelled in the wrong direction. He channelled his frustration at Multiple Sclerosis and anyone in the line of fire; although he tried not to offend anyone, his truth was hard for some people to swallow, including me. I asked if his visitors ever took him out of the ward and his reply has haunted me ever since.

"My wife couldn't care less about me. She's shagging my best mate and there's nothing I can do about it."

As his explanation unfolded his eyes became laboured and his demeanour shrank like a dying violet, this man was already mentally dead. He then tried to defend his wife's actions by describing the reason behind her extra-marital activities. Apparently he'd lost control of his bladder some months before being admitted to hospital and wore a catheter making it impossible to continue a physical relationship. He didn't blame his wife for seeking some sort of a physical relationship elsewhere but what was damaging was the trust he had obviously placed in his best friend. He just couldn't handle being kicked while he was down by the two people he cared for most. I didn't posses the tools or the experience needed to give him some comforting words, so all I could do was to offer to release him from his prison for a while and let him taste fresh air again. I placed a blanket over his legs and pushed the wheelchair towards the ward entrance, where we were stopped by one of the nurses,
"Err, where do you think you're going?"
"I'm just taking Stuart down to the car park for some fresh air."
 The nurse was having none of it; saying that we weren't allowed out of the ward. I convinced her that I'd just push Stuart down to the next ward and back just for some different scenery.
She agreed in principal but watched us walk past the lift. As soon as she was distracted I pushed the button to call the lift but continued to walk down the corridor ignoring her watchful eye. I turned to return to the ward, then about ten yards from the lift the doors opened. Looking straight ahead I could see the nurse was busy so I steered the wheelchair into the lift. The doors closed trapping the chair and then they opened again allowing me access. I turned and pushed the button for the ground floor hoping that the nurse would be distracted long enough for the doors to close. As soon as the doors closed I turned to Stuart with a huge conceited smile,
"Right where do you want to go?"
It was a silly question because he was already further than he'd been in months. I could have taken him down to the morgue and he would have been content! Without

any prompting he told me the tragic circumstances surrounding his professional and personal demise. He had been a manager and had ended up without the control of his bladder and legs. We must have done two laps of the hospital grounds before making our way to the car park. We came out of the rear entrance only to be faced with some building work and a sandwich van selling bacon butties and that distinctive taste of the 'polystyrene' cup coffee. Eating that sandwich and drinking that coffee on a freezing March morning was like being on holiday.

While we drank our coffee, Stuart reiterated the anguish he felt at no longer being in control of his basic bodily functions. He told me of his torment; coming to terms with his wife becoming the breadwinner and having to deal with the possibility of never being able to work again. He told me how his sex life had deteriorated because he could no longer maintain or sometimes obtain an erection. The stress of these events had clearly taken its toll for as he sat in that chair he looked so vulnerable. Returning to the ward I just had to sit alone with quiet reflection. None of the doctors had made any indication towards the possibility of me suffering the first symptoms of MS. This was quite simply because the attacks at this stage were too long to be associated with Meniere's Disease but considered too short to be related to Multiple Sclerosis.

I knew nothing about MS so I sat on my bed watching each of the MS sufferers. I needed to prepare myself for the worst. Stuart's wheelchair was at the forefront of my mind and it was then that the reality of what I could be facing really hit me. How could I continue with a physical job if indeed it was MS? I watched the three men intently, paying particular attention to how each of them coped with their varying disabilities. Although each of them differed from the next the underlying problems were plain to see; physical disintegration. It scared the hell out of me. Under such circumstances it's very difficult to remain optimistic when the history surrounding my being there was severe enough to warrant a week of intense scrutiny under a leading neurologist. These facts alone point to something seriously out of the ordinary and I was now at its mercy.

Monday morning we were awoken at the crack of dawn and as usual forced to join the rest of the other patients at the table for breakfast, after which I went to shower. While I was in there one of the nurses knocked on the door and started having a go at me because a porter had been sent to take me for the first of many neurological tests. I uncharacteristically snapped back that I wasn't a mind reader; nobody had bothered to tell me. The aggression came from not knowing where to direct my anxiety and frustration that had now consumed me purely because I felt in the dark as to where these tests were leading. I'd been given no information as to what these tests consisted of so I felt like a lamb to the slaughter.

As I walked back into the ward I was greeted by one of those clumsy looking hospital wheelchairs and ordered to sit in it before being taken for the first of the tests lined up for me. A technician attached electrodes to my temples and to the top and back of my head with 'glue'. The test involves watching a black and white checked pattern on a TV screen. The black and white squares alternate on a regular cycle which generates electrical potentials along the optic nerve and into the brain. These can be detected with electroencephalographical (EEG) sensors placed at specific sites on the top of the head. Each eye is tested independently while an eye patch is worn on the other eye. When I arrived back at the ward, one of the nurses gave me a bottle of nail polish remover and told me that the only way to remove the 'glue' was to apply the contents with cotton wool. I smelt like a whore's handbag by the time I'd finished!

Later that day, I told Stuart where I'd been. He told me that he knew that they were investigating for MS. Twice a day I would take that man out of the ward for half an hour; no matter how much fear he'd managed to administer into my conscience. The more I got to know him, the more sympathetic to his situation I became.

On Tuesday morning I was taken for a brain scan. This was completely different from the previous day's experience. The room was huge and brightly lit with a machine that resembled a large polo mint. I lay on the machine, my sleeve was rolled up and my arm was injected with dye to show up on the x-ray. There was an awesome feeling of calm as the dye raced around my body sweeping it with the warmth of the sun reappearing from a cloud. The machine rose nine times by inches as it groaned and clicked, taking vital x-rays of slices of the brain in the search for abnormalities. Having spent a couple of days in the ward I built up a relationship with most of my fellow patients and each time I returned to the ward they would enquire as to what the tests entailed. When I told each of them that I would be having a lumber puncture the following day, their grimaces and tales of their experiences put the fear of God into me. Warnings of the immense pain and an unbelievable headache made me wish that this was already over but I had twenty-four hours to mull it over.

Wednesday afternoon and the female doctor that had performed the examination the Friday before, entered the ward alerting the attention of a ward nurse. Together they made their way towards my bed. My heart sank and my arse started twitching, the lads started to 'take the piss' and all I could do was smile defiantly. A local anaesthetic made the lumber puncture completely painless, I didn't realise the doctor had even started to extract the fluid from my spinal cord until she pulled the curtains open. I was instructed to drink plenty of fluids and to remain lying down for the rest of the day; this would prevent the severe headache I'd been warned about. That night I was inundated with visitors and no matter how vulnerable you feel the sight of your closest friends and family walking down the ward lifts the weakest of spirits. The strain on Jennifer's face was plain to see and she knew there and then that she wouldn't be getting a call from me that night.

Thursday was when Dr. Vaughan made his ward rounds and with that came the possibility of a favourable discharge. Anticipation was running high on the agendas of a couple of us wanting to return to the comfort of our own homes. Boyish banter between those seeking the magic signature helped to retain some sort of semblance. Expressing to the others that I couldn't handle another week in hospital lead to 'tongue in cheek' taunts. It wasn't too long before Dr. Vaughan made an appearance and as he made his way down the ward the other lads started shouting across the room,

"You can't go home Ant, you're too ill!"

My eyes met his with the same look as a mischievous puppy. With a gentle broad smile he placed his right hand upon my right shoulder and gently squeezed it, this gesture needed no spoken words of comfort; I knew then that I was going home.

An understudy of Dr. Vaughan showed me the x-rays of the brain scan carried out earlier that week and quite visible was a black spot that appeared on all nine sections of the x-ray film. I quickly pointed out the mark and enquired as to its significance. I was then told that this was probably scar tissue from a virus and that they intended to treat this with a course of steroids. Somehow I wasn't convinced of this man's explanation because he couldn't look me in the eyes; I felt he was hiding a valuable piece of information. In his defence he quickly added that I would be sent for a M.R.I. scan which was a relatively new x-ray machine that could detect abnormalities in the nervous system.

My whole body sank as yet again no real answer to this nightmare had presented itself. With a prescription slip signed, that was all the ammunition needed to return to the comfort of familiar surroundings. My bag was packed and lay on the bed waiting for my father to collect 'us' both. When he finally arrived, my father took my bag and with a wink he said,

"Come on son, let's go home."

As I said my goodbyes and good-lucks' making my way out of the ward, Stuart had wheeled himself to the end of his bed. He'd been very weak and I smiled to myself at his determination to say his personal thanks for the short-lived relief from his metaphorical prison. With a smile and a firm handshake I wished him luck. He looked me straight in the eyes and said,

"It's you who needs the luck."

With such a profound parting statement the journey home was deafeningly quiet. I never saw Stuart again after this and I've often wondered what happened to him.

Chapter 5

The calm before the storm

With all the events of the previous week, I found it extremely difficult to concentrate. My mind would keep replaying those conversations with Stuart. In my mind's eye I held the image of the black spot on the x-rays but I felt optimistic at starting on the steroids; I'd become extremely weak and I was longing to return to work. When I left hospital I weighed a little over seven stone and the illness had added a decade to my face; my complexion was now ashen and my cheekbones had become more prominent adding to the illusion of a walking skeleton.

The effects of the steroids were swift and within days I was eating like never before. Depression was beginning to creep in again and the return of the vertigo attacks was leaving me weaker for lengthening periods. After one such attack I was lying in bed one night when my mother came to sit with me; sobbing having witnessed the suffering of one of her cherubs. For a little over an hour she'd tried to persuade me to take a holiday to help speed my recovery. My mother was turning into an old woman with the worry of the last few months. Not wanting to leave the running of my business I declined, trying to convince her that I was fine. My father's small frame blocked a proportion of the landing light illuminating the room.

"Well is he going Andie, or what?"

As my father moved closer to the bed, the light illuminated tears as they slowly trickled down my mother's cheeks.

"Antony, son, can't you see what this is doing to me and your mother." There was a short pause before he continued with,

"I love you son." There was a sputtering sound as my father tried to quell a sob.

My mother's soft voice pleaded with me once more; as I raised my left hand to wipe away the tear making its way down her right cheek, I quietly said,

"Don't worry any more Mum, I'll go."

My dad reassured me that my business would be well looked after before rushing downstairs to telephone our friends in France to confirm my well-needed holiday. Our Darren told me to enjoy myself and chill out because he was going to take care of everything until I got back. The following day Jennifer excitedly rushed home to tell me that she'd explained the circumstances to her boss and he'd given her two weeks compassionate leave. That was it; all we needed now was to make arrangements to be picked up at Calais. We were leaving the very next day.

We were going to catch the four a.m. ferry; my parents drove us through the night. After collecting our tickets we all stood hugging each other outside the ticket office. Jennifer and I made our way to the bus and I was now relishing the thought of spending a fortnight with Jennifer away from all the problems. As I stood on deck watching the white cliffs of Dover disappear into the darkness of the spring sky, it took me away from the nightmare of the unanswered questions.

Waiting to collect us from Calais was Christian, a friend of the family. I was also looking forward to seeing Jacky - a French bloke who had lived with my family for eighteen months. Jacky shared my bedroom during his stay with us and I ended up employing him. We became as close as brothers. I couldn't wait to see Jacky again because I wanted to tell him all the fears I had, I just knew he'd understand.

As Jennifer and I walked down the corridor towards the foreign faces, it wasn't long before I could pick out Christian. He was an ex-rugby player with broad shoulders, menacing cropped hair and to complete the picture, a brown leather jacket straining to hold his immense frame. As I spotted him he was scanning the crowd. My broad smile greeted his glance; his returning smile was halted with a look of total mystification. Not only did I know what he was thinking but also what he wanted to say and it was one of those rare occasions when you say absolutely nothing, the look says it all.

We set off for Armentieres (the twin town to Stalybridge, Cheshire). The sun struggled to rise in the sky but its warmth quickly heated the car and it helped to accelerate the feeling of leaving my problems behind. I watched Jennifer through the passenger mirror and she was smiling, something I'd not had the pleasure of witnessing for what seemed an eternity. Our first few days were spent relaxing and 'recharging the batteries' and trying to communicate within this alien environment.

This affliction had kept me awake night after night wondering about the outcome and the long-term effects of the vertigo attacks. For the whole two weeks I slept for more or less twelve hours a day and with the opportunity to sleep, I took full advantage of the situation. It was really refreshing just to get away from all the stress that had been building up over the last six months.

Before I could appreciate my fresh surroundings, I found myself being brought back to reality sat back on the ferry; Jennifer seemed to stare into space, I wondered just what thoughts were going through her mind. The reality was quite simple: we now had to face up to whatever was ahead of us. How long and hard will our next journey be? It wouldn't be another holiday. We were facing a journey of destiny and I just knew it wasn't going to be easy. I tried to imagine the thoughts floating around Jennifer's head. Was she as apprehensive as I was and further more would our relationship survive?

My parents looked as though the fortnight was as kind to them as it had been to us. My mother's youthful looks had returned – she was glowing. Hopes of a definite appointment for the scan were dashed. Mum's disappointment showed in her eyes when she said that there hadn't been a letter from the hospital.

It was now early April; a month after the week that I spent in hospital. If the vertigo attacks turned out to be a passing phase the profoundness of the events would surely change my attitude to life. I rang Dr. Vaughan's secretary as soon as possible and pleaded with her to find me an appointment for the scan. I besieged her with phone call after phone call but she was unable to give a definite date. The greatest obstacle was quite simply that there were only two Magnetic Resource Imaging (MRI) scan machines in the northwest. One was at the Manchester Medical School and the other was in Liverpool.

All I could do now was to patiently wait for the letter to fall upon the *welcome* mat. Working within this limbo period was virtually impossible. Not only was my physical strength non-existent but I was feeling depressed because of the frustration of not being in complete control.

The letter finally arrived for my scan. The date I'd waited for was now in black and white – 4th June 1990. To prevent further worry to Jennifer and my family, I decided to go alone for the scan. As soon as I'd reported to the receptionist I was instructed to remove all my clothing and wear a blue gown. I waited for my name to be called and I looked around the room at the other patients. Before too long I was asked to follow a nurse to the scanning room. The nurse gave me a reassuring smile before handing me a list of music. The nurse told me that I could pick a tape to listen to whilst I was in the scanning machine. This was supposed to relax you enough to allow an uninterrupted x-ray. I chose Phil Collins purely because he was one of Jennifer's favourite pop stars and it allowed me to imagine she was by my side.

As the nurse and I patiently waited outside the door we exchanged pleasantries and I gave her a brief description of exactly why I was in the hospital. Midway through our chat we were interrupted by the screams of a young boy coming from the other side of the door. The nurses and the boy's parents tried in vain to calm him down from the claustrophobic tension built up within seconds of being placed in the machine. I heard the nurses explaining that they would have to return at a later date with an anaesthetist to allow them to carry out the scan effectively.

On entering the room I could sense the fear that boy must have felt just at the sheer sight of the machine. I thought the brain scanner was intimidating but that was 'a walk in the park' compared to this huge metal tube shaped device. The MRI scanner is a huge cylinder in which the patient is placed via a conveyor belt. I lay on the bench with my head next to the machine and when I was comfortable the belt sprung into action and I slowly became surrounded by the darkened tube. It was so tight that if I'd have stuck out my tongue I'd have touched the inside of the metal surface. The nurses had given me instructions not to talk and to relax until the x-ray was over. It was the most claustrophobic I'd felt since I was locked inside a coffin by kids at school when I was in the play 'Oliver!' I could now fully understand the boy's fear. I'd been lying there for about five minutes listening to the droning of the machine before I impatiently cried out,

"Hey nurse, where's my music?" with a disgruntled moan.

The instruction not to speak was reiterated and then the sounds of Phil Collins. Driving home from the scan was one of those occasions in which you can't remember half of the journey; you seem to be driving on 'auto-pilot'. The results were expected within the next ten days. All that was left to do was to try to maintain some kind of normality.

Chapter 6

Two little words that changed my life

Wednesday the 13th June 1990; this was it the day I'd been waiting nine long months for, I felt sick to the pit of my stomach. The morning dragged, I was in a world of my own. I just knew that today was going to change my life forever and there was nothing I could do about it. I simply had to except the inevitable and face head on whatever was coming. And in a paradox, I was relieved to find out the truth.

Me and Ronnie walked into the reception. To the right a coffee shop held host to three patients decked out in pyjamas, slippers and the obligatory dressing gowns. They chatted away with friends and family as they drank coffee and ate chocolate brownies. To my left two women sat at either end of a long table like bookends, one was on the phone the other typed away on a keyboard. Ronnie flanked my side like a bodyguard as I introduced myself to the receptionist,

"Hello love, Antony Kelly for Dr. Vaughan".

She glanced down at her list before confirming the two o'clock appointment.

"Ok Mr. Kelly, follow the yellow line".

At the entrance to the corridor three coloured lines stretched off into the distance leading you along the passageway and into a catacomb of anatomical departments. Red, blue and the yellow line lay to the right hand side. I walked side by side with Ronnie and the silence was tangible. The yellow line would take us through a maze of corridors and to Dr. Vaughan's receptionist. I introduced myself once more and was invited to take a seat. I sat there with a twisted stomach as I prepared myself for what would almost certainly change my life forever. Episodes flashed before me as I felt a huge rush of adrenaline flush to my face.

Ronnie chatted light-heartedly to ease the tension. I couldn't make eye contact with any of the other patients. As other names were called before mine a nervous heat radiated within me. It seemed cruel to keep me waiting twenty minutes. Ronnie tried to distract me but I just wanted the consultation over and done with so that I could just get on with my halted life. The previous patient reappeared and my heart sank, a nurse called my name; I turned to Ronnie,

"Are you coming in with me?" I said needing a child's reassurance.

"I'm here to give you support, of course I'm coming in." He said with comfort.

We followed the nurse to the consulting room where Dr. Vaughan sat behind a huge desk. Our eyes met and his familiar broad smile tried to ease my anxiety but I was far too tense for that. The nurse closed the door and Ronnie and I sat down. Dr. Vaughan asked about my health since we last met. I explained that I'd had nine more vertigo attacks and was still unable to fully return to work. He sympathised with my frustration. Dr. Vaughan started talking about the results of my scan. I sat rigid and braced myself for whatever it had revealed. Ronnie crossed his legs and began to shuffle around uneasily. Dr. Vaughan leaned forward interlocking his fingers as his elbows rested on the edge of the table. Looking me straight in the eyes he calmly and precisely said,

"I've got some good news and some bad news."

A familiar dryness of the palate, only this time I knew it wouldn't be a vertigo attack. It was a nervous reaction to his words. It's *MS*, I thought. The room suddenly became stuffy as an uncomfortable wave of warmth heightened my senses and made me gasp for air.

Dr. Vaughan looked at Ronnie to get his attention too. He then explained his findings to both of us. There was a pause before Dr. Vaughan continued,

"First of all the good news. We thought that the brain scan was showing a tumour but I'm pleased to say the MRI scan has confirmed that this is **not** the case. If that would have been the case then we would have given you three months to live." He added.

His directness and execution of building up to the bad news made me feel as if the bad news wouldn't be so severe. The implementation of softening the blow was well rehearsed yet done with great attention to his 'patient's' feelings. Once again I felt the wings of an angel wrapping themselves around me; they belonged to Dr. Vaughan.

An atmosphere of respect filled the room as he continued to explain in great detail the severity of a brain tumour. He added that if indeed it had been a tumour, it was in a very delicate part of the brain and surgery would have been out of the question. Dr. Vaughan's approach had worked because my only thought at this time was '*I'm going to live!*'

"Now the bad news." He said, looking again at Ronnie, who continued to shuffle around in his chair.

"I'm afraid to say that all the tests now point to *Multiple Sclerosis*." He said in his gentle Scottish manner.

This was what I'd prepared myself for. Now confirmed by my consultant it struck home. Fear gripped me like a forest fire. I began to panic and sweat profusely. I glared at Dr. Vaughan and tried to listen but his recommendations for future treatment were muffled. I was in a complete daze.

"Are you OK" he said.

I nodded vacantly. Dr. Vaughan had a whole conversation with Ronnie and I do not remember any of it. Ronnie told me afterwards that although they couldn't say for sure what brings on MS they think there could be a link with me suffering from Shingles as a child. My mind reeled with the conversations I'd had with Stuart in hospital. The image of his wheelchair holding him prisoner was at the forefront of my mind. The terrifying reality was hard to take. I drove Ronnie back to his farmhouse where we had a cup of tea and told his wife Marion what he'd said.

As I drove home I thought about all the sacrifices I'd made to make a success of my business and to enjoy the finer things in life. I now had to face my biggest challenge by far. I felt as though I'd already climbed a mountain and just as I'd reached the summit there was another mountain to climb without rest. As I pulled onto the drive my parents were waiting for me.

"*I've got MS,*" I said wearily, "and I have got to go and tell Jennifer". My mother burst into tears.

I waited outside Jennifer's place of work to tell her the news. She appeared and her sweet smile greeted me. I smiled back at her but she instinctively knew I had bad news.

"Jen I've got MS." I said unintentionally abrupt.

She burst into tears; *My whole world had just caved in.*

Chapter 7

Facing an uncertain future

The first few weeks after seeing Dr. Vaughan were surreal. I had to tell everyone what the scan had revealed and the more I told the story to friends and customers alike, the more the reality struck home. Voices would echo, "What you've got MS!" Quite a lot of people had heard of MS but most didn't really know what it was and neither did I. The more I began to learn about the illness; the more disheartened I felt.

I was prescribed a tablet called Tegretol Retard to try and stop the vertigo attacks. In order to find a suitable dosage for me, Dr. Vaughan prescribed two hundred milligrams a day for the first week and then gradually increased the dosage until the attacks stabilised or stopped. Unfortunately these tablets caused headaches, nausea and exaggerated the Tinnitus. Weeks would come and go. My health didn't improve so I couldn't work.

Depression gnawed away at me and frustration played a big part in that. The sheer fact of not being in control was something that I couldn't deal with. Trying to gain control of an illness that differs from person to person has been virtually impossible but something any person with MS must deal with. I allowed myself to think that after diagnosis things would return to normal; I underestimated the power of Multiple Sclerosis.

At this particular time I didn't know that in order to conquer the effects of this illness, you first must learn to respect it. For the sake of Jennifer and my family I had to remain optimistic. This became an obsession. The attacks returned every three days. The side effects from Tegretol meant that this form of treatment was an unrealistic option.

On the 19th September 1990 I went along to Tameside General Hospital to have my 3-month consultation with Dr. Vaughan. His broad smile instilled a confidence in me even though it was short-lived. My account of the previous three months left him confused as to how he could ease my dilemma. He suggested a short course of Prednisolone to be taken to help me gain strength and weight. The dosage started with sixty milligrams a day for the first week and gradually reduced over 3 weeks. The steroids had some effect in reducing the attacks but they also gave me an unbelievable migraine.

My head was in absolute bits. I couldn't work full time and when I did I was so weak that I had to get the lads to do all the ladder work. My patience was non-existent and this caused me to eventually end up sacking Tiggy and employ a guy called Terry. I set off to work with Jimmy one Saturday morning and I felt tired but nothing too out of the ordinary; but five minutes into the journey that familiar dryness to my palate returned. I knew I didn't have long before the effects of the attack would render me helpless but I didn't panic too much at this stage. Past experience told me that I had around thirty minutes before my day came to an abrupt end. A mile further on and I was hit with a really violent attack.

I slowed down to try and concentrate on the road ahead, trying desperately to steer in a straight line. Jimmy couldn't drive and I knew my only chance of getting home quickly and salvaging the day's commitments was to reach Terry's. Another mile on and I had double vision. I was the first car in the queue at the traffic lights and as the cars filtered past me from each side, disorientation played games with me as I saw cars pass me by two by two, one on the road the other floating in thin air. As I pulled cautiously away from the lights the road seemed to be rotating anti-clockwise. To compensate for this I found myself tending to over steer to the right causing Jimmy to cry out,

"Ant, you're in the middle of the road."

I slowed down to a little over a crawl and tried to drive as close to the curb as I could, allowing the queue of cars behind me to overtake. I don't know what was going through Jimmy's mind but the next thing I remember was pulling up outside Terry's house. Jimmy reappeared with Terry and as the tinny thud of the van door slammed shut, Terry looked at me with bewilderment and said,

"Fuckin hell Ant"! Are you alright?"

I looked at him with piercing fear in my eyes and said,

"Tez; just get me home."

Deadly silence spoke volumes, *what can you say*? As we neared home I burst into tears, sobbing uncontrollably with frustration. All I wanted to do was to go to work with the lads but once more I was going to lose another valuable day. The torment I was going through spilled out in Terry's driving became it became more urgent and erratic. It was quite clear that Terry wanted to get me to my parent's house as soon as possible. Sobbing like a child in front of mates was highly embarrassing but at the same time it was comforting to know that my friends had the compassion to assist me in any way they could. Once I was in the familiar surroundings of home my fear faded. I had to concentrate on 'riding the storm'. The time span of the vertigo was so inconsistent that it was impossible to use a standard method of recovery. The only distraction was to simply focus on the television screen.

A little over a year had passed since this nightmare had begun and still I could see no end to the attacks. I also found myself in total dismay and asked the same old question, *Why me?* Can anyone answer that question? One of the most annoying things that happened was whenever I was out with Jennifer people would approach us and ask her if I was alright, as if I'd suddenly gone deaf! I felt like saying, "I've developed MS not become a vegetable!" My consultations with Dr. Vaughan were a repeat of previous meetings. His frustration at my predicament was clear and after a short period he said,

"I'm running out of options, I'm going to try you on Epanutin, which is commonly prescribed for Epilepsy, this may stop the attacks."

My morale was so low that if he'd told me to eat shit for a week to stop this nightmare, I'd have done it! *I was that desperate.*

Within weeks of taking Epanutin the attacks had stopped. I felt as though I'd finally got my life back. A permanent smile replaced the frustrated frown. Every working day was a joy and I could now continue with the quest that I'd set myself all those years ago. Dreams were beginning to transform themselves into reality.

Darren had started to work for me again with a view to him becoming a partner and expanding the business. Darren and I worked well together but our personalities are so alike that we frequently clashed. I was so relieved getting back to managing my business that I didn't realise that I was putting Darren under so much pressure. One morning Darren told me that he'd bumped into Gitts (Ian Gittins) the night before. He used to work for a competitor of mine and I knew he was reliable. Darren told me that he was looking for work. I had plenty of work so he started working part-time alongside me and Darren. I'd finally found an employee that had the same care and attention to customer demands as us. With things seemingly back to normal, Jennifer and I started to look for a house.

Christmas and New Year came and went and still I had no attacks. It was January '91 and I found a semi-detached, two-bedroom bungalow, tucked away in a quiet cul-de-sac; it was perfect. Easter was the time we moved into our new home. That was the proudest, happiest day of my life. From the living room window panoramic views of Manchester and the surrounding areas just added to its beauty. We soon settled in, the neighbours were great and everything seemed flawless.

With months of normality I became complacent of the MS and treated life with little regard for the future. I had a successful business, a woman I adored and a dream house.

Unfortunately an argument with Darren saw us parting ways and Gitts working for me full time. With him by my side I thought that I was 'bullet-proof'. Jennifer's 22nd birthday was imminent and everything was going our way. The MS was virtually in the background and so I decided that this would be a very special birthday for her. Jennifer's dream car was a Mini Cooper and Rover had started reproduction of this 60's classic in August 1990. A couple of weeks before Jennifer's birthday we were passing a Rover dealership and we stopped to have a look. There, in the showroom, was a gleaming black Mini Cooper. Jennifer expressed a wish that she'd love to own one; one day. With that very same 'bullet-proof' attitude I walked into the showroom the very next day and placed a deposit on it. I was to pick it up on her birthday.

On the morning of her birthday I gave her a card and a token birthday present to disguise my true intentions. We parted for work with the usual, "see you tonight." but knowing all along that I would see her again in her lunch hour. Around an hour before she finished for her lunch I went to her works car park and armed with the spare keys I drove her car away for the very last time.

I returned just five minutes before she would walk into the car park to go to her mother's house for lunch. I pulled up in the car and placed a big red ribbon around the roof before driving the car to her parking space. As I drove into the car park some of the lads she worked with were loading a wagon and recognised me. Panicking that they would 'blow the whistle', I raised my index finger to my lips and gestured a childish "Shush." I locked the car and hid at the back of the warehouse and patiently waited for her.

I didn't have to wait too long before she appeared. I watched as she made her way with total bewilderment toward the car that was parked in her spot. She cautiously walked around the car, eyeing up the bodywork and pondering why this car was there and hers wasn't. One of the lads shouted,

"I think it's yours!"

Jennifer seemed to focus all her attention to the red ribbon wrapped around the roof. I couldn't wait any longer; I marched toward her with purpose.

"Happy Birthday sweetheart."

"Have you hired it for the day?"

"No. It's yours," I said, "and there's the key."

As I looked into her fulfilled eyes it was worth every penny. Through thick and thin that girl was there encouraging and supporting me and this was my way of saying thanks for being there. She drove me back to work; her hands trembling each time she changed gear. As she pulled up at the side of the road, her radiance made me the proudest man that day. For the rest of the afternoon, I floated up my ladders.

By the end of August I visited my dentist because I was experiencing bleeding gums when brushing my teeth. This became very uncomfortable. My dentist explained to me that this was a side effect of the Epanutin. I had to go back to my doctor to address the problem. My doctor explained that the Epanutin was causing gum enlargement and that I would have to come off the tablets. This couldn't be done instantly - I had to be weaned off them. It was suggested that I try a tablet called Mysoline. In order to make the change in medication and reduce the possibility of side effects; I would start with a low dose of Mysoline (slowly to increase) and a regular dose of Epanutin (slowly to decrease).

That night I took the required dosage and within half an hour I was stumbling all over the place as if I was drunk! Jennifer had to undress me and put me to bed because I was totally off balance. Fear gripped me again because the symptoms were exactly the same as that first fearful day when this nightmare began. I just couldn't believe what was happening because I'd not had an attack for months and I'd sort of put the MS to the back of my mind. I suppose that was some sort of denial but it was just too hard to think about what lay in store if indeed the MS got a grip of me. My muscles were so weak that I couldn't even turn over in bed; I just lay there on my back waiting for the room to stop spinning. I eventually drifted off.

Jennifer and I awoke to the weather report on the radio alarm clock, informing its listeners that today would be sunny and dry - a window-cleaners dream. The birds could be heard squabbling above the sound of the radio and the sun's rays filtered through the thin curtain material. Jennifer asked me how I was feeling. I couldn't even lift my head from the pillow, the Sand Syndrome had returned.

Jennifer said that she wanted to stay at home with me but I convinced her to go to work because there was nothing she could do. She protested the whole time she got ready to leave but still I insisted she go to work. There was a knock at the door; it could only be one person, Gitts. I was suddenly swept over with the most amazing guilt because Friday was the busiest day of the week and I knew Gitts would have his work cut out trying to do it alone.

I was a prisoner in my own body once again but you never get used to it or accept it fully. It was with a sinking heart that I heard Gitts say to Jennifer as he entered the house,

"Oh no, not again."

Every nerve and sinew in my body cried out in despair as the tone in his voice sympathised with my plight but at the same time realising just what that day had in store. Lying face down with saliva dampening the pillow I called Gitts to join me in the bedroom because I thought that I owed him an apology. I felt his presence before I went on to say,

"I'm sorry Gitts I can't move."

"Don't worry Ant, I'll sort things out."

It was with those words that Gitts transformed himself from an employee to a friend that I needed so desperately. I was filled with relief, as I knew that I could rely on him. I heard the van's engine start and then fade away over the volume of the television and shortly afterwards Jennifer planted a gentle kiss on my forehead before leaving for work. The door closed and the house fell into a deadly silence, bringing a feeling of complete and utter isolation. Never in my whole life did I think for one minute that it would ever come to this. My body was so limp that I had the unenviable feeling of being set in quick drying cement. As I lay there a gentle breeze filtered through the opened window, ruffling the curtains like a flag. With the breeze came a calmness that filled the room, reiterated by bird song. The fragrance from the flowers intensified each time the breeze was strong enough to displace the curtain and this brought the tranquillity needed for me to fall into a deep sleep.

On the following day these symptoms had entirely disappeared much to my surprise. I then contemplated the future and the effects I would suffer at the 'hands' of Multiple Sclerosis. With such an unusual illness I knew I had an incredible fight yet to come. It was at this point that the seed of determination was sown. I simply couldn't give in (although I had no control whatsoever over these attacks), I knew that I had to fight it and try and make the best of the days I was ok.

With the side effects of Mysoline, it no longer seemed an option to transfer from the Epanutin. However, I couldn't use the Epanutin to control the attacks because of the problems I had with my gums bleeding when I brushed them. A solution had to be found quickly. In early September I returned to Dr. Travis's surgery to ask what could be done to combat the side effects from Epanutin; I was given no alternative but to try to come off them. I was overwhelmed with fear of a reoccurrence of attacks but it was necessary in order to avoid all my teeth falling out. Dr. Travis suggested I wean myself off the Epanutin slowly and after 6 weeks I was finally free of them.

To my disbelief I had no further attacks for 12 months! Life had returned to normal.

Chapter 8

The return of the nightmare

I had returned to running my business and had little time to do anything else. After the success of the late eighties came a recession; it shook the very foundations of my business. Every penny was now accountable for. With each new contract available came a steady stream of window cleaners ready and willing to do the work for next to nothing. Existing contracts were stretching payments from a thirty-day period to a ninety-day period; this caused major cash flow problems and a new headache for me to contend with. Although I was still managing to pay the mortgage and the wages, there was little over for Jennifer and I to enjoy. Throughout 1992, I was owed thousands of pounds with little chance of a cheque dropping on the 'welcome' mat. This period brought a new kind of stress and the return of the Tinnitus.

In June of 1992, Jacky was getting married to Catherine a paramedic he'd met. Not only did Jennifer and I receive an invitation but so did half a dozen of his other friends in England. I desperately wanted to go but with the cash flow as it was, it would have been an expensive trip. Jennifer was superb when it came to household finances; all the bills were paid promptly. When I suggested that we go to the wedding she rightly brought to my attention our cash flow problem. I didn't care about the bills I just wanted to be there for Jacky; after all he was like a brother to me. Jennifer refused to budge on the subject and a stubborn rift between us began to widen.

Because the Tinnitus had returned so did my fears, this brought back horrific memories and I began to look at life in a different light. The Tinnitus was wearing me down; my sleeping pattern was disturbed leaving me mentally fatigued with little patience. One of the most difficult problems to arise was trying to explain my feelings. There are simply no words to describe a nightmare that can't be awoken from.

When the weekend of the wedding arrived I sulked like a spoilt bastard. I gave Jennifer shear hell. It's one thing that I'm not very proud of but something that anger took care of and of course I was lashing out at the MS. I wasn't the easiest person to live with when the Tinnitus was in full swing.

A couple of weeks later Jennifer and I went to the cinema with some friends of ours. We bought our tickets and waited in the foyer for our film to start. There was no seating available so we made our way toward an empty space along the back wall of the complex. I was about to sit down when with absolutely no warning whatsoever, a violent vertigo attack struck and quickly reduced me to my knees. My pupils began to involuntary rotate, inducing a squeamish reaction from all those around me. I couldn't believe that this was happening all over again. The spinning sensation brought on by the vertigo was far more severe than with previous attacks; the only saving grace for me was that this attack only lasted around five minutes. *The nightmare had returned.*

On Monday morning I phoned to make an appointment to see Dr. Travis yet again. As usual I couldn't get an appointment until the following week due to his popularity.

Out of shear desperation I asked what time Dr. Travis finished his surgery,

"Four o'clock," said the receptionist with a confused and inquisitive tone of voice.

"OK, thanks".

The receptionist asked if I wanted to make an appointment but I declined saying that it didn't matter. I lied. I had every intention of seeing him. I was so desperate that I unethically took the situation into my own hands. I arrived at the surgery just before four o'clock, knowing full well that Dr. Travis never has the chance to finish work on time. I announced myself to the receptionist.

"I really need to see Dr. Travis, if you tell him that I'm here and I've suffered another attack I'm sure he'll see me." I said with despondency.

The receptionist phoned through and sure enough with the replacement of the handset the receptionist smiled,

"OK Mr. Kelly, down the corridor and..." she was in mid sentence when I rudely interrupted her,

"...to the right!" I said with humorous relief.

Within a few minutes of sitting down the receptionist appeared with a familiar brown envelope bulging with neatly folded paper. I guessed that they must have been my medical notes. It wasn't until I realised how many patients were there to see my doctor that I felt guilty about what I'd done. I could see no alternative than to revert to the 'miracle' of Epanutin despite the consequences.

Dr. Travis prescribed Epanutin again and asked me to return in 2 weeks to monitor any side effects. We decided that putting a stop to the vertigo attacks outweighed any side effects. Within the 2-week period between consultations with Dr. Travis, I was at the mercy of random attacks that came without warning. A new twist developed within this period when my hands and feet would involuntarily cramp up, rendering them useless. The first time this happened I was at the top of a ladder when my toes curled downwards and I was stuck clinging on for dear life. I began to question my safety and reverted to being grounded, shying away from the obvious dangers of climbing ladders. I spoke to our Daz and we agreed to put our differences aside and he'd start to work for me again.

As I left the doctor's surgery I thought that I would go and see how Darren and Gitts were getting on with the work. I don't know why but I ended up in the middle of the local indoor market. I felt claustrophobic and needed air so I made my way toward the exit.

I'd almost made it to the door but before I could get to the exit a vertigo attack knocked me off my feet and I fell to the floor. Treating the situation as if accidental, I tried to get my feet but the vertigo had hold of me. A woman stepped over me and as our eyes met she quickly turned away making me feel as if I looked drunk. I clung to the framework of a market stall using it as a staff in which to get to my feet. Then through the glass of the counter separating the customer from the stallholder, two horrified women peered at me whilst transfixed to their stools.

I desperately looked at them for a response but their look of disdain shocked me. I simply had to get out of there because I felt as though they were looking at me with an 'Is he on drugs?' accusation. I was now upright on my unsteady legs. Although the ground appeared to be like that of a rotating barrel, I stumbled toward the exit and out of the market.

I had to get to one of my customers so that they could fetch Gitts or our Daz. I ignored passers-by as they stared at me stumbling my way across town. Feeling embarrassed wasn't an option, I was ill and I just needed to get home.

I ended up at a shop where the two girls who worked there used to brew up for us when we were working in town. They were chatting as I got to the door, Sally's motherly instincts came with such spontaneity that she sat me on the staircase where I placed my head in my hands and desperately tried to hold back tears of frustration. She was fully aware of the history of this erratic illness but she wasn't prepared for what sat in front of her. Darren and Gitts appeared within minutes and once more the comfort of home was moments away.

It was incidents like this that brought home to me the true demolition caused by Multiple Sclerosis. I thought that my diminishing stamina was due in large part to the interrupted sleep pattern caused by Tinnitus but there was one particular incident that verified my worst fears. We went to a contract that needed the use of a three-sectioned ladder which was quite heavy. Since the onset of MS this had become increasingly strength sapping and because the contract was every two months, it became a good indicator as to how my strength and stamina was holding up. On the previous visit to the mill I had little difficulty in lifting the ladder once it was leant against the wall but on this occasion it sapped all my strength. Immediately after extending the ladder to its forty-foot summit I doubled over with my hands on my knees breathing as heavy as an athlete who'd just run a marathon. It was at this precise moment that Dr. Vaughan's comment echoed in my mind

"Window-cleaning, you'll have to give that job up."

I looked at the top of the forty-foot ladder. I breathed heavily as I placed one foot on the bottom rung and thought, *"Who are you to tell me that I can't do this job? I'll show you!"* I hesitated at the thought of having to climb to forty feet a dozen or so times. My legs were crying out to my brain *"NO!"* I slowly climbed the ladder but by the time I reached the top my legs felt as if they were on fire.

I had a strange sense of achievement when I reached the top and instinctively I reached down to my side to pull the applicator (used to soap the window) from its sleeve. It was much heavier than I remembered from the day before. All this made me realise that my strength and stamina was so important to me now. It was with the very same determination that I have fought many battles with this Invisible Stranger. Sometimes I've lost, but I've won more battles than I've been defeated. Winning a battle comes at a price; it may be that your legs fail to carry you for a couple of days but in all honesty it is reward enough to know that you're not giving in.

Each morning when I woke up my immediate thought was "can I move my legs?" I would lie in bed for a couple of minutes, timid, before allowing my brain to 'motor' my leg muscles. This would help me to evaluate whether or not my legs felt heavier or stiffer than the night before. As I anticipated the day ahead I carefully took my first few tentative steps towards the bathroom. This feeling of continuing weakness became an obsession and began to gnaw away at me like a cancer. With this preoccupation, my mind was in complete disarray. My mood swings were just about bearable to those around me.

On many occasions just eating took a great deal of energy and this almost always led to not being able to finish a meal. Swallowing became a problem and sometimes painful adding to the perplexities of living with MS. My appetite soon diminished and I wasn't getting enough energy and felt fatigued all the time. Along with the fatigue came impatience and severe mood swings. My job was now beginning to lose its appeal because without the energy to carry ladders in the same manner as before the job quickly changed from being a pleasure to being a physical nightmare. I knew that I couldn't relax I had to go on fighting and I was determined to do so.

I'd turned Jennifer's dream into a nightmare. No more was I the carefree, happy-go-lucky boy she fell in love with. I'd become a zombiefied shell of a man, far too preoccupied with Multiple Sclerosis that inevitably pushed her aside. I'd try to talk it through with her but just end up defeating the object. I knew she loved me but I don't think that she was *in love* with me. Our physical relationship had deteriorated so much so that on the rare occasions when sex was on offer, it was like making love to a ferry; roll on, roll off, pull my nightie down when you've finished. I became very disillusioned with life and questioned almost everything. All sense of rationality was drifting away. I'd walk into a room and completely forget why I'd gone in there in the first place. Once I poured Vimto over my food and poured Ketchup into a glass. It must have been hell for those around me because I was irritable, indecisive and depressed. My attendance at work was fast becoming erratic but still I was determined to continue until the bitter end.

One of the most comforting aspects of my job was that the majority of my customers became acquaintances; when contracts were due to be done I looked forward to exchanging pleasantries and keeping up to date with their lives. There was one particular contract I did on a daily basis and one of the girls' who worked there started to catch my eye. Amy was a ray of sunshine in the mornings for she was always smiling and very flirtatious with me. I'd always stopped and had a little chat with her but one morning she looked as if the whole weight of the world was upon her tiny shoulders. I asked her what was troubling her and she told me that her boyfriend was neglecting her and she wanted to finish the relationship but she was afraid of hurting his feelings. I told her about my situation and the stress I was under. This became a regular occurrence each time I saw her and we became firm friends easing each other's dilemmas and frustrations.

One morning I bumped into her just as she was going into work and before I knew it we were in a quiet spot kissing. The minute our lips locked together my body rushed with adrenalin and tingled with blood rushing uncontrollably to a particular part of my anatomy. It was over far too quickly and it took me a while to recompose myself and wait for the swelling to reduce; I let her disappear before I made my entrance into the building. When our eyes met we shared a shy smile and I knew there and then that I wanted more.

I was in a daze all morning and then it hit me; Jennifer. I couldn't remember the last time I'd kissed Jennifer in such a way and that evening I tried to kiss her in the same manner but to no avail, she simply wasn't interested. I lay awake into the early hours mulling over my life and how it had turned into a complete and utter shambles.

The next morning I just couldn't resist meeting Amy again for an action replay and this time the bitter sweet feeling made me feel like a man again after such a long absence. I felt totally alive.

The relationship with Amy took on a new dimension as we continued to flirt with each other and meet up from time to time. Our conversations were always filled with trepidation as to our respective partners' feelings but yet their lack of interest in keeping the relationship alive pushed the two us together. We didn't want to hurt our partners but if we continued to see each other away from the workplace it would be inevitable that it would quickly become a physical relationship.

We both continued with the charade but time was adding to the desires. As the weeks merged into months I desperately needed the comfort and feel of a woman who was in love with me and the physical aspects that go hand in hand. I certainly wasn't getting it from Jennifer and an opportunity arose that changed things forever. I met up with Amy on one of her days off and we ended up consummating our relationship. From that moment on we couldn't bear to be apart but we were still with our partners and I was heavy with guilt yet light with the feeling of being loved. It blew the M.S. into orbit and I once again tasted the testosterone of being a red blooded male.

The summer arrived and we both went on holiday with our partners' only to return and confess our love for one another. The strain on the relationship with Jennifer was coming to a head and to add weight to the situation Amy split up with her now very repentant boyfriend.

Once back from holiday the battle commenced between me and the MS. At this point MS was beginning to win the battle much to my despair. Darren and Gitts had been 'holding the fort' whilst I was away and on my return they had shown great compassion by allowing me the lighter tasks to conserve my energy. They too must have had time to reflect upon my present predicament. I fought vigorously for a month but this invisible stranger had me in its grip and once more extracted the energy from me like the juice of a grape in a winepress.

This was the start of a five-week stint at home and a massive bout of depression brought on by the feelings of inadequacy at not being able to 'bring home the bacon'. Absolutely no one truly knew how I felt. I received lots of sympathy but I didn't want sympathy. I wanted someone to understand the constant whirlwind of emotions. I couldn't explain the feelings of a man unable to work. I took on the task of painting the house and some days this was nigh impossible.

It's important to note that after discussion with other sufferers that I realised I was not alone. Quite often MS sufferer's can look or appear to be lazy or lethargic. This is because anti-bodies have to work overtime attacking the areas of damage to the nerve coating (myelin sheath). How one looks and feels are two entirely different entities. I would lay awake at night in immense pain looking at the streetlight defusing through the curtain thinking to myself 'I'm a man with everything and yet nothing at the same time!' This was particularly frustrating because all I could think about was that I was trapped inside my own body and I was losing my grip on normality. Amy became my escapism from the turmoil but I still went through a mesmerising process of change.

During the five weeks at home I'd finished painting the house but it was with great difficulty. I remember one day I painted the bathroom doorframe and spent the rest of the day on the sofa watching TV. The energy it took just doing this small task drained me and the pain was much more than just an ache. When Jennifer arrived home she asked me what I'd done that day but when I showed her that I'd only managed one small doorframe she said,

"Is that all you've done?" sarcastically.

She didn't realise what she'd said but it whipped me into a fit of verbal abuse. I was realising that she didn't understand my illness and that was partly my fault for not opening up. I felt let down and resentful but I didn't know how to share my problems, trying to protect Jennifer from my mental anguish had exploded in my face and it was I that ended up with egg on my face.

After five weeks of battling against constant pain and fatigue to paint the house, it was a great relief to return to work but the damage had been done. I could no longer climb ladders with the same vigour as before. Gitts was getting married in early October so I had to be able to cover the work while he was away.

I'd only been back at work a week when yet again I was unable to find the energy to even walk around the house unaided, leaving Darren and Gitts to cover for me once again. I could sense that I was coming to the end of the line, not only with my job but also with my relationship with Jennifer. I was now becoming very desperate as Gitts would be on honeymoon for a fortnight and I had to find somebody to cover me if I was unable to work. Darren instilled confidence in me as he assured me that he would take care of things and ask some of the other window cleaners to help him as and when the need arose.

Gitts had decided that he was going to hold his stag night in a hotel in the Lake District and when I told Jennifer she made it quite clear that she didn't want me to go. I really couldn't get my head around this obsessive behaviour. In many ways the poor girl didn't want me out of her sight longer than was necessary, for fear of my attacks coming in unfamiliar surroundings and her not being there for me. Strangely enough I could understand her anguish but I couldn't understand her motives, I was so desperate for some sort of normality. Jennifer was a girl who was very insecure and unfortunately my MS exacerbated this. The pre-occupation fuelled by weeks, months and now years of just how fragile the best laid plans can be, had us both losing sight of the reason we had been together in the first place; plus I was having an affair.

Multiple Sclerosis was a major factor towards our break-up but it wasn't entirely to blame. Yes, it's true that once you're suffering from a life changing illness your attitude to life alters and at a remarkably quicker pace to that of a partner. Words fail you as you try frantically to tell your partner what's going on in your head. I felt suffocated. On the one hand, I had Jennifer wrapping me in cotton wool and on the other, I had to face one of my worst nightmares: *not being able to do the job I loved.*

This was the final nail in the coffin. We decided to split up the week before Gitts and Rachel's wedding but for the sake of our friends we turned up at the church to show our happiness for them. Attending the wedding together exaggerated the split and brought us both to accept the inevitable with immense maturity. I was now free to pursue a future with Amy.

I was facing the most difficult part of my life as all my dreams over the last few years were slipping through my fingers like the rope on the losing side of a tug-of-war. All the fight had gone out of me. This 'invisible stranger' gloated at the sight of my life falling apart at the seams. The stress of breaking up with Jennifer and trying to run my business exaggerated the symptoms of the MS. I found it impossible to work with any form of regularity. The attacks came back again to haunt me with vigour. I couldn't plan anything because of the irregularity of the attacks. The vertigo would spin me right off my feet and I would try to fight the effects. Vertigo could come on in five minutes. Each attack would bring on the anguish of "I hope its quick" but even short attacks lingered like a toothache. It would always leave a bitter taste in the mouth as I came to realise that *it* was in control and not *me*.

Battle-scarred from these attacks I would dust myself down and try to do something; even trying to make a cup of tea was like running a marathon. I was also experiencing a tremendous amount of pain and discomfort and this has been the worst part of the MS; and something that I had no choice but to live with. I lost control of my bladder and frequent bed-wetting gave me the feeling of complete and utter inadequacy. I'd just turned twenty-nine but I felt like a senile old man.

By the end of November 1993, the battle to continue working was well and truly lost. However, I felt a strange relief at not having to go through the constant pain barrier of trying to remain on my feet all day. After a couple of weeks leading up to the Christmas rush, I became very frustrated at the thought of not being able to help the lads but I was powerless to do anything about it. Tinnitus had returned to such a degree that the left side of my face was numb. The 'test-card' noise was so loud, that each night I would use an earphone using music to try to mask the sound torturing me. I felt nauseous all the time and trying to eat anything was almost impossible.

I quickly lost about a stone in weight. Once more I became irritable, indecisive and had little concentration. My eyeballs started to flicker from side to side following the attacks and my hands started to swell. I seriously thought that most of these symptoms were due to the stress of splitting up with Jennifer and not being able to return to work but little did I know that a deep depression was on its way.

Christmas and the New Year came and went. I wasn't looking forward to it and I just wanted it over and done with. Jennifer and I continued to live in the same house but we led completely separate lives. I was so wrapped up in self-pity that most of the time I ignored her. I ignored the phone when it rang. Nothing or nobody can prepare you for the changes you have to face. It's up to the individual to come to terms with the problem before conquering it.

At the beginning of 1994, I wondered what the year would bring. Was I going to be able to return to work? I knew that it wouldn't be soon for I could hardly function around the house, never mind anything else. I really couldn't handle being at home all the time. Going into town via taxi just to put a cheque in the bank was like receiving a pass from prison. One morning I returned home and decided to wash the dishes from breakfast. I turned on the hi-fi and stood at the sink looking through the kitchen window at the light illuminating the living room of Trish and Dave's.

Trish would call for coffee sometimes and I thought I'd go to visit her as soon as I'd finished what I was doing. I was half way through doing the dishes when I felt a tightening in my throat causing me to gasp for air. The more I gasped for air the more light-headed I became creating the sensation that I was going to collapse.

I made my way to the front door to get some fresh air. One of my neighbour's sons was walking his dog, as he did most afternoons. He didn't notice me and I couldn't raise a murmur to let him know the stress I was experiencing. My anguish at not being able to call him over heightened my fear.

My breathing became more erratic causing my throat to rattle. Feeling dazed and unsteady I was drifting towards unconsciousness. Then the lights went out.

The next thing I knew I was lying face down on the driveway. My legs were uncomfortably raised and the edge of the doorstep cut into my skins. A throbbing sensation in my elbow confirmed where I'd broken my fall. I tried to get up but I was so dazed I could only manage to get onto my hands and knees. I was fighting to breathe. I raised my head and the cul-de-sac was deserted but the light in Trish's living room across the road was like a beacon.

The ground was still wet but I didn't have the slightest concern about getting wet I just had to reach Trish's door. I'd only crawled a few yards when I dropped to my elbows and continued. My right elbow was still burning from the fall but I had to reach that door.

As I was crawling down the drive my heavy breathing echoed off the cold tarmac. The wind was going straight through me and I was shaking uncontrollably. I reached the top of Trish's driveway and lifted my head trying to maintain the momentum to reach help.

I eventually found myself at the door and my whole body slumped to the ground. Instinctively my arm raised, my fist clenched and I knocked on the glass at the bottom of the door.

I'd got there with fight and determination and I was exhausted. As the door opened I only had the energy to whisper,

"Trish, get me an ambulance."

Trish bent over, placed her hands under my armpits and pulled me into her house. She asked me what had happened. I couldn't answer her. She had to use all her strength just to get me to the chair. I was unable to help her because my body was so limp. With blind panic she tried to get some sense out of me but I was cold, shaking and hyperventilating.

I fought for air and my eyes were now glazed. I looked Trish in the eyes and her startled expression chilled me like a horror movie. Two other neighbours appeared in the doorway. They had seen me crawling along the driveway and at first thought that I was playing a joke on Trish. When Alan and Marion had seen Trish struggling to pull me into the house they realised that something was wrong.

Marion held my hand and spoke to me in a calming manner whilst Trish phoned an ambulance. None of them knew what to do.

They could see the distress I was in and they all tried to put me at ease. I now realise what it must be like to be asthmatic. The feeling of your throat closing scares the hell out of you. I tried to calm myself down and breathe with some sort of regularity. My whole body was tingling and still I was shaking. My vision was blurring and a sense of tunnel vision was frightening. I was aware that I had to keep breathing with slower and longer breaths in order to try to stay conscious.

Trish was pacing the room not knowing what to do whilst we waited for the ambulance to arrive. She came to face me and asked for the phone number where Jennifer worked. This was a welcomed distraction but I searched around my head like a man sitting at a desk looking under a pile of paper's saying to himself "I know it's here somewhere".

When Jennifer arrived she'd seen this on numerous occasions before but still her expression was the same as the first time, as if we were no further forward. As she regained her composure she asked,

"Is it my fault?" her eyes heavy with self-reproach.

What went through that girl's mind God only knows but strangely enough I knew exactly what she meant by the question; for any form of stress would greatly exaggerate symptoms. I placed my hand upon hers and looked her in the eyes,

"No, I'll be okay."

I didn't want the others to pick up on this because the moment and the comment belonged to us.

An ambulance from Rochdale, some fifteen miles away had to be deployed to deal with my emergency. In the meantime Jennifer had handed me a plastic bag so I could breathe into it and the carbon monoxide from expelled air brought sensation back into my body.

It was forty minutes before the ambulance arrived.

When the ambulance men arrived they put me on oxygen straight away and I took large gulps, my body soon woke up. I was taken to casualty where I was kept on oxygen. My family followed Jennifer to the side room in which I was placed but the look on their faces made this yet another unwelcomed incident.

After examination I was allowed home and as Jennifer and I drove up the driveway, the intruder light lit up the side of the house; followed very quickly by lights in the neighbours' doorways. As I got out of the car, Trish and Dave stood side by side in their doorway,

"Are you alright, Ant.?" They shouted across the road.

I turned to face them,

"Ye, I couldn't be better. Check this out!"

With that I started doing star-jumps on the drive just to show them that this bastard MS wasn't going to get the better of me. The other neighbours were brilliant with their genuinely concerned offers of help. I felt surrounded by warmth. This was to be our last nightmare together.

Some weeks later Jennifer moved out.

Although this was inevitable, when it actually arrived it hit hard and once again those so-called words of wisdom I received from Stuart in hospital came back to haunt me. The final embrace before she walked through the door was of friends and not of lovers. A strange sense of relief filled the air as I could now relax and lick my wounds.

My head was in absolute bits and around this time I was put on Dothiapen (anti-depressants), because I would cry at insignificant events. Even an advert with the slightest hint of empathy could set me off.

With no return to work in sight and the fact that I couldn't get out during the day just exaggerated the feeling of inadequacy. Looking at four walls all day was no tonic for recovery. So I set about renewing my love for the hobby that I never seemed to find the time for whilst working.

My love of art would be the saving grace for me and to spend most of my time with a pencil in my hand gave me something else to concentrate on. I was still suffering from Tinnitus and found it increasingly more difficult to sleep at night, I would while away the darkened hours with a sketchbook and headphones for company.

Due to my irregular sleeping pattern I was very irritable and my concentration span was reduced to clumsy and irrational behaviour.

It was now almost six months since I had last worked. I woke one morning to realise that I'd met my soul mate, Amy - a person who accepted me 'warts and all'. It seemed that for the first time in my life I'd met someone who heard *exactly* what I was trying to say. Prior to this I felt as if I'd been speaking a foreign language since the nightmare began. It felt like spring all over again. A smile replaced my stony, worried expression. I began to grow stronger but unfortunately not strong enough to return to work. I felt completely comfortable around her and my baggage was neatly put away.

I was given a Disability Living Allowance form to fill in. Unfortunately I decided to complete these forms alone. When you're faced with personal questions your immediate reaction is to deny needing the help that your family and friends give you unconditionally. Almost every section asks the question "How many days a week do you need help with...?" How the hell can anyone with MS predict that? Nevertheless you must generalise your symptoms and ask for the help when you need it. The advice I needed was to get someone who knew what they were doing when filling in the forms in order to receive the maximum help available. Through no fault of my own I was now faced with having to try to live on the 'invalidity benefit' (as it was then). This was only a tenth of my previous earnings. I was notified that a doctor from the social security list would call at the house to assess my claim. When the doctor did call I was having a 'good day' and I saw him alone. This was a fatal mistake. A quarter of an hour after walking in through the door he was walking out. I sensed he'd refuse my application. I was right.

Chapter 9

A new beginning

On the 22nd May 1994, I was given the news that Jacky and Catherine had become parents and I was asked to be godfather for the second time to their beautiful little girl (who they named Laura) was a very welcomed distraction. I'd also started smoking Cannabis to help with the relentless pain I was experiencing. I'd heard stories of fellow sufferers using Cannabis to help relieve pain and when a doctor suggested that it just may be beneficial, I decided that drastic measures needed drastic action.

It worked within the first few weeks and I was experiencing relief from the pain and I was beginning to sleep for longer periods. My mobility started to come back and I was using my walking stick less.

I'd always had an adventurous spirit and this was nurtured and encouraged by Amy. She gave me a renewed zest for life. I'd always had an interest in hang-gliding, which led me to book a small course. Monday morning arrived and I was up with the larks! This was something I'd got out of the habit of. I used to love that fresh feeling first thing in the mornings.

The office of the flying school was in the heart of the Peak District - a beautiful place, whatever your interests. As I entered the office, my apprehension was soon dispelled when low and behold Melvin, a bloke I'd known for years was standing there with the same bemused expression as me. The safety talk that ensued was a prelude to the signing of a disclaimer form. Clearly stated on the form was "Do you have any form of disability?" I thought to myself, 'they'll never know because they'll never see anything'.

We were given directions to the launch site and a convoy of cars set off. As Melvin and I caught up with each other's news, the instructor promptly joined us in the car park with a glider strapped to the top of his car. There were four of us that had signed up for the course and we were given the task of carrying the glider and all the equipment to the top of the hill. When we reached the top of the hill the instructor demonstrated how to erect the glider before giving us another safety check. The instructor then turned to me and with a little smirk he said,

"Seeing as you're the smallest, do you want to go first?"

I didn't need asking twice and with that I put on the helmet and Melvin helped me into the harness. I was now about to fulfil an ambition I'd had for a long time. I stood under the glider and hooked the harness to the main frame before assuming the flying position to test the harness was working correctly.

As you lift the glider to waist height, adrenaline pumps through your veins like the fuel in an injection system and the breeze takes the weight of the glider. The moment had finally arrived! For the first time in years I felt really alive and living life to the full.

I was given the go-ahead to launch whenever I was ready. I waited momentarily for the breeze to lift the glider with the same ease as lifting a feather. As the breeze grew stronger the glider was trying to lift me into the skies, I knew it was time. I was totally focused on my landing target, then the breeze touched my face and I set off running as fast as I could. I wasn't aware of just how easy it is to take to the air; with half a dozen steps I was air-borne. I was still focused on the landing site and then it hit me, I was flying!

The adrenaline seemed to expel the illness that had plagued me for so long and suddenly I felt a million miles away from all my problems. The adrenaline rush was awesome as I felt the air holding the glider aloft and with the slightest push or pull of the bar the response from the glider was gracefully exhilarating. One thing that left a lasting impression on me was the way in which the glider gave me a feeling of control. It floats through the air with such ease, all I had to do was enjoy the ride and make slight correctional steering adjustments. As the glider eased through the air pockets my stomach tingled as if in a fast moving lift. The flight was over before I knew it and my first flight and landing was faultless.

As I stood to undo the safety clip I could hear the others applauding and shouting. As I reappeared from behind the glider I looked up the hill towards the others and raised my arms in triumph. Then the reality struck home as I realised that I had to walk up to the launch site. The gradient of the hill seemed to have doubled whilst in mid flight but luckily for me this was a beginner's glider and it came complete with wheels thus making transportation child's play.

I couldn't allow the instructor or the others to see me struggling to walk up the hill and fortunately the others came to help me for it would speed up their flight. I'll never forget this day for it was the first time (for what seemed an eternity) that I felt normal. Normal; in the sense that I totally blocked out my aches and pains and had a natural fatigue instead of the usual MS fatigue.

Melvin was up next and we were both buzzing from flying. At the end of the day we went to the nearest town to develop the film in his camera. We waited the hour in a pub and caught up on life and loves since we last met. This bloke was an extrovert and liked to be the centre of attention. His job (as an entertainer) suited him down to the ground and the stories he told me of his conquests of the assistants he employed made my toes curl.

That night, I re-lived every second of the flight with Amy and she hung on my every word with a broad smile. The weather had taken a turn for the worse and each day we would have to phone for the weather report to check the wind speeds.

As the week unfolded we had the opportunity to fly once more but this time we went to a different location. The scenery was breathtaking; just to have visited this place would have been enough. The hill levelled off after about a hundred meters and was peppered with thistle bushes. A line of trees restricted flight distance but still allowed enough space for a decent flight. We were landing the glider on its wheels and allowing our legs to drag along the ground to act as a brake, this proved rather stupid landing in a field of thistles.

On one particular flight (seeing as it was one of the hottest days of the year), I didn't wear any gloves and had a T-shirt and jeans on. I took off and within seconds I was about thirty feet in the air. My Instructor asked me to descend over the radio and on doing so the wind eased, reducing the flight length. As before I landed on the wheels but this time I went straight through the thistle bushes. I can't even begin to explain to you how that felt. The thorns instantly imbedded into my knuckles, my chest and my thighs, I'm just glad they didn't stick into my *you know what!* I sat on the hill pulling the thorns from my knuckles and anxiously awaited my turn to fly again.

When the glider was erected the left-hand wing tip was slightly bent causing the glider to lean in the same direction during and after takeoff; so we all had to compensate for this by leaning slightly to the right. It wasn't long before I was clipped into the glider once more and off I went. As I left the ground a gust of wind lifted the glider to around forty feet within seconds,

"Yahoo" I shouted at the top of my voice.

This was something that the instructor amused himself with, each time one of us took to the air. He made us shout this and if we didn't he would tug on the rope in order to make you descend.

The wind raced up the hillside lifting the glider above the thermal. The glider was now leaning precariously to the left and my flight pattern was heading away from our flight path. The instructor started screaming down the radio for me to lean to the right, which I did immediately. It takes a couple of seconds for the shift in body weight to take effect but due to the panic I didn't wait long enough and subsequently leaned to the left once more with devastating consequences. I plunged to the ground but luckily for me the wing tip of the glider hit the ground first. I was shaken but not stirred.

It was over in seconds but I now found myself grounded with the glider on its side. Only my pride was hurt as I tried to get to my feet but because I was strapped into the glider I could only place one foot on the ground. Just by chance the wind direction changed and blew the glider onto its belly allowing me to place both my feet on the ground. I stood up and undid the harness; one of the lads had reached me just as I appeared from behind the glider. I gave the others a wave to let them see that I was okay. At the launch site we could see that I'd snapped the wing bar rendering the glider unfit to fly, thus ending the day's flying for everyone and leaving me feeling really guilty.

We all had a few more flights after it was repaired but because of the poor weather conditions the course ran into weeks and I was going to France for a month to see my new god daughter. I never flew again after that.

At this point in my life I was doing exactly what I wanted to do. I was ecstatic about living life again and having a girlfriend that allowed me to be myself; she was very understanding and one hundred per cent behind me. On learning that I would be going on holiday for a month the majority of woman would kick off and give you grief about even contemplating leaving them for that amount of time; but not Amy. She understood that after everything I'd been through this was exactly what I needed. This woman had the ability to make me feel renewed of self worth and an awesome feeling of being wanted; I didn't want to let go of this incredible rush.

Laying eyes on Laura for the first time was quite emotional and a great distraction from the void left from the undertones of inadequacy. I'd only been there a couple of short days before we went to the south of France for three weeks of sun. We stayed in a family apartment just outside Cannes which turned out to be pretty much central to our tour guides plans. Jacky revelled in taking us all over the area allowing an insight into the cultural differences compared to the north.

Day trips indoctrinated me to the delights of the Cote D'Azur from St.Tropez to the majestic Monaco and Monte Carlo. Standing on the hairpin bend of the famous Grand Prix course looking down the hill into the mouth of the tunnel was surreal to say the least, but that's just how my life had manifested itself, burning legs as a reminder of the journey there; I'd suffered more than most but the reward was unequivocal.

The three weeks of sun replenished aching limbs but more importantly the zest for travel and adventure. The holiday gave me a well earned rest and set me up to face life without working.

Although it had been almost twelve long months since I'd worked, I'd still not accepted it mentally.

Being pre-occupied by the physical and mental exhaustion made me lose sight of the important things and I was returning home to a woman that had helped with the healing process.

Chapter 10
Deception

I returned from France with that butterfly feeling in my stomach, the kind one gets from a full-on relationship. I'd missed this girl's company so much. The illness was beginning to fade thanks largely to the way she made me feel. It was as though all the negatives were turning into positives. This angel had eased my suffering and rekindled the spark of life that was once there. The inadequacy that had become so dominant drifted away into the distance and self worth and contentment filled the air.

As the weeks passed we became inseparable. She was feeding my confidence thus creating defiance toward the MS and a blatant v-sign in its general direction. It just wasn't allowed to resurface although it kept on trying to rear its ugly head. Amy's support and conviction was enough at this point to halt any further disruptions to my ever increasing quality of life. I'd re-established contact with Melvin and we began to go out in a foursome enjoying life's pleasures and each other's company and we became socially intertwined as we continued to treat life as one big party.

At the end of September I received notification from the Disability Board that my application had been turned down on the grounds that I was considered (by law), not to be eligible for the benefit. It seemed that a fifteen minute visit from a doctor (who just happened to call on one of my good days) and the misleading information in the numerous forms I filled in was considered just. I was so relieved that I had my own business to fall back on for the only benefit that I was receiving was a tenth of what I was taking home before I was struck down with this inconsiderate illness. I had absolutely no help whatsoever with filling in these forms and now I felt as though the symptoms I was experiencing were said to be considered a figment of my imagination.

With the onset of Christmas excuses for partying came easily and along with the continuous drinking binges brought such fatigue that many of my symptoms were exaggerated. After the Christmas period I started to suffer terrible bladder problems; I felt as though I needed to empty my bladder all the time. This became a running joke amongst my friends and they would count how many times on a night out that I would go to the toilet. On one particular evening I was informed that I'd gone to the toilet seventeen times. The lad's new nickname for me was Slackbladder, which I found quite amusing because they knew that I'm a massive Blackadder fan.

It was really embarrassing having to stand at a urinal and not being able to pee. Men would come and go while you're still standing there but it was something that I had no control over. When I did manage to pee there wasn't enough to fill an eggcup! Bed-wetting became more frequent and it left me feeling totally dejected each time I woke Amy to change the sheets. My strength had begun to diminish and I had to go everywhere with a walking stick. I developed tremendous pain in my legs and lower back each time I tried to walk anywhere, making it difficult to do anything too strenuous. The only relief came from smoking Cannabis.

I began to notice Melvin's attention toward Amy; he fancied her and went out of his way to make sure she knew it. This forced me to question his motives and the seed of doubt was sown. Amy oozed flirtatiousness, which was her nature. I had begun to question whether or not she really could handle being involved with a partner that would in all probability become a burden on her young life and self doubt re-emerged its ugly head.

I felt that Melvin was constantly trying to gauge a reaction from their games of flirtation. He'd begun the process of trying to persuade Amy to help him out from time to time with his work. Amy was young and easily impressed by the bullshit Melvin told her. Amy eventually began to work with him and I was wracked with jealousy. Or was jealousy the wrong term? Insecurity was definitely present; I couldn't decipher between the two. I just kept replaying the conversations I'd had with Stuart in hospital and I hoped that I wouldn't end up in his situation; all bitter and twisted.

Those conversations began to haunt me even more because I was having problems with my erections. Many a night I couldn't obtain or maintain an erection and to add insult to injury I'd often piss the bed. Great! a bloke who can't get it up or hold his bladder.

One evening I told Amy how I was feeling and she listened intently. The following morning she asked me to marry her. I said yes quicker than Linford Christie could leave his blocks in a hundred-meter sprint. Amy made me feel as if the MS was an inconvenience and not a hindrance. I'd now found someone that I could completely open up to. I felt that I was finally home.

I walked around in a daze, feeling guilty about doubting Amy's loyalties and passed off the flirting as just that. I was ecstatic that not only were Amy and I to marry but that she was willing to except me with the possibility that I would probably never work again. This was a huge obstacle for me to overcome.

The more Amy worked with Melvin the deeper their relationship grew. I could sense her drifting closer to him. Was my insecurity pushing Amy away or was it inevitable that this would happen? In any case Melvin didn't help matters and I began to see through his charade. The work they were doing was exciting and a young girl can be soon impressed, so in all honesty why would she want to be burdened with all my problems? It's a major decision for anyone to take on and it was something that I constantly asked of Amy.

She always said that she loved me and I suppose that was enough for me. I originally thought that we were strong enough but neither of us expected the problems we now had to face. The mental aspect of the illness outweighed the physical limitations and I found this to be the hardest aspect to deal with. Not only did I feel inadequate beforehand but with the loss of my erections all self worth as a man disappeared. She seemed to forget that we'd had an affair to be together and I saw the same behaviour pattern in her. Deep down I just knew they were lovers and in a sense I deserved all I got.

My temper flared up on many occasions and I lashed out in frustration breaking crockery and ornaments as a strange sort of release valve. This unacceptable behaviour was all the excuse Amy needed to call it a day and turn to the "Chameleon" with the sympathetic ear. Amy dismissed my claims of diminished responsibility and coldly walked away from the dilemma that had taken some time to settle.

I was left a broken man. My whole world had collapsed around my ears and I reverted into myself. I refused to answer the phone or the door. I hid away and wallowed in unashamed self-pity.

I was gullible enough to think that this could never happen to me but Stuart's indiscriminate truth took me to the living hell all MS sufferer's fear; and like a naughty puppy I had my nose rubbed in it.

I'd been to see my doctor on numerous occasions to see what could be done about my bladder problem and before long an appointment for the urology clinic came through the post. On the afternoon of the tests I went along to the hospital not really knowing what to expect. My most imaginative nightmare couldn't have prepared me for this absolute torture. While I was in the waiting room a nurse sadistically filled me in on all the gory details of what I was about to endure. I tried to convince myself that she was an actress and Jeremy Beadle would walk into the room followed by a camera crew. But on entering the examination room I was greeted by four men with that 'if only you knew what's going to happen' expression on their faces. The doctor who would perform the torture smiled cautiously at me. We all knew before commencement that I was incontinent. The doctor callously requested that the computer technician remain in the room. I agreed.

I was asked to lie on the examination table and assume the foetal position. It took me right back to the very unpleasant rectal examination I'd had a couple of weeks before. My buttocks tensed tighter than a Camel's in a sandstorm. A tube was delicately pushed up my rectum and into my bladder and then unceremoniously taped to the cheeks of my arse to hold the tube in place. A further instruction came for me to lie on my back and this was completed with total fear as my eyes fell upon the tube that was going on a very dark journey down my modest manhood to its destination; my bladder. The doctor held my penis with his left hand and then rubbed anaesthetic gel around my 'Jap's eye'.

I froze as the doctor pushed the tube in millimetre by millimetre. The grip I had around his forearm tightened and he grimaced as the blood flow was drained from his left hand. I made sure that he knew just how much pain I was feeling. Then yes you've guessed it; this tube was also taped around my penis.

I was then informed that the tube in my rectum would feel a little cold, as water would be pumped through to the bladder to artificially inflate it. As the water was pumped through the tube, the cold exaggerated the urgency I now felt, as I wanted to urinate. I informed the doctor that I now needed to empty my bladder but he insisted that I try to hold on as long as possible in order for them to induce a correct reading from the computer.

When eventually I was allowed to sit up, my stomach seemed to swish around like that of a cartoon character. On rising to my feet a bucket was placed in-between my legs. I just opened the floodgates but nothing happened. As I looked down into the bucket, I swear in front of my very eyes my penis swelled like a doubled over hosepipe. With four men in the room I developed a 'shy willy'. The assistant and the male nurse in attendance found it amusing to turn the taps on full in the sink behind the computer technician and in all honesty the sound of the water flowing was enough to allow the floodgates to open.

My mind was convinced that the bladder was now expelling urine but I passed nothing for a couple of seconds quite like a delayed reaction. When I did start to pass water the pain was unbearable; it's probably the closest I'll get to the feeling of passing burning glass. This by far was the most unpleasant of all the diagnostic tests I've had to endure. The tube that was inserted had grazed the walls of my urethra and the urine had now turned this tube into a red-hot poker. I had to force myself to hold back tears of pain.

After all that, I then had to adopt the foetal position once more and as the tape was removed the hairs on my buttocks were being ripped out by the roots causing my eyes to water. I lay on my back once more and as the tape was removed from my penis the flesh was being stretched like that kids toy 'Stretch Armstrong'. Removing the tube was worse than when it was inserted. The pain was far greater than before.

The doctor thanked me for my patience and advised me that I'd receive the results in due course. I was led away to the changing room where I tried to get dressed but the pain wouldn't allow me to put my undies on so I slipped them into my coat pocket.

As I walked past the reception area the nurses said their goodbyes with a strange smirk, I thought it was because of the urodynamics examination so I left sharply. It wasn't until I delved inside my coat pocket for my car keys that I realised that my underpants were hanging out of my coat pocket.

Everything around me had run aground except for my business but it was heading for a coral reef and as the captain, I was ignoring the cries of Darren and Gitts in the 'crows nest'. Despondency had taken control. I saw Amy one morning and I asked how she was. She replied with a broad smile and the same radiance I'd seen before,

"I'm on top of the world".

I was gutted to think that she could be so calculatingly callous with my fragile feelings but this just confirmed to me that she was lost to me forever; and I now knew what it felt like to be on the receiving end of an affair, cast aside and forgotten.

I made my way home only to be met inside my four walls by contemplation. The events of the last five long years had left me physically and mentally exhausted. As I looked to the future, I solemnly couldn't see one for myself. I took consolation in the bottles of beer chilling in the fridge. As the effects of the alcohol and an empty stomach quickly took me to a stupor, thoughts of a *permanent* sleep seemed so inviting.

The future was frightening the hell out of me and I didn't think that I would ever be content again because of the way things had turned out. I was distraught at my relationship ending in such a fashion but above this I just couldn't face the desecration of my body and the rapid demise in my quality of life. I pulled another bottle of beer from the fridge and as I placed it on the worktop next to the sink, I stared at the array of tablets sitting on top of the bread bin. As I prised open the bottle top, all I could see was a way of easing the anguish.

I opened a jar of tablets and washed some of them down in an almost negligent manner, not giving a second thought as to my actions. I sat with tears rolling down my cheeks when there was a knock at the kitchen window, it was Barbara; a close friend of mine. As our eyes met her expression adopted a puzzled look.

As the latch on the door clicked to the open position Barbara barged her way into the hallway with urgent concern.

"What's the matter?" She said in a disgruntled tone.

I explained exactly what had happened while she poured the beer down the sink and made us both strong coffees. Her chastisement of the situation I'd taken myself to had a distinct sympathetic reprimand. Her motherly instincts came to the fore as the distress I was in needed immediate attention. I felt that fate had sent me a message.

Barbara's appearance was a pure fluke. She just happened to be passing and thought she would kill a little time before going to school to collect her daughter Stephanie. As Barbara handed me a cup of coffee there was a knock at the door. It was Trish, she'd seen Barbara's car on the drive and decided to call. Trish was a little under the weather and had taken the day off work. Once again fate had reiterated its intentions. The two of them set about trying to reassure me that things are never as bad as they seem and although at the time this was no consolation, with each coffee they insisted I drink, I began to see sense.

My judgement had been clouded by the events of the previous couple of months. I can't honestly say whether or not I'd have done anything stupid but all I wanted to do was sleep and I had no desire to face another day.

The weeks following this were difficult to cope with and afternoon drinking binges became a common occurrence for me to help mask the realities I had to face up to. I wasn't finished here with the stupidity. One evening after a night out with the lads, I'd finally allowed myself the luxury of smiling but when I opened the door all that changed as the house felt cold, empty and deafeningly quiet. It struck me with the silence of an arrow.

Anger at the situation I now found myself in wiped away the smile. I poured myself a glass of wine and switched on the TV for company but I wasn't really watching it. I just stared into space. I didn't remove my coat because I felt as cold as the wine I was drinking.

I drank the wine as if it was water. I took the wine from the fridge and grabbed the jar of sleeping tablets before returning to the sofa. I washed a handful of tablets down my gullet with the wine. I was lower than a snake's belly. The TV was beginning to annoy me by now and I decided to listen to some of my favourite tunes as I slipped away and gave in to the MS.

I tried to rise to my feet but I stumbled to my knees. The alcohol had accelerated the effects of the tablets. I was overcome with self-recrimination and the thought of my mother standing over my grave sobered me into a complex emotion of remorse and guilt at being so brazenly selfish.

I tried to reach for the phone because I'd seen Trish's light on and I knew she could help me. The phone was on the window sill, I couldn't reach that high but I could reach the one in the bedroom so I crawled into the bedroom, it was probably around one a.m.

Trish answered within a couple of rings. I told her that I'd accidentally taken a sleeping tablet with the wine and that I could no longer stand up. I lay on the bedroom floor face down. I heard her key in the latch and when Trish switched on the bedroom light, it illuminated my guilt.

Her concern seemed clear enough with the way in which she spoke, with a soft and quiet voice. I think deep down she knew the real reason behind my desperation. She had to undress me and once again she had to struggle to lift my limp body.

"Will you be alright now?" She enquired; unconvinced of any answer I'd give.

I didn't want to be left alone but I felt that I'd be asking too much if I asked more of her at such an hour. I smiled reassuringly trying to ease her distress and the remorse for my uncharacteristic actions, which kept me silent. She hesitated for a few seconds before turning toward the door and switching off the light. As she closed the door behind her, the house filled with an eerie calm. The tablets saved me from another frustrating restless night.

Chapter 11
Living in Limbo

After the madness that had taken me to the depths of despair, it was really difficult to deal with life itself. I just existed.

I didn't have any motivational direction whatsoever. I was still wallowing in unashamed self-pity following the break-up with Amy and this seemed to overshadow the problems I was having from the MS.

Amy had arranged to call one Saturday night and I'd told Paul and Carmolina that she would be calling. They asked me to phone them and let them know what happened. When she finally arrived she was cold, unapproachable and completely remorseless. We chatted for a short while before she made her excuses and left without any hope of reconciliation. I watched her drive away; I knew I'd never see her again. I felt betrayed, cast aside like something you've just stepped in. I phoned Paul and Carmolina almost immediately. The connection rang as I saw Trish walk across the road towards my driveway, then Paul said,

"Hello" In an expectant voice.

"Let me answer the door, Trish's here."

As Trish entered the hallway she asked me what she'd said. I told her that Paul was on the phone and I would tell them both at the same time. I picked up the phone,

"Paul"

"So Ant, tell me what happened."

I burst into tears, sobbing so much that I couldn't speak a word. I dropped the handset and placed my head in my hands. Trish grabbed the phone and told Paul that I was too upset to talk. It was at this point that my emotional baggage became just too heavy to carry and the bitterness overwhelmed me. Paul told Trish that he was going to come up to collect me and take me down to Evesham. If ever I needed a friend it was at this moment.

The thought of Paul having to drive for at least two hours at nine thirty on a Saturday night just to be with me, made me feel really guilty about my emotional weakness. Trish phoned David and asked him to join us both until Paul arrived. I was really embarrassed about them babysitting me but their un-phased attitude was a great relief. I didn't want to be alone. Trish and Dave made light of the situation: I didn't want to burden my friends with the need for more sympathy; I'd already burdened them too much.

Shortly after eleven thirty I heard a car pull onto the driveway. "It must be Paul," I thought. I couldn't get to the door quick enough. There he was standing in the doorway with a big grin on his face, curly hair blowing in the wind and larger than life. I just threw my arms around his neck. I was astounded that I had such good friends and the sheer fact that Paul had driven all the way from Evesham at a moment's notice humbled me to the point of shame. We set off the following morning after drinking into the early hours.

A few weeks later I went along to see Dr Travis because I was still experiencing a lot of pain. When I actually sat down in his office and he asked what he could do for me, I broke down. I couldn't really explain why. Circumstances had got the better of me and I think subconsciously that I was crying out for help. I knew this man would do his utmost to help me as he'd always tried to do in the past. Dr Travis suggested that maybe I would benefit from speaking to the surgery's counsellor. I didn't hesitate because I wanted to move forward so desperately.

It was really difficult to try to open up to a complete stranger. The first couple of sessions were spent trying to find a way of expressing my feelings but once I'd got used to the person sitting at the other side of the desk; I spilled my guts to him.

In a way, talking to a complete stranger helped me to re-evaluate a new mental approach to getting on with my life and not to dwell on the past. The counselling I received helped me to place everything into a 'mental filing cabinet'. It could be shut away and revisited at my command but it didn't quite work out like that. My biggest problem was that now that I couldn't work and my personal life had failed, I felt inadequate. I also learned in these sessions that my vulnerability was a form of mourning for the life I once had and that it would take some time to adapt to a new way of life.

I had to fill the void left and I turned to the comfort of art. I started going to a local art class and I found this to be very therapeutic.

In the November of 1995, a family friend from France came over to stay with me for two weeks to do some athletics training with my father. Sandor could only speak a few words of English so I had to accompany him quite a lot of the time to translate for him. This was a great distraction, so much so that for two days I'd forgotten to take all my medication. When I realised what I'd [not] done I decided to try to get through without taking any more tablets (the side effects were wearing me down). I just wanted to use the Cannabis to help relieve the pain. Luckily, I didn't suffer any major side effects much to the bemusement of Dr. Travis. This was a major turning point because the tablets had begun to rule my life. I felt really free and unrestrained. Using the Cannabis also enabled me to adopt a much-improved sleeping pattern. Although I never slept completely through the night, I enjoyed not having to lie awake night after night. My mental state improved a little but the daily battles still left their mark. I began to stabilise somewhat and my stamina started to improve leading to me leaving my walking stick at home.

In the spring of 1996, I bumped into an old school friend of mine whilst out fishing. Sean and I had some serious catching up to do and we carried it on in his local. Gaynor, his girlfriend was into yoga and I expressed a desire to give it a try because a friend of mine with MS told me of the benefits. I started to accompany Gaynor to the classes regularly and within a couple of months the strength in my muscles had improved tremendously, especially in my legs. For the last couple of years I'd always had difficulties climbing staircases and now, thanks largely to Marion (the yoga instructor) and her patience, I was able to tackle stairs with far less problems.

The summer came along and my mental state had improved slightly but I was barely able to manage my business with the same conviction and enthusiasm purely because I couldn't be hands on. I was losing interest and also the stress kept on flaring the symptoms of the MS. After much deliberation I decided that in order to move forward and live a less stressful life I would sell it and try to enjoy life more. I approached my brother Darren and asked him if he would be interested in taking over the business. He jumped at the chance and so the wheels were set in motion.

The business was easy to sell, it sold itself. But what was I going to do with the money? I thought long and hard about this and my conclusion to this dilemma was quite simply this: if by chance I did end up in a chair, I want to live with *Reflection not regret*. I decided that I would live for the day and worry about tomorrow when it came, that's a philosophy I wanted to stick to.

The driver's seat of a Porsche fitted like a glove. Since childhood I've dreamed that dream and the dream became a reality. The buzz I got from driving that car remained the same.

By November of 1996, I put the house on the market because Jennifer rightly felt it was time that her name was no longer on the mortgage. I applied to the Building Society to be sole mortgagee but I was refused because of my MS. I didn't tell them that I'd had to give up work. They wanted some sort of guarantor and although Ronnie offered to do it, I decided it wasn't worth all the stress.

I now had to think about what I would do and more importantly where I would live. My whole world was changing and it seemed that I had absolutely no control over it. Until the sale of the house I was now living in limbo.

Chapter 12

Making the most of it

It was December, winter had arrived. My cousin Grahame (who lives in South Africa), phoned to say that in four days time he would be in Windsor with the junior South African gymnastics team and would I like to go and see him. I jumped at the chance; I'd not seen him since he moved out there some seven years earlier.

Whilst we were having a meal on the first night, he said that they were going on to Hungary for a competition. I told Grahame that I had a friend who lived in Budapest and that I'd been there a year earlier and if I could get a flight I'd see him there. Sure enough I got a flight and I phoned him from Budapest saying that my friend Tibor would drive me to the gym the following day. The tone of his voice was unconvinced. He thought that I was winding him up.

As I walked into the gym the very next day the look of amazement on his face was something to savour. I witnessed my cousin nurturing raw talent into precise polished performers and I knew it wouldn't be too long before his name would become synonymous with South African gymnastics. That came two years later when his gymnast Simon Hutcheon won the first gold medal a South African gymnast had won in a major games at the Commonwealth Games in Kuala Lumpur. Grahame's parting words were an open invitation to go to Africa for a holiday as soon as I'd sold the house.

By the end of April of 1997, I'd sold the house to a young couple who showed the very same enthusiasm as Jennifer and I did back in January 1991. The date for transferring the keys was the 22nd June. All that was left for me to do now was to organise the mother of all parties.

The previous November I bought some fireworks that had been left over from bonfire night. I told everyone to be there at midnight to see them go off. On the day of the party (Saturday) my brothers came to help out with moving all the furniture and removing all the internal doors (except the bathroom of course), to make the house open plan so we could squeeze as many people in as possible. As eight o' clock drew nearer, I felt a massive twinge of sadness and fear at the same time; for in less than twenty-four hours I would be giving up my dream house and living in unfamiliar surroundings.

I simply had to put this behind me and concentrate on giving my friends a night to remember. My head was swirling but I put myself in party mode and made sure that those thoughts weren't revisited until the next day. I treated the party as my wake and all the friends who couldn't make it were there in spirit.

By ten o'clock everything was in full swing and with around a hundred people there the overspill onto the driveway and the garden, it got noisy. Before long the police turned up and told us to turn the music down. I was overwhelmed by the turnout and I was determined to join in as partygoer and not host, which removed all the anxiety of making sure everyone enjoyed themselves.

The evening was passing above and beyond all expectation and as I looked around the house it was full of laughter, warmth and happiness proving beyond any doubt that everyone had left all their problems at home. This gave me the dignity to leave the house with my head held high.

At the stroke of midnight (as promised), I began to empty the house and everyone congregated at the bottom of the driveway. Earlier that day I'd taken a plastic mop handle and removed the head to use as a launch pipe for the rockets. People asked with amusement whether or not I was planting a tree to live on when I left. They all became aware of its purpose when I appeared with a rocket the same height as me. People were still arriving as I lit the fuse paper of the first rocket. As I retreated, I looked around in every direction; everyone's eyes were firmly placed on the fireworks and anticipation of a night to remember. Whoosh, the sound of the rocket climbing into the darkness had every pair of eyes following its progress and waiting for the whole sky to light up. With each firework came a new delight and even I marvelled at the fireworks I'd managed to get my hands on. I'd gone out of my way to buy a Chinese firecracker for the grand finale; it must have been around four feet long and I'd unravelled it and hung it over the "for sale" board. With the grand finale poised, I heard a forceful male voice,

"Who's Mr. Kelly?" I looked over my shoulder and three policemen and a policewoman were walking towards the bottom of the driveway.

"I'm Mr. Kelly." Said my brother, Darren.

"No, I'm Mr. Kelly." Said my brother, Shaun.

"No, I'm Mr. Kelly." Said my friend, Dean.

"No, I'm Mrs. Kelly." Said Joanne, (Dean's girlfriend). None of them were telling lies because we all share the same surname. As you can imagine we were all really drunk by this time and this just aggravated the policeman's patience and with that,

"Right no more fireworks!" He said.

He was standing with his back toward the "for sale" board and the other police officers' were by now circling me. How they knew that I was *the* Mr. Kelly they wanted to speak to, God only knows. As the policeman was just about to read me the riot act, I noticed a shadow moving toward the firecracker with an outstretched arm. As the figure fell into the light I could see that it was Gary Derbyshire. He lit the fuse of the firecracker and all hell broke loose. Over a hundred people were in hysterics, something that definitely didn't go down well with the police. The policeman told me that he was going to arrest me for "a breach of the peace" but unfortunately for him he did this within earshot of Ronnie, who said,

"Are you going to arrest us all? Because if you're going to arrest Mr. Kelly, you'll have to arrest the lot of us. We're all causing a disturbance!"

The policeman tried in vain to quell Ronnie's outburst but he was humiliated when Ronnie quoted the section number and the contents as if reading from the law book. Ronnie is definitely no push over when it comes to legal matters and with Ronnie's continuing bombardment of rules and regulations the policeman had no alternative but to ask me to turn the music down and keep everyone inside.

From midnight to around four in the morning, everything was a blur but around that time Tommy my next door neighbour came to the party to have a farewell drink. I told him about the fantastic firework display that he'd missed and just at that moment I caught sight of an unused firework sitting innocently on the windowsill. I turned to him and said with an enormous grin,

"Tommy I've saved you one. Come on let's wake some neighbours up." I said.

There were still around twenty people at the party and we all went into the front garden. It was around 4.15am and it was beginning to get light. I placed the firework in the centre of the lawn with such mischief that I giggled like a silly schoolgirl. This thing had sixteen tubes taped together to form a square, I didn't know what it did.

I lit the fuse and made a hasty retreat and then I thought, "I hope this isn't too loud". The first tube burst into life; it was a screeching air bomb repeater with three repetitions per tube. Boy was it loud and there were fifteen more to go. But just like a tube of Pringles, once you pop you just can't stop. It was lit now and there was absolutely nothing I could do about it. I just doubled over laughing at our predicament; we were definitely going to upset somebody. As it happened we upset too many of my neighbours but it would be without doubt the last time I'd upset them, for later that day I would leave for good. A guy from up the road came over complaining about the noise and he squared up to our Darren. He just laughed at him and told him to chill out and have a beer. He stayed for over half an hour and had a good laugh with us all before bailing out back to his wife. By seven o'clock there were three of us left, me (of course), Darren and the party animal Max; first to arrive and last to leave.

I only slept for some four hours before being awoken by Trish who brought me a cup of tea. I now had just over six hours to clean up all the debris from the party. Trish and Darren helped me to clean the aftermath of the firecracker and clear up all the bottles and cans from both gardens and the driveway. Darren and Shaun were moving the rest of my things to my new home so I had to get organised.

I was going to live with Andy Harrison - a childhood friend of mine who offered me the spare room and the freedom of his house. We're very close friends so I knew that this move would work for the both of us. When Darren and Shaun started to clear the house they asked if I needed any help cleaning the house but I wanted to be alone, inside the cocoon that had witnessed so many emotions with me.

I needed to put ghosts to rest before stepping out into the big wide world. It seemed to be an immensely lonely couple of hours especially after the unconstrained happiness I'd felt only a few hours before. My head was bombarded with memories amassed from the last six years spent in this house and in a strange way I knew that I could now walk out of that door and move forward leaving it all behind me.

I stood by the window staring at the view with my head full of nothing. I became aware of somebody looking at me. I looked across to Trish's and she was stood at her window looking at me. She gestured "are you alright" with her typically gentle manner. I simply smiled and nodded. She knew what I was feeling at that time and her concern brought well-needed reassurance.

Before too long the new owners were knocking at the door; my heart missed a beat and I had a hot nervous flush at the thought of 'what happens now?' I thought I'd lost everything; my business, my house and even my right to work. How the hell do I move forward from this situation? As Mike and Joanne walked through the door they were beaming and I felt at ease. It took me right back to the time Jennifer and I first walked through that door as the then new owners. I was happy for them.

Once all the pleasantries were out of the way it was time for me to walk out of that door with my head held high and a smile to face a daunting uncertain future. During the last few months I'd decided that I was going to have fun until my money ran out and to hell with the circumstances. My car was full of things from the house and before I drove to Andy's and my new home, I had one last thing to do and that was to say a big thank-you to two truly exceptional neighbours and friends.

This wasn't a goodbye but a reluctant ex-neighbour's recognition for the unselfish support received throughout my darkest days. I'd cried on both their shoulders and laid my heart on the table like a deck of cards. They knew how difficult this was for me but still Trish was powerless in her attempt to hold back the tears that rolled down her cheeks, as the realisation that I would no longer be just across the road sank in. This was definitely the most difficult part of leaving and I laughed nervously as I climbed into my car.

I glanced over at the house I once owned and the living room light illuminated new life into it. One last smile for my friends before I drove off was all I could take. I was full of gratitude towards this woman because of what she'd done for me. I'd needed the reassurance that Trish had given me, for that I'm truly grateful. I rounded the corner and headed off to a new life which would surely be full of uncertainty and excitement at the same time.

Chapter 13
To the Victor the Spoils

Four days after moving in with Andy I was off to France to see my god daughter. I was taking Ronnie's son Nick, who was in-between jobs and we were set for a week of chilling and exploring.

The first day of our holiday was hectic; we'd driven through the night to catch the four a.m. ferry and with just a couple of hours sleep we headed south to Valenciennes to see Laura an hour and a half's drive. She was now three. I knocked at the door; a child could be heard screaming excitedly. The door swung open, I was greeted by Jacky's beaming smile,

"Hello my bruva". A tiny figure, an angel dressed in a doll's petticoat style dress pushed her way past her father's legs.

"Bonjour parrain" came from her lips.

My translation was immediate, 'Hello godfather'. I lifted her up and her arms wrapped around my neck like a python trying to squeeze the life out of me. I was cured for a few moments until the burning sensation in the legs and back reminded me she'd grown. I was home once more; my French family has always lavished me with unconditional love.

 We all sat around the table eating chocolates, drinking coffee and catching up with one another. I was full of my trip to Africa. All the while Laura never left my side. As always when I visit the Everaerdt household my time there is precious and ends far too quickly, within it seemed no time at all we were on the road and heading northwards back to Armentieres.

We'd been invited to dinner because some of my friends were going on holiday and this would be my only chance to visit them on this trip. Christian (uncle to the Dancette children), had just acquired a farmhouse complete with forty-five acres of land in the Dordogne region of France. Eight members of the family were leaving the next day for a three week holiday. As the evening progressed Christian insisted that Nick and I should go with them for a week or so and the others egged us on. The more beers they plied us with the more the invitation appealed to us and especially me. It had been an ambition on mine to drive to the south of France in a Porsche and now the opportunity was staring me in the face, the Dordogne beckoned.

We got up early the next morning and drove to see Laura again, I simply couldn't resist. By the time we got back to Armentieres I only had a couple of hours to sleep. We were setting off at eleven p.m.

I was absolutely knackered and it was raining when we set off and we had eight hours of driving to do. It was a nightmare trying to negotiate six lanes of traffic at half past one in the morning on the Paris ring road, especially in the rain. Half the journey was spent on single lane roads to avoid paying the tolls. It was a good job Nick had passed his test or I would have been stuffed. By the time we got to the farm I just wanted to sleep. The rain had followed us all night.

We arrived to a building site with puddles everywhere, the toilet and bathroom had no ceilings, just partitions. If you farted, everyone knew about it. We stood at the front door drinking tea then whispered to each other,

"What have we done?"

We just felt at that time as if we'd made a huge mistake taking up the invite, purely because of the state of the house and the fact that we all had to 'doss it'. After breakfast Nick and I decided to go and sleep for a few hours, we were sleeping in a caravan that was in the barn. I slept for the rest of the day. I got up as the sun was going down and Nick took me to explore the farm. It was absolute paradise and I just stood there and took it all in smiling to myself. Although I was tired and in pain, it didn't matter because I felt a million miles away from the life I'd just left. I was stood there in the middle of a wet Dordogne and all of a sudden it hit me, I was now as free as the birds I was watching.

We ended up staying there for eight days because I convinced Nick to stay an extra week. We didn't regret it because it was a privilege to see the Dordogne Valley through the eyes of the French. We had the privilege of visiting a vineyard owned by Christian's friend and had the opportunity to see the process from start to the obligatory wine tasting. Chateau's stood proud in the middle of rolling hills manicured with lines of vines. We visited the world famous 'Grotte de Lascaux', which translates to the caves of Lascaux. This is a pre-historic cave painting site deep within the hills of the Dordogne and an important archaeological site. It was discovered just after the Second World War, when heavy rainfall caused minor landslides in the area opening up an entrance to the cave. Four young lads were out walking their dog and it disappeared down a hole. The dog's owner followed the dog to rescue it but to his absolute amazement he discovered a cave littered with the most incredible array of cave painting ever known to man. The four young lads entered an Aladdin's cave full of facts and creation left by our ancestors. Absolutely overwhelmed by what they had just discovered they decided to make a pact to keep it secret amongst themselves. One of the lads just couldn't contain his excitement for a few days later he shared his secret with his father who went to the site with a local archaeologist which in turn led to mass hysteria in the archaeology world. Within no time at all, the entire place was alive with people desperate to witness for themselves this astonishing find. The cave paintings were amazing and I tried to imagine living back then without MS, Aids, Cancer, Disease or Illness but not even my imagination runs to that.

I fell in love with the place and in all honesty it's a place I could see myself living. I took Nick to see the war graves at the Somme on our way back north, which was quite poignant when you read the ages of the dead soldiers.

A couple of days with Laura and then it was time to go back home. On our last night one of Christian's sisters asked me if I would take her son back with us for a couple of weeks. I asked her how he would get back to France and she said he could get the train. When I pointed out that the lad was only twelve and she couldn't even contemplate him travelling through a foreign country on his own, his face resembled a slapped arse. He looked like he'd lost a quid and found a penny. I don't know why but I really felt as sad as he was and somehow I ended up offering to take him back.

Two weeks later I was taking Jerome back home and I ended up begging my god son's mother Belinda to take David with me. While I was away it was going to be David's ninth birthday. He'd hardly even been away from his mother overnight never mind for the weekend but in the end she agreed. This was a real magical moment for me and I was in my element.

Within two and a half weeks of leaving the house I'd been to France twice and more importantly been able to drive on both occasions.

Africa was on the horizon. It still hadn't hit home that would be taking this trip to South Africa. Each time I mentioned it, it was as though I was talking about somebody else. I'd only been at Andy's for a month and he'd hardly seen me at all. Africa was just around the corner and I was going to grab it, take it and enjoy every last minute for this was going to be the start of my new life and the new me.

The flight was the longest I'd undertaken and to relieve the boredom of the ten and a half hour journey I sketched, much to the amusement of the couple sat beside me. When it started to get light I stared at the gaps in the clouds just catching glimpses of the brown sun kissed landscape in sheer disbelief that I was flying over this massive continent. I didn't know what was in store but boy was I looking forward to it. As I closely monitored our position on the screen the realisation that I would soon be stepping on South African soil was becoming more apparent with each occasion the update reduced the landing time. The only way to comprehend the sheer size and scale of Africa is to fly over it during daylight, the landscape changes dramatically from region to region and you begin to feel the beauty of this dream destination.

The seat belt sign illuminated indicating that landing was imminent, I could now begin to appreciate that the dream was fast becoming a reality. The ground was brown with the effects of limited rain fall but still it was stunningly exquisite. Urban overspill indicated that the journey was nearly at an end. Waiting for me at the airport was Grahame and his son Mitch, who I'd only seen immortalised on photograph but he was much cuter than the picture portrayed.

I was in a bit of a daze as the reality hit me that I was now stood on African soil. I'd always dreamed of going to Africa, ever since I was a kid and used to watch Tarzan on TV. I was expecting the sun to shine but the moment I got out of the airport I had to take my coat and jumper off; there's no better feeling than it being warm enough to just wear a tee-shirt at ten-thirty in the morning. I thought to myself 'I can handle two and a half months of this'.

Driving down the motorway soon changed my perception of Africa being a third world country, for all the global corporates' displayed wealth in a condescending manner. On the surface it's anything but third world it's the infrastructure that remains third world. One of my first lasting impressions of South Africa is that at every traffic light you come to there's always two or three indigenous South Africans trying to sell their wares, anything from oranges through to top up cards for mobile phones.

As we exited the motorway and headed to Aunty Ruth's (my dad's sister), I was stunned to see every house peers over a six foot wall with a smug "you can't get me behind here". We turned left just after another global symbol, the Spar supermarket and headed up the hill. I was taking everything in just like a child in new surroundings; Grahame turned to me and said,

"This is it!" with a wry smile.

With that he pressed a button on the key fob and the electric gates invited us to enter the sanctuary. The house door opened and out came Aunty Ruth armed with her camera and a comment that always pisses me off,

"Oh, I thought it was our Harry for a minute".

Yes I'm afraid my dad would never have gotten away with maintenance payments where I'm concerned. Aunty Ruth and Uncle Ken's house blew me away; I thought I was in Spain for a minute in a luxury villa complete with swimming pool in the back garden. It came complete with a maid and a gardener, no wonder Huddersfield was left well behind. Next stop was Grahame and Jane's place that overlooks a valley; no electric gates here but the plot they own is fifteen hundred square meters, the house looked lost in the space provided for it. The first few days were spent catching up with the family and getting my bearings. One of the first purchase's I made was to invest in a field guide to the birds of South Africa. Once it was out of the bag that I was an ornithologist Grahame and Aunty Ruth told me about a Black Eagle's nest that's in a botanical gardens. Apparently it's the only one in South Africa that's within a residential area.

The next morning Grahame made bacon and eggs on toast a flask of tea and we were off for the morning armed with binoculars, telescope, camera and a video camera. Grahame kept laughing at me saying, "Spot the tourist". The pathway leads you through manicured gardens and lawns, a stark contrast to the dry brown landscape that surrounds this oasis. A snack bar caters for the dozens of visitors and it is at this point that the true beauty transforms into a breathtaking vision that is firmly locked in my memory and has become the screen saver on my computer. A burnt sienna rock face raises high above the tree tops and is split by a waterfall cascading into a rock pool at the foot of the hill.

A line of trees are segregated by the pathway that snakes its way to the waterfall. Once level with the trees you cross a small bridge over a stream and once over the bridge you're slapped in the face by what I can only describe as paradise. The lawns quietly creep up to the hillside with a few trees scattered in an erratic fashion. With its splendour and just to the left of the waterfall is a huge nest occupied by Africa's largest eagle. My telescope was fixed upon the nest as quickly as being given the nod from a horny woman with you on her list.

I could just make out an eagle chick and then as if right on queue one of the adult birds landed in the nest. Wildlife is such a wondrous thing and this was no exception, it was at this point that the dream became a reality and I relished every minute of it. Just by the rock pool another pathway winds its way up the mountainside to a viewing point, giving the viewer almost unequalled intimacy with the eagles. The view alone is spectacular enough to make the climb well worthwhile but to be able to look down into a nest that until now had only been accessible to me via a TV screen was priceless.

Our presence near the nest site brought both parents to investigate our unwelcomed intrusion and these majestic eagles flew within fifteen feet above our heads and landed together in one of their favourite trees that allows them to survey the whole valley and us. I was overwhelmed with these truly wild birds that decided to co-habit alongside the constant invasion of privacy. The female seemed to be scrutinizing us from around the rock face that conceals about a third of the nest. To just finish the experience off, the bacon and eggs on toast got devoured and in between my camera was clicking faster than a group of Japanese tourists.

At the other end of the gardens was a huge pond with a raised wooden walkway around the lower part of the park where you can obtain close views of nesting birds. Fan-tailed Cisticolas and Masked Weaver's made the garden a regular haunt for me. The icing on the cake was being in close proximity with Red-winged Starlings and Brown Hooded Kingfisher; I only had one thing to say to my cousin,

"When can we come back?"

The first Sunday of my holiday and a trip to a man made dam was organised, it's about a forty-five minute drive from Honeydew. Hartbeespoort Dam sits in the Magaliesberg mountain range at the confluence of the Crocodile and the Magalis rivers and is where the TV programme 'Wild at Heart' is filmed. The family had a caravan and a speed boat for the odd weekend's entertainment. The dam was built in 1923 for irrigation purposes and has a surface area of 20 million square metres. When we arrived Uncle Ken was busying himself with organising the bar-b-que and I couldn't wait to see this boat that I'd heard about.

On the site of the Hartbeespoort Sailing Club, the boats are locked up behind the clubhouse and a tractor is at your disposal complete with driver to take the boats to the dam and then back to the lock-up. We arranged for the tractor to bring the boat to the caravan so it could be cleaned before we got on the water; when the dust cover was removed this horny looking boat was hiding underneath. I cleaned that boat with almost the same enthusiasm as I had cleaning my Porsche, I couldn't wait to raise anchor and speed around the dam in it.

Once the boat was gleaming we launched directly from the trailer and with the slight breeze the boat rocked gently from side to side. Captain Grahame Fidler took command and as he pulled back the throttle we were all thrown back in our seats. The compartment at the front of the boat had a small hatch enabling me to stand up with just my shoulders and head peeping out of the bodywork. This was perfect for me to set up my tripod and watch the birds in the nature reserve that adjoins the bottom of the dam. The tripod was at eye level thus giving me the opportunity to get extremely close to the water birds frequenting the dam. Watching the Pied Kingfisher hovering like a Kestrel before disappearing beneath the water was magical. African Darters (a slim version of a Cormorant) sat with wings outstretched drying them in the sun and Bee Eaters flitted from perch to perch as they caught insects on the wing. Once we'd left the reserve Captain Fidler turned to me,

"Would you like to drive?"

"Oh, go on then". I replied.

My attempt at driving the boat was so amateurish that I resembled Captain Pugwash.

The way I felt only a couple of days into my holiday was as if the MS had gone, disappeared, I couldn't find it anywhere but I wasn't in the slightest bothered about finding it. My mind always seems to be in a contradictory state but the one thing Africa did for me was to appreciate my surroundings, the scenery, the wildlife and first and foremost living; here you live, whereas back home in my second class citizen state benefit culture, I just exist.

No self worth, robbed of my right to manipulate my future. It was on this very trip that I found wealth, not material wealth but mental wealth. It is true to say that if I'd have continued with my business I'd have certainly had all the trappings that go with it, after all I did have a good start and I was still in my mid twenties. Money brings its own problems but I think we could all safely say that we would live with that, I'm no different. Money should be used to experience life and travel, broadening one's perception and interpretation of the world we live in. How many times have you heard about someone close to retirement with shit loads of money and they're either too ill to do anything with it (and therefore its left to the kids who squander it on BMW's and the latest mobile phone every time the weather changes), or they die just before the check hits the carpet.

The family that I'd not seen for years were unpatronising towards me; a disposition I found extremely welcoming for MS was hardly mentioned and I got on with things allowing me to temporally forget the affliction unwillingly bestowed upon me. Although no matter how far you travel there's no getting away from your physical disability but mentally I was far more detached than the 6000 miles between home and what I now regard as sanctuary.

Around the time that Jane and Grahame moved to Jo'burg, one of my friends from school Gavin Jackson moved there with his girlfriend Louise. Gav had got a job with BMW so off they went but returned some years later when Louise got home sick. About a month later Griff the Spliff also moved out. Just before I set off on my adventure, Gav gave me the number of one of his and Griff's mates who could get in touch with Griff. Dave Botha was married to Julie who originally lived in Cheadle Hulme, Stockport, so I felt very comfortable about ringing up out of the blue. When I spoke to this guy within no time at all he'd invited me over for a braai (the term used in South Africa for a bar-b-que) and gave me the number where Griff worked. Griff didn't have a clue that I was in Jo'burg so I couldn't wait to phone him. I dialled the number and within four rings a voice answered,

"Hello, Quick Quick can I help you?" I thought I had the wrong number because Quick, Quick sounded as though it was a take-away.

"Err, can I speak to Steve Griffin please?" I said hesitantly. There was a pause and in the background I could clearly hear the noise of a car's engine, which indicated that I had indeed found the young lad from Ashton.

"Hello, Steve speaking".

"Ste, its Ant Kelly. How ya doin?"

"Ant, I don't believe it. How's it goin Bru?" His accent tainted.

I explained that I was there to visit my cousin and maybe we could get together for a beer. He suggested that he'd come and collect me that very night after he'd finished work, sounded good to me. Later that night a car's horn sounded at the gate, I went outside to greet the man who remained in my memory as a boy racer in his Peugeot 205.

We greeted each other with the widest of grins, the firmest of handshakes and a masculine embrace and then it was off to catch up and drink copious amounts of beer.

We drove to a pool hall where we were going to meet up with Griff's girlfriend. We talked about people back home and who did and who didn't have kids. I turned around and saw this vision of beauty with long dark hair, slim figure and the widest of smiles, before I could say anything Griff introduced the girl as Nikki his girlfriend. Nice one I thought Africa's been good to him.

While we were at the pool hall, there was an electrical storm, the likes I've never seen before. I went outside and stood under the canopy at the entrance to the pool hall armed only with a beer to watch this lightning storm illuminating up the skyline of Johannesburg. Next minute Griff came outside to see where I was, he told me that I shouldn't be outside on my own because I may get robbed. I did see a couple of blokes walking past but they just looked in my general direction and then ignored me, I didn't feel at all intimidated.

A popular attraction to visit is a place called Randburg Waterfront, which is a manmade lake surrounded by shops, bars, restaurants and all sorts of entertainment for all ages. It would become a place frequented regularly. On one Sunday we'd all been to watch Daley (my cousin Janet's son) play football and afterwards about ten of us went to the waterfront, firstly to eat and secondly to fulfil one of my lifetime ambitions, to do a bungee jump.

Once we were all strategically placed to see the bungee jump in its entirety I made my way to the office. I was weighed and asked if I wanted to have a waist harness or an ankle harness, I opted for the ankle harness because that's what bungee is all about. The crane like platform was about thirty meters high which was reached by a cage lift giving extended views overlooking the whole of the complex and the Johannesburg skyline. My dream was finally being realised as I patiently waited for instruction to make my way toward the jump site.

I had a mixture of feelings, yes I was nervous but not to the extent I imagined beforehand. The adrenalin rush was amazing, it made me feel alive and totally detached from the physical restraints I lived with daily. The long wait was almost at an end. My patience was rewarded when the two attendants ushered me forward to take the leap into my personal history book. It was strange that all the fears disappeared I just wanted to launch myself off the platform to show everyone watching that MS didn't have the power to quell my personal quest for victory. This was it, the moment had arrived.

"5, 4, 3, 2, 1, bungee". The attendants shouted.

The attendants' final word had hardly registered before I was propelling myself forward into a dive reflective of all those in the Tarzan films I'd watched as a kid. The air rushed past my ears creating a similar noise when you're stood at the top of a hill in a brisk wind. The water came up at me with break neck speed and just as you begin to doubt the bungee cords strength it pulls you back with the same velocity creating a renewed decent, each bounce shorter than the previous one. It was over before I knew it but that split second adrenalin rush was enough to fulfil my expectation of exactly what I'd imagined it to be. As I hung upside down slowly being lowered onto a platform I became overwhelmed with jubilance that I'd conquered yet another confinement of MS and to make it extra special, I was in South Africa. When my feet were on terra firma I wanted to do it all over again only this time from a greater height.

A few days later a phone call from my mother brought me news I was hoping not to hear. My mother's voice trembled, holding back tears as she told me that Mike had passed away. Mike Roden and his family have been family friends for over twenty years and my father had coached his son Paul. Paul trained with my dad for some five or six years and in that time he finished sixth in the 1980 World Cross Country Championships in New York.

When I set up business on my own at the tender age of twenty one, Mike would stand on the balcony at the back of his café (The Koffee Pot) with me and give me very sound advice on how to run a successful business. I can still to this day remember his words as though he'd only told me yesterday. I, as well as many others spent many a happy hour in his company, he was a true gentleman. When the inevitable does come around everyone always says of a person "He was a good bloke". In Mike Roden's case there are no words more truthful, he was a man I admired for his principles and his devotion to his family. I veraciously miss this man's wisdom; he was a friend who is often in my thoughts. To this day his wife Norma keeps his pipe next to his chair and when I'm in the room I find this very comforting for it's as though he's just popped out of the room for a moment.

This made me realise that I'd made the right decision to seize the day and I didn't want the hard work I'd done to go to waste. If the circumstances arose that I was in a wheelchair with pots of money in the bank, that wouldn't matter one bit if I couldn't enjoy it. I would much rather be able to sit there and tell people about the things I've done and seen. Africa was certainly opening my eyes to the real significance of life, relish each opportunity and grab it with both hands.

Two days later on Sunday the 31st of August 1997, we were awoken to the news that Princess Diana had died in the early hours of the morning in a car crash in Paris. As the day progressed more sketchy news of how the accident happened was being transmitted on two of the three terrestrial channels all day long, making the significance of the previous nights events all the more surrealistic. What made the incident even more comprehensible was the fact that not only were all the ex-brits phoning one another but the South Africans were also relaying their disbelief that this angel of humanity had been taken from us. We all felt robbed.

My sadness for Mike intensified with the realisation that no matter who you are, there's only one thing certain in life and that's death. These two deaths brought home to me that no one knows when it's your turn and this trip should be cherished. It took me a few days to muster up the courage to phone Norma to convey my condolences but after speaking to her I felt more at ease with the grief. The last time I saw Mike he was sat in his chair smoking his pipe and looking forward to getting the operation over and done with and returning to his beloved café. He looked in fair health and had no concerns that he wouldn't make a full recovery which makes his passing away even more painful.

It was after this weekend that Griff asked if I'd like to drive to Victoria Falls in

Zimbabwe with him because he'd been offered a job in Zambia helping to build a tourist campsite. I jumped at the chance with no regard for finding my own way back to Jo'burg. The thought was totally undoubting as I now had the chance to fulfil yet another dream of mine, to bungee jump off Victoria Falls Bridge (at the time the highest in the world). Death had breathed new life into me.

The very next weekend would see a turn in emotions for I was to attend the engagement of Griff and Nikki. The Saturday night arrived and Griff came to pick me up, it was awesome to be at his engagement six thousand miles from home. We went to Nikki's parents before going on to the restaurant where we were steadily joined by Griff and Nikki's friends. The party was in full swing and with the beers flowing and the music playing the party atmosphere over spilled into moving on to a club. With all the volunteers rounded up, allocations to cars were given out and the race was on to reach the club before this atmosphere fatigued. It was raining heavily that night and the roads were treacherous after being baked in the sun all day. I was with a guy who thought he was Mikka Hakennen and as he raced through the streets of Jo'burg I deliberated whether or not I would be joining Princess Diana, taken in the same way. The lightning was spectacular which took my mind off 'will this idiot make this corner or not?'

I've never been so scared in all my life. As soon as I entered the club I ordered a double brandy and coke to brandish my nerves. Through the window near the entrance I could see the lightning illuminating everything in sight, it only lasted a split second but I was drawn to it like a fly to an insect-o-cut. I took my drink outside and stood under the veranda staring across at the skyline patiently waiting for the next marvel nature had to offer. A tap on the shoulder woke me from my trance, it was Griff,

"Ant, what have I told you about standing outside bru?" With that we rejoined the other's and partied into the early hours.

Chapter 14

Victoria Falls

The following Friday morning I got up at six, put the kettle on and prepared for Griff to collect me for a six-thirty start to the greatest adventure of my life. Six-twenty eight displayed on the video and then headlights shone through the living room window that overlooks the driveway. It was Griff followed by the rising sun. Griff was in Nikki's car, we were to drive to Nikki's to collect Griff's four wheel drive Toyota Hilux. We got to Nikki's and the gates opened.

Nikki's dad had a Rottweiler with a mean streak that made me very vary of its movements. I'd been there the week before and it had tried to bite me. We drove into the driveway and I could see the dog appear from behind the garage. I sat in the car not wanting to be in close proximity to those ferocious jaws but Nikki beckoned me out of the car assuring me that it wouldn't go for me with her there. So cautiously I got out of the car watching the dog's every movement. Nikki said,

"Stroke him and say good morning".

I tentatively outstretched a clenched fist and then 'bang', my fist was buried in its jaws. I pulled my arm back with the speed of the lightning I'd seen the week before and simultaneously Griff wrestled with the dog's collar. When the dust settled my hand had a small flesh wound that was beginning to bleed. What a start to my adventure but nothing could arrest my voyage. Nikki's mum instantly became all motherly toward the sight of blood and took control of cleaning and plastering what in all honesty was a mere scratch. As soon as she'd finished my hand the kettle went on.

Nikki's emotions were building into a crescendo as the moment drew nearer to when she would have to say goodbye to her new fiancé as he set off to Zambia in an attempt to create a new future for them both. I felt as though I was intruding on a very personal and private moment but I've been in love and knew where they were coming from.

It was now time to go and as I was sitting in the passenger seat I remembered Griff as a youngster at Hartshead High school and then as an apprentice car mechanic at Quicks with Gav Jackson. I contemplated our expectations of life as school kids (and although my life was mapped out as a window-cleaner from an early age and Griff had an interest in mechanics), we couldn't have in our wildest dreams have imagined where we would be at this stage in our lives.

I watched intently as Griff and Nikki's final embrace had me fighting to hold back tears. It was too much for her as floods of tears made their way down her cheeks before being wiped away by her sleeve. Nikki's parents could only look on as innocent bystanders, for I could sense their anguish as they had no choice but to wait their turn to comfort the broken heart of their precious daughter. Griff and Nikki's father were being typically male chauvinistic by nervously smiling in a vain attempt to make light of the girls despondency. It simply wasn't cool for the men to cry.

It was time, the embrace finalised as Griff had to drive out of sight and be absent for god knows how long to find a future for him and his future wife. I felt awkward yet privileged to witness such a tender moment. Griff climbed into the driver's seat and wound down the window, leaning out for one final kiss before placing the gearbox into reverse. Nikki's father pressed the button on the remote control and the electric gates opened behind us. Apprehension wrapped itself around Nikki's aura as slowly the car moved from the security of her love and affection onto a journey with no immediate end which was fraught with danger. With the car now on the road the gate was ordered to close, Nikki stood behind it with uncontrollable anguish. She was joined by the dog wearing a smirk and giving me a "got you, you bastard" look of defiance. She watched us until we were out of sight. The highway is just around the corner from the house so we were soon joining the steady stream of traffic making its way to work and I'd embarked on a journey I'd never have thought possible.

I looked over at the illuminated green digital clock on the dashboard, it was seven thirty four. We headed north towards Martins Drift, the border control between South Africa and Botswana. Even in and around Jo'burg there's plenty of space but the further north you travel the more open and spectacular the scenery. Upon each horizon reached and crested a new and breathtaking landscape presented itself. This had been my first opportunity to travel around in Africa and to be heading to a destination I'd only dreamed of visiting was overwhelming. By around lunchtime we'd reached Martins Drift and already the excitement was like that of a first date.

The border crossing has a small building and within it a bank teller's style counter, where you're presented with the obligatory customs form to fill in. Under the section for your occupation, I entered Artist, I couldn't resist. A check of details and a payment and you're on your way to explore a new country with wildlife in abundance but not before the customs guard questioned my intentions for the visit, he wanted to know if I'd be working whilst in the country. I told him,

"Hell no bru I'm on holiday". With that we were on our way.

The countryside opened up to give you a sense of insignificance in the expanse of this incredibly diverse continent. The array of wildlife held me spellbound and speechless at the same time as I looked up each new species of bird in my reference book. Before too long we were coming across small groups of mud huts slightly set back from the road and with it typical images of African scenery were real, but unlike the TV screen I could touch it and smell it. My eyes scanned in every direction making mental notes for future extraction.

The small villages that we came across became further and further apart making the sheer size of the country more imaginable. One such gap between villages that I can remember was over 60km and walking at the side of the road (somewhere halfway between), was an African woman with a baby on her back wrapped in a blanket and carrying a parcel on her head that I definitely couldn't have lifted. I turned to Griff and made a comment about where she may be going and what she may be carrying in the middle of nowhere. She walked with purpose, something that I found completely baffling. I was now beginning to see Africa in its typically spellbinding raw natural beauty and it's become one of the most important experiences of placing life's simplifications into perspective. This woman didn't worry about the gas bill or going down to her local on a Friday night, so I asked myself who's the idiot?

As we drew nearer to Francistown (one of the larger towns in Botswana), we decided to buy petrol and something to eat. We had to go to the bank to change our Rands into Pula. Just as we entered the bank I noticed a small group of black youths scrutinizing the car and paying particular attention to our activities. There were a few people milling around the small shopping area so I didn't worry too much. As we came out of the bank we had to walk passed them to get to a fast food place three or four shops further down from the bank. The fast food joint did chicken so that's where we went, besides there was nothing else. With our backs to the entrance, we didn't notice a table being taken by the youths as we ordered our food. Griff and I sat at a table near the door trying not to make eye contact or antagonize them in any shape or form. We tried to ignore their attempts at intimidation but they wouldn't settle until they'd had their fun. Just before I'd finished eating Griff turned to me and said,

"Ant, wait here for me. Don't move. Don't look at them lot. I'll be back just now. Okay".

"Ye, okay mate no probs".

As Griff left the shop I could feel five or six pairs of eyes burning into the back of my head but I carried on eating trying desperately to use my body language to act undeterred. It seemed like an age but within a couple of minutes Griff reappeared wearing his denim jacket and then sat opposite me once again.

"Have you finished Ant?" I nodded.

His second sentence had more concern to his voice,

"Go to the car and don't look back until we're there, I'll be right behind you".

I did just that and I hardly raised my head until I was stood with my hand poised to open the passenger door handle. The indicators lit up and the familiar sound of the door locks unlocking was more than a relief. I jumped into the cocoon of safety and as I looked back in the direction of the shop, six youths stood outside leaning on the railing watching our every move. He just smiled pulled his gun from under his jacket,

"I showed them this baby. One of them passed a knife under the table so that's why I went back to the car".

I knew he had a gun but I'd never seen it, I didn't know whether to feel relieved or a renewed nervousness at seeing the gun. It all seemed like the Wild West but in all honesty we're not dealing with a western democracy so guns are an everyday occurrence in Africa. I was just relieved that the incident passed off uneventfully.

We made our way north towards the Xai Pans region of Botswana and the mountain region hid in the now darkening sky. We changed places and I drove for a while changing back minutes before we came across a checkpoint, where they check for potentially infected meat being transported north. A flash of Griff's I.D. card and his driving licence and the guard waved us through; he lifted the barrier and we continued into the darkness. Another stint in the driver's seat for me and within thirty minutes of taking over, we were once again confronted by a meat restriction point. Once again a guard in an army uniform stood in the middle of the road with one hand outstretched gesturing for us to stop. As we approached I noticed the barrel of a rifle reflecting in the headlights above his right shoulder. As I pulled up, I wound the window down,

"Can I see your documents please" Said the guard. I passed him my passport and he examined it with the aid of his torch.

"Where is your driving licence". He added.

"I haven't got it; I've left it in Jo'burg".

"Please step out of the car". I did as he asked.

At the side of the road was a small hut with the door ajar, the light illuminated the bars of a cell. The guard was going off his head and I now found myself arrested for having no licence and no insurance. All that was going through my mind was images of my mates back home laughing at me getting arrested. The rifle left the guard's shoulder and pointed in my direction, I was now ushered towards the hut. At the side of the hut sat a woman with a child asleep in her arms looking in our direction without paying too much attention to what was going on. The situation had now changed from a frivolous inconvenience to a surreal nightmare but fortunately for me I was travelling with a man who has travelled extensively through Africa and knew that a packet of cigarettes, a couple of cold beers and that mornings newspaper would end in a telling off and sent on our way provided we change places in the driving seat. I made my apologies and we were on our way getting increasingly closer to our destination.

Soon after leaving the checkpoint the road changed from what was a poorly tarmaced road barely wide enough for two cars to a dirt track that was carved through a mixture of shrub and woodland, making driving hazardous. Although the full beam of the cars lights lit the route admirably, the owl that hit the windscreen came as a complete shock and left us silent for a while. We were heading north for the Pandamatenga border crossing which would take us into Zimbabwe when suddenly out of the bush appeared my first truly wild elephant. We were travelling along at around fifty miles an hour but the elephant wasn't fazed by our presents it continued to walk into our path and across the track. Griff jumped on the brakes and a dust cloud temporarily hid the elephant from view. As the dust cloud settled the headlights strained to illuminate this magnificent beast. Gravity cleared our obscured view to reveal the elephant's lackadaisical stroll, a glance in our direction indicated that the elephant was totally undeterred by our near fatal collision and it just pushed its way through the undergrowth snapping branches with consummate ease. My delight at seeing this magnificent African creature seemed to arrive briskly although we'd been on the road for some fourteen or fifteen hours. My delight was shared equally by Griff (who having this pleasure on many occasions), revelled in the delight of this majestic member of the big five.

Friday was almost at a close but it had been a day full of exceptional encounters, especially from a wildlife point of view. When eventually we arrived at the border point it was shut so we decided to pitch camp about a hundred meters from the crossing and be the first through the following morning. We unfolded the roof tent, climbed into our sleeping bags and slept. The wind had picked up that night and with the tent perched on the roof of the car it was now swaying from side to side. I was woken in the early hours to the unmistakable sound of shoes scraping on the aluminium steps that allowed access to the front of the tent from the bull bars followed by the noise of a zip. In a semi-conscious state I turned my head to face the front of the tent, a shadow blocked the moon's reflective light and I realised that the shadow was the figure of another human. My heart missed a beat,

"Griff there's someone outside". I said as I shook him vigorously.

"What".

I repeated the sentence only this time with a more nervous tone to my voice. Griff sat bolt upright,

"I've got a gun pointed straight at you and I'm not afraid to use it". He said.

With that the shadow disappeared and all we could hear was the sound of rustling bushes. I shit myself but Griff just lay back down pulled the sleeping bag over his shoulder, rolled over and said,

"It's alright Ant, you can go back to sleep, they won't come back".

I didn't sleep another wink all night; I just lay there motionless listening to the wild boar's grunts interrupting the wind whistling through the trees. As soon as it became light I lay on my front and unzipped the rear of the tent and rolled a spliff. I lay there watching the sun coming up whilst Griff snored beside me. Birds busied themselves flitting from bush to bush as I felt contentment at being in such a stunning place. A border guard walked past with a rifle tucked under his left arm,

"Good morning Sir".

"How's it?" I replied whilst nudging Griff in order for him to check him out.

We heard a gunshot interrupt the bird song followed by a brief silence before the singing resumed. Moments later the guard appeared some fifty meters away excitedly hurrying back to the border point carrying a young wild boar by its back legs. As he passed he just smiled and we just nodded nonchalantly. It was now around a quarter to seven and we decided to pack up the tent and make our way over the border. The sign that welcomed us at the crossing read 'opening times eight am till six pm' we were an hour early and was made to wait in the car park. A young boy of about ten appeared at Griff's window wearing little more than a smile. Griff wound down his window,

"How's it?" He said welcoming the boy to feel at ease.

"Do you like Manchester United?" this boy's English was well within comprehension. I interrupted Griff,

"I do, do you?"

The boy just nodded before adding,

"Have you got a shirt for me?"

Griff took control,

"No we haven't but I've got some gum".

The boy's eyes lit up as Griff rummaged around in the glove box, he gave the impression that it could have been his birthday and we were well and truly humbled by this youngster. The boy's father appeared in his uniform at around five to eight and handed us both a piece of paper that read,

'Mr Suchabody (whose name I couldn't pronounce even if I could remember it) is retiring at the end of the month and all donations for his party will be gratefully received'

I smiled thinking of how many people they'd tried this on with. Griff asked where the named man was but the game was up when the guard told us that it was his day off. Scam busted but the guard wasn't finished there, he then wanted to search the car and opened the rear door so he could see what was in the cooler box. This was his domain and he wanted us to comply reversing the dominance role. Griff not wanting him to find the bag of Swazi Gold and running the risk of being arrested gave him six cold beers for the so-called party. That was all it took to be ushered through the customs gate without a hitch. The three guards on duty were more than friendly and were delighted when Griff gave them a cheap black pen. The boy's father opened the gate with a huge smile and waved us through; we reciprocated. The track carved its way between the trees and it reminded me of the enclosures at a small wildlife park.

A similar scenario greeted us at the Zimbabwe crossing but twenty cigarettes and a packet of chewing gum gave us an uncomplicated border crossing. We were now in Zimbabwe and another stamp adorned my passport. It had taken twenty-four hours and already the adventure was fast becoming memorable. The road that leads from the border camp was tarmaced for a couple of hundred yards before becoming yet another dirt track; we were now north of the Hwange National Park. The wind was still as strong as the night before and we could see vultures in the distance. We'd been driving for about half an hour when to our left the trees were littered with what we guessed to be about two hundred and fifty Whitebacked and Lappetfaced Vultures. The amount of vultures in the vicinity suggested only one thing 'a kill'.

"Shall we go and have a look Ant?"

Before I could think about the implications of my actions I'd left the safety of the car armed with only my camera. I was like a man possessed trampling through the bush like a guide. I was on a mission and when I eventually looked back Griff was some thirty yards behind me videoing the vultures and 'Ant the tracker'. The ground near the car had been burnt leaving only dead trees in its path, this stretched for about sixty yards before the grass became waist height. As we got closer to the vultures they started to disperse to higher and safer vantage points quickly followed by the birds on the ground. The wind was testing their ability to fly to the full and distracting me from potential danger. Griff was only yards behind me when he spotted the dead Zebra lying under a tree with its stomach ripped open. This was an incredible sight especially without my armchair, you soon get caught up in the buzz of the adrenalin. This was the defining moment that my childhood dream actually introduced itself as reality, I was in my element.

"Just keep your eyes open, I think this is fresh kill, I don't think I wanna hang around much longer. My hearts pounding". Said Griff, knowing that his gun was firmly tucked under his driving seat.

"Ye, mine too".

I'd never felt so alive, the adrenalin was pumping life into my weak limbs. We didn't waste any time getting back to the safety of the car. It was only when we got into the car that it really hit us just what could have happened. As we celebrated by pulling the ring of a cold can of a Black Label lager, I turned to Griff and said,

"Cheers mate, that was a top buzz".

"Crazy bastards aren't we?"

I had to agree.

We decided to return to the kill only this time with the security of the four wheel drive. As we parked a comfortable distance from the Zebra, from absolutely nowhere a beige open top Jeep pulled up complete with Japanese tourists and their khaki clad guide. He parked up beside us,

"Have the lions been back yet?"

"No" Griff replied.

"One of the other guides was here last night, there were two lionesses here. I'll come back in a bit. Good luck". With that they disappeared into the bush. I turned to my bewildered friend,

"Fuckin ell mate, what have we just done?"

We sat there motionless and silent until we'd finished our beer contemplating our near fatal mistake. This was the adventure that I'd longed for and when it bestowed itself upon me it was greater than any childhood fantasy.

After a couple of hours of following days old tyre tracks and feasting upon the abundance of animals we came to a tarmac road that ran parallel across our path, we turned left, the noise of rubber on tarmac took us straight back to urban sprawl. A sign re-established that by telling us that Victoria Falls Airport was only twenty two kilometres away. I was almost there.

We passed the airport and the population increased, these were the first people we'd seen since the Japanese tourists some three hours earlier. At the railway crossing crowds mingled and some distance away a cloud sat on the ground. The cloud is created by the spray from the waterfall and even before you see the scale of the falls you simply know it's going to be huge. A train delayed us momentarily; it was old and added to the charisma and charm of the ever smiling population. People waited patiently for the train to pass and time stood still for a few moments. The crossing cleared and everyone resumed their lives. A cluster of buildings advertised the fact that we had now reached the end of our journey but not the end of the adventure. A Wimpy stood proud on the corner of the crossroads and invited us for lunch. We sat at a table outside overlooking the hustle and bustle of the indigenous population desperately trying to scratch a living from the many tourists that seemed to have taken over the whole place. The cloud was hypnotic; I simply had to see for myself the grandeur that lured Dr. Livingstone.

We booked into the Victoria Falls camp site which consisted of hut type chalets and spare ground for tents. With a place to camp secured we drove to the entrance to the falls. Ten Zimbabwean dollars granted access to what I can only describe as mind blowing natural beauty. The pathway winds its way around several viewing points, each as spectacular as the previous one. The first viewpoint is at the side of the mighty Zambezi River, constantly overlooked by the statue of Dr. Livingstone. This first impression is everlasting as the Zambezi flows into the canyon, a vain of Africa and a lifeline for millenniums. The sheer volume of water is overwhelming.

At the lowest viewpoint is the permanent rainbow that sits in the spray. There's a place where you can stand right on the edge and look into this hundred and forty meter canyon, it's at this point that the bridge connecting Zimbabwe with Zambia is in full view. The arc of the bridge is home to the bungee jumping platform from which my dream would come true. The bungee rope hung seductively enticing me to sample its delights. It would have been awesome to have made this my first bungee jump but I didn't know that I would be standing here. I remember seeing the jump on television some years before and thinking how I'd love to do it not thinking for a second that I would ever get there but life's full of surprises. You can't actually get to the bridge from the falls; you have to walk round by the road so Griff suggested that we go to the bridge on the following day which was Sunday.

We made our way back to camp and lit a bar-b-que and an Australian couple called Greg and Sue introduced themselves and joined us. They asked if we would join them in the Explorers bar where all the backpackers congregate. The campsite is situated next to a row of shops that stops at the Wimpy, there's a pathway that acts as a short cut to absolute mayhem. During the day this place is busy but when night falls people appear from every nook and cranny. The shops consisted of the obligatory souvenir shop complete with caps and t-shirts with Victoria Falls bungee jump written on them, an adventure centre and a foreign exchange.

The minute you step onto the pavement you become fair game for all the beggars, con men and muggers; you've got to have your wits about you. The road is only lit where building stand so extreme caution is needed. We were approached by a bloke who asked if we wanted to change money, he offered unbelievable rates but there was a catch. The economy was in disarray at the time and the Zimbabweans would do anything to get their hands on Rands, Dollars and even Sterling. This guy wanted our money up front and wanted to do this in the unlit alleyway, away from prying eyes, Griff told him where to go. We'd only walked a couple of yards before a voice said,

"Excuse me lads". It was a white man in his mid forties.

"My name's David, I'm with the undercover police, be careful who you do business with. Ok lads". With that he disappeared into the shadows.

In-between the souvenir shop and the adventure centre is the entrance to an Italian restaurant and the Explorers bar which are situated on the first floor. The bar was rocking, it reminded me of Christmas because it had the same atmosphere; everyone was talking to everyone else, laughing and drinking. Greg and Sue introduced us to another Australian couple, there was more Australians here than Zimbabweans. We carried on the party mode back at camp, beers flowed and so did the rain but that didn't dampen our spirits, Griff simply pulled out the awning from the side of the car and we all huddled underneath it and cooked sausage on the bar-b-que. Along the fence line was an electricity box that would arc each time the water hit it and the sparks made a spectacular impromptu fireworks display.

When I woke up on the Sunday morning I knew I'd done too much walking the day before because my legs and lower back felt like I'd just ran a marathon; the journey was taking its toll but I was having such a buzz that I ignored the signs and continued to enjoy every minute of my escapade. After we'd organised ourselves I put a rucksack on my back and we headed off to fulfil my dream. The bridge is quite a walk from the campsite but the winter warmth pointed my legs in that general direction. A steady stream of people lined each side of the road and the faces of those returning from the direction of the bridge where full of life, my pace quickened.

The road snakes its way towards the bridge, it's flanked on both sides by trees and a herd of Buffalo about twenty strong lay idle in the sun. With no fences of any description this part of the walk was fraught with danger and everyone observed the herd particularly the males; this for me is what being in Africa is all about, the danger adds to the excitement. The border crossing in-between Zimbabwe and Zambia is just a formality and you can stay in no-man's land all day if you wish. The bridge was now in sight; the buzz I felt was enormous. The left hand side of the bridge from the Zimbabwean side holds the train tracks whilst the right hand side has a road and a walkway.

The wrought iron structure arched across the canyon from a by-gone era leaves only one exclamation 'How the hell did they build this?' On the road side of the bridge is the green canapé that's home to the platform for the bungee jump, we made straight for it. The security of terra firma fell behind but the view of the canyon from this position is totally bewildering. The t-shaped canyon holds you spellbound as you stand some one hundred and forty meters above the rapids that have helped to carve out this spectacular sight. I looked over the rail only to have my legs turn to jelly as my fear of heights returned (whether this is some kind of inbuilt survival mechanism I don't know but that didn't quell my desire to join the list of jumpers of the world's highest bungee).

I asked the attendant (yet another Australian) about the jump and he explained that there was an Iron Man competition and the jump was booked all day but he would put my name down in case of a cancellation. Griff and I stood and watched as one by one these adrenalin junkies threw themselves off the bridge with just a 111 meter bungee cord strapped to their ankles. The sound of the water rushing through the canyon is amazing and the only sound that rises above it is the crowd counting down the jumpers. Each time a bloke left the platform I could count to six before the recoil brought the jumper back towards the bridge. After a couple of hours of hanging around a voice shouted,

"Antony, do you still want to jump?" It was the Aussie attendant.

"Err, ye." I said nervously.

I was then sent to the office to get weighed for the bungee cord. The office was on the Zambian side of the canyon but before the border crossing so no stamp from that country entered my passport. The steps that had been dug in the ground sapped the energy from my legs and they began to burn with pain and it was like walking upstairs with lead boots on. Two women sat behind a desk in a bus stop type hut, two men were filling in the disclaimer form whilst the previous two jumpers sat and watched the video of their jumps. I waited patiently for my turn and stared at the TV screen. I struck up a conversation with the two lads and they didn't have to explain the sensation of the jump it was written all over their faces. The desk became vacant and I approached,

"Hi Ladies, the Aussie said that I can jump".

"I'm sorry the two before you are the last two jumps of the day we have to stop at five." Said the older one of the two.

I made the very next available appointment which was Tuesday morning at eleven a.m. The walk back to the camp site was a crippler, Griff had taken the responsibility for the rucksack long ago but still it felt as though it was still stuck to my back. A coppice near the road looked far to inviting not to rest for a while and enjoy the pain relief of a joint. We sat on the trunk of a fallen tree, drank a can of Carling Black Label. A Zimbabwean appeared from nowhere,

"Do you want to buy a carving?"

He didn't even wait for a reply before shoving two bust carvings of a man and woman under our noses.

"I don't want to buy anything". Replied Griff.

I looked at the figures, they were made of ivory.

"You couldn't give me one of them you sick bastard, an elephant has had to die to make them". I said with venomous contempt.

His price came down rapidly to a quarter of his original price. My patience was running thin but it was Griff who got the message across. It is sad that these exceptionally friendly people have to resort to trying to sell one of their commodities to feed the family. Eventually we got rid of him but not without cost, he bummed a beer from us then disappeared into the bush.

"Look out for the Buffalo". I yelled.

That night Greg and Sue came by our tent and asked if we wanted to go to watch the video of their day's adventure, white water rafting on the Zambezi. We went to the only other bar in the village near the railway crossing and joined the rest of the group from that day's three rafts. Everyone huddled around a screen and the video started. Almost straight away Greg and Sue appeared on the screen, all smiles. Griff and I found it highly amusing watching the pair of them being thrown around the raft and occasionally into the Zambezi. It was around two in the morning before we decided to carry the party on at camp.

Griff sat on the wall at the side of the car armed with his didgeridoo, he blew into this delicately decorated instrument made famous by the Aborigines and the sound hung in the air creating a haunting vibrancy. I was by this time functioning on adrenalin alone and Greg told me that he was doing the bungee jump later that day and

I should go along and see if I could get a cancellation, I agreed.

Dawn came quickly, for it was only some four hours previous that we called it a night. Griff woke me but to my complete dismay the Sand Syndrome had returned with a vengeance. This came not really as a shock because I knew I was taking my body to its absolute limit but this just emphasizes how much this illness has no regard for inconveniencing the sufferer. This time though the effects were rather like being in a bath of Golden Syrup and I didn't even have the strength to turn over to alleviate the immense pain in my lower back and thighs. I'd definitely gone overdrawn in the energy account. Griff didn't have a clue what to do, his expression took me back to the memory of that fateful day back in August 1989 and the expressions on the faces of Jennifer, Darren, Kathi and the doctor.

Griff had asked me what to expect if I was taken ill but I never told him about these attacks because I'd not had one for ages and I was determined not to fall victim to it again. Griff had gone to fetch breakfast, a cheese and tomato toasted sandwich from the Wimpy but the energy needed to eat it eluded me. Greg and Sue turned up to go to the bungee jump and his comment upon discovering that I was in bed was like pushing a knife into me, for when he said "Is he chickening out?" I wanted to climb out of the tent or shout to him but Griff fought vigorously in my defence. I'd have given anything to accompany Greg to the jump and not only show him that we Pommies can out do the Aussies but then to turn to him after the jump and tell him that I did it with MS. Maybe one day I'll stand on that platform with my stomach in my mouth, sweating palms and legs like jelly waiting for the wind to rush past my ears. Yes I was scared of jumping, who wouldn't be, it goes against in-built self preservation but it all comes down to overcoming ones fears and facing the unknown, something that's essential in the fight against a formidable enemy known as Multiple Sclerosis.

I was totally spent, it had taken everything I had and more just to see one of the most spectacular sights of nature and I almost fulfilled one of my dreams but it wasn't meant to be. Yes the MS had won this particular battle but my victory brought its own rewards; this was the most exciting trip I'd ever undertaken and the reward for me was standing on that bridge at Victoria Falls and seeing for myself what I'd seen on television some years before, the canyon, the falls and of course the abundance of wildlife.

When Griff returned he told me that Greg had lost his bottle and turned back from the jump, only to return a couple of minutes later and jump off backwards. I was elated for him and I lay there with a wave of contentment over me.

I'd been offered a lift to Harare the capital of Zimbabwe by yet another Aussie who drove trucks full of backpackers around Africa. He told me that he would take me there for $20 and I'd have to wait in Harare for two days until his friend set off for Cape Town, and I could get a lift to Jo'burg for $90. The trip would take ten days taking in some spectacular scenery. This would have worked out handsomely because only a few weeks earlier a gymnast from Harare stayed with my cousin and I would have had a place to stay. This would have been awesome but I simply didn't posses the energy to take on such a trip so I had to be content with the jaunt and accept defeat and lick my wounds ready to fight another day.

Griff arranged a flight back to Jo'burg the very next day at 12.30 pm and brought breakfast that once again I couldn't eat. Griff was going to make sure that I was going to get the most from this trip and set about getting a bloke from the camp to help to lift me out of the tent and into the passenger seat to take me for a game drive. We sat for a while and watched the Baboons rummaging in the bins before driving down the side of the Zambezi River looking for game.

We came across a small herd of Elephants giving a perfect opportunity to photograph these magnificent mammals at close quarters. The bull Elephants started to force their way through the undergrowth and in-between us and the juveniles making their way along the river bank, we had no alternative but to follow with the car. It wasn't long before we lost them in the thickening bush; it amazed me how easy it is to lose a herd of Elephants. We returned to camp with a stranger, the man who stayed in bed all day had gone.

I was determined to enjoy my last night in Vic Falls and go to the Italian restaurant and the Explorers bar. The restaurant was bustling but a couple of Aussies offered us the remaining two chairs at their table. Within no time at all we were in the comfort of new found friends each sympathetic to my weakened state. As the meal drew to an end rumours of a lunar eclipse circulated around the restaurant, it emptied with the speed of a fire drill. The owner was undeterred by this evacuation of his premises; instead he left one of the waiters in charge and joined everyone else at the entrance to the shops to witness this unique sight. Two of the Australian girls put my arms around their necks and assisted me to my feet before helping me down the staircase.

The Explorers bar was also empty and it seemed as though the whole temporary population of Victoria falls stood at the entrance, silently looking to the skies. These two girls pushed through the crowd and sat me on the step next to the road and sat with their arms around me, needless to say I was in my element and a lunar eclipse into the bargain. As I sat, the moon was already a warm orange colour. Griff appeared with a welcomed beer and the moon orbited behind the earth's shadow; the crowd cheered and clapped but the cheer was electric when just over an hour later the moon reappeared with its distinctive white and grey glow. This in some way made up for my absent day and ended my last night with some compensation, especially as someone pointed out the planets Saturn and Jupiter at ten o'clock and four o'clock respectively. This sight eradicated all the aches and pains I had, for everything in Vic Falls stopped in awe of the changing colours of the atmosphere on the moon's surface. An eclipse party ensued at the Explorers bar and I sat at a table watching everyone dancing and drinking copious amounts of alcohol. If you're going to be ill, you may as well be ill here.

Wednesday morning came far too quickly but with all good things that come to a premature end the memory never leaves you. I'd had the trip of a lifetime and been rewarded for my persistence ten times over. Griff drove me to the airport and as I got out of the car a guard asked if any of us was Antony Kelly. When I told him it was me he told us that the plane was waiting for me. I was ushered to the gate but I couldn't gain entry until I'd paid the $20 airport tax. I was escorted through the gate, I didn't get the chance to thank Griff properly for the trip all I could do was to shout, "Griff, I'll write to you".

I was helped onto the plane, I sat there looking at the micro lights on the tarmac and I promised myself that one day I would return to complete the bungee jump and to fly over the falls in a micro light. The plane journey was a nightmare, it felt as though I had a knife stuck in my lower back and my breathing changed to a shallow, short inhalation in an attempt to ease the sensitivity of the nerve ends. It would take ten long days to fully recover but given the same opportunity again I'd have done it all over, even from the restraints of a wheelchair. For the following ten days the pain didn't generate its usual grimace, for a smile of fulfilment replaced the frustration.

Chapter 15

Kimberley

A couple of weeks after my return to Jo'burg at the end of September 1997, Grahame's hobby took us on a convention to the sleepy town of Kimberley, situated in central South Africa. This was the first South African juggling convention and I was there as official photographer. Kimberley is home to the largest disused diamond mine in the world. The story goes that in 1866 Erasmus Jacobs found a 21.25 carat diamond by the banks of the Orange River at Hopetown and in 1871 Colesberg Kopje found a diamond which created such a stir that it started the diamond rush and the manual digging of the famous 'Big Hole'.

In 1873 Hopetown was re-named Kimberley in honour of the Earl of Kimberley, the British secretary of state for the colonies. The town had sprung to life and the diamond rush created the same problems as the gold rush of America. Each prospector had a surface area of thirty by thirty feet, so tensions were high as one prospector dug deeper than his neighbouring counterpart leading to fights and riots. In 1888 Cecil John Rhodes took control of the mines and Kimberley thus controlling the diamond markets of the world generating untold wealth for this one time sleepy town. By the time digging eventually stopped on the 14th of August 1914, the hole was 215 meters deep with a surface area of 17 hectares and a diameter of 1.6 kilometres. 22.5 million tons of earth was excavated yielding 2,722 kilograms of diamonds; the biggest of which was 83.5 carat's, which was later known as the 'Star of South Africa'.

Kimberley was the first town in the southern hemisphere to install electric street lighting. Just outside the town is a dam called Kamfersdam, which is internationally recognised as a wetland of great importance because of the large flocks of Greater and Lesser Flamingo's that make for a truly magnificent spectacle. Our first day was spent at the mining museum overlooking the 'Big Hole'. It's not too difficult to imagine what life was like at that particular period for you are transported back in time so remarkably that the only thing you don't sense are the smells of the time.

Saturday morning was spent in a supermarket car park whilst the jugglers did their thing much to the amusement of the ever increasing crowd of bewildered onlookers. It was the hottest day of my holiday so far at a staggering 36 degrees centigrade. I'd forgotten to wear my cap; I could feel the sun cooking my brain. The display lasted a couple of hours and I could feel the energy being sapped from me rather like attempting to take a sauna with all your clothes on. I wanted to visit the town's art gallery because of its collection of 16th and 17th century paintings by the old masters, which included Flemish, Dutch, English and French painters. Everyone else was going to picnic in the local park so I decided to meet up with them all later.

Armed with a map of the town I set off in search of the art gallery. Unfortunately for me the map did not include all the side streets so I was a lot further from the gallery than I thought. I'd been walking for about 15 minutes, the heat radiated from the pavement so I stopped at a shop to buy a bottle of water. As I patiently waited my turn at the counter, I noticed a man in his early to mid twenties walk into the shop wearing a t-shirt, shorts and no shoes, his feet were dirty. As I paid for the water I asked for directions to the gallery, the voice of a man behind me said,

"She doesn't understand you, not many people around here speak good English because we all speak Afrikaans". It was the man with the dirty feet.

He offered me a lift to the gallery. Being rather sceptical of strangers in Africa I hesitated fractionally with my answer. He reassured me because he said his wife would think it a pleasure to show an Englishman around their town, so I accepted cautiously. The man lead me to a Cavalier exactly the same colour and trim as one I owned back in 1987, I was ushered to the rear offside door. He opened it and beckoned me in; there were two passengers in the car a man in the front and a woman in the back seat. I climbed in; the woman was also not wearing any shoes. It's a very Afrikaans thing not to wear shoes but in this instant the pavement was so hot that you could have cooked an egg on it. I was introduced to the man's wife and his school friend and a conversation about Manchester United ensued.

After my experience in Botswana, you tend to be a little more careful but I was so fatigued that I thought 'stuff it'. The gallery wasn't that far and the road leading up to the entrance boasted neatly trimmed trees. The car pulled up at the foot of the steps and I expressed my thanks. The driver conveyed a wish that I enjoy the rest of my stay in Africa and extended his hand out of the open window; I shook his hand and smiled at the others. I turned toward the gallery and admired the architecture. I could still hear the car's engine, I turned to wave goodbye but there was no car to be seen; I freaked. The foliage on the trees were trimmed to a height of around six feet so there was no way my view was obscured, it was as though I'd seen a ghost.

I took a swig of water and walked up the steps, my legs were burning and I was drained from the sun. The reception was manned by three elderly gentlemen who welcomed me once they'd heard my accent. One of the blokes was originally from Bath and we chatted for a while before he told me that the gallery was going to close for lunch and I only had an hour to look around. The air conditioning was shear bliss after being in the sun for so long. When I walked away from the reception they must have thought that I'd plopped in my pants. Kimberley's wealth displayed itself upon every available space on the walls and pedestals within this magnificent building. As I was walking around the gallery, I felt as though I was being watched and every now and again I caught sight of two of the men (but not the guy from Bath), hiding in the shadows slowly following me from room to room. It was really un-nerving; this town was beginning to 'creep me out'. I stayed until I was politely asked to leave because I was determined to appreciate the art that had cost millions of Rands.

Later that night we all met in reception to make the short drive to 'The Star of the West' which has held a licence since 1870. It's the second oldest pub in South Africa. The story goes that an English woman started the pub when she used wood from a shipwreck and the surviving sailors brought the wood to Kimberley with carts and Oxen. She started a bar downstairs and a brothel upstairs. She was known as 'Diamond Lil' and it's said that she would only sleep with men for diamonds. I guess Diamonds really are a girl's best friend.

The jugglers had hired the function room upstairs so each of them could show off their juggling talents; I was there for the beer and oh ye as 'official photographer'. When we pulled up outside the pub I had a bad case of déjà vu but we'd drove past it earlier that day so I didn't think too much about it.

I can't really explain the following but I had a reoccurring nightmare as a youngster where I was in a saloon in the Wild West and I end up witnessing a shooting from a balcony, which overlooked a piece of spare ground. I would always wake up as I shouted down from the balcony for the shooter to stop. I used to have this dream periodically from an early age.

Nigel pulled up outside the pub to let me out; he parked the car on spare ground across the road. We were asked to use the side entrance that lead to the back door of the pub and as we started to walk up the side alleyway I just instinctively knew the layout of the pub.

We filtered up the alleyway in single file and as I entered I could hear laughter, overlapping conversations and Can Can music. It was the same start as the dream I'd had and the music sent a shiver up my spine. In my dream an iron partition was attached to the wall making a squared off section with the back door in the middle of four bench tables. Before I reached the partition I could clearly hear a couple laughing, my heart sank because that was the next sequence to the dream. I reached the iron partition and I stared at the couple in shock; the laughter stopped and the couple stared at me, I turned away in embarrassment following Grahame into the rear of the bar. I stood at the side of Nigel as he introduced himself to the landlady and asked where the room was. I looked around the pub strangely expecting to see a certain layout. I stood motionless watching intently as people stopped their conversations to return my unwelcomed glances. I felt really vulnerable and I was feeling really ill because my head was burning with sunburn.

The landlady pushed up the hatch at the corner of the bar,

"Follow me".

I stared at the floor directly under the hatch; I knew exactly what I was looking for. The corners of the square lino tiles were held in place by brass studs, the lino had worn away around the stud from decades of wear. I broke into a sweat.

We were led upstairs. I pulled myself together and followed the rest strangely knowing that the staircase doubled back on itself with a high level sash window. I knew we were going to turn left and the door at the end of the corridor on the left was the only door from the three that led into the function room. I was right.

The bar was on the right as you walked into the room with a doorway in the middle leading to a kitchen, again the same as my dream. My eyes scrutinized the positioning of the furniture; brief relief came as the tables were set out differently to the dream. I began to relax a little until everyone started to move tables to make room for all the juggling paraphernalia. Before my very eyes the room transformed to the room I remembered, my head was up my arse.

This was too much for me so I sat on the balcony drinking fresh orange and trying desperately to pull myself together. I looked down across the road at the spare ground used for a car park. It looked familiar to the fatal shooting from the dream. It was surreal. I tried to calm myself but the dream played over and over in my mind. I suddenly remembered something that would settle the uncertainty for me. Under the window that overlooked the staircase had a piece of floorboard missing in the corner of a plank, making a rectangular shape. I got into a conversation but my mind wouldn't let this last piece of the puzzle linger. I asked Nigel to go and have a look for me without telling him why. He came straight back and asked me if I was taking the piss. I couldn't speak for a few moments and he kept asking me if I was OK. I didn't know what to think.

I pleaded with Nigel to take me back to the digs. On the way back I told Nigel to look after Grahame because I was sure that something was going to happen. Nigel gave me a 'that must be good shit your smoking' look and I went straight to bed.

Around midnight Grahame walked into my room to check on me, he said things were fine so I went back to sleep. I was told the next day that some woman grabbed Grahame's hat in the bar downstairs as they were leaving and there was almost an altercation and the woman had pulled a knife and threatened my cousin but the landlady intervened.

I still to this day can't explain what happened but all I know is that Kimberley had a profound effect on me. I was relieved to head back to Jo'burg, I felt as if I'd travelled back in time and I wasn't at ease with this god-forsaken town. I've never had the dream since.

My last Sunday in Africa was spent at the Randburg Waterfront only this time to do a reverse bungee whilst strapped inside a caged metal sphere. The sphere is locked into place on a platform before you're strapped into the seat and your legs are strapped onto a metal plate. Two bungee cords are connected to two poles and each side of the cage and then are stretched hydraulically to fifty meters.

As soon as the cords are taut the operator releases the sphere by stepping onto the release pedal and then you get one of the biggest adrenalin rushes ever. Glenn had told me all about this new feature and I simply just had to have a go, it would be a great way to end this amazing adventure. Glenn volunteered to be my accomplice and before being strapped into the seat the macho side of us came out by daring each other to hold our arms outstretched throughout the ride. The operator warned us not to do this but we chose to ignore him. The noise of the hydraulics fell silent signalling the inevitable launch.

The attendant stepped on the release pedal; the air rushed passed our ears and the momentum left our stomachs' behind. Before I had a chance to think about the fastest assent I'll ever experience in my life (unless invited on a shuttle launch), we had a bird's eye view of the car park behind the many shops, bars and restaurants. My arm smashed against the metal bar leaving a multi-coloured bruise for my fortitude. The sphere hung in the air waiting for gravity. The cage spun violently as it descended, the recoil granted another brief glimpse of the Jo'burg skyline. A backward somersault resulted in the cage falling to earth with us parallel to the landing platform; my heart was in my mouth as the cords seem to do their work at the very last second. A dozen or so bounces later the sphere begins to regain stability and you can now breath normally again. The sound of the hydraulics begins the lowering of the sphere to the platform and all you can do is wait to be peeled off the seat. Those first few steps on terra firma were a little shaky until the brain can catch up with the events of the last couple of minutes.

This was one of the most disorientating self induced encounters of my life as I experienced 0-100mph in 2 seconds and a G-force of 3. Glenn enjoyed the experience just as much as I did and it was a commendable way in which to cement our friendship. Just days left to departure from the experience of a lifetime, I'd met some amazing people and saw some amazing things. I had a bucket load of stories to tell my friends back home. I was sad to leave but I was in some ways looking forward to seeing everyone back home especially my young nephew Jamie, who was only nine months old when I left for Africa.

The time had come and the airport departure terminal was by far the worst encounter I'd had in Africa. Grahame, Jane and Mitch sat patiently with me waiting for that moment when the announcement comes over the Tannoy to attend the designated gate. My gratitude towards them was immense and I hope that they realise just how much Africa and my time spent with them had rekindled life into a once dying soul. When it was eventually time to make my way to the gate the farewell was difficult but I managed to hold back the tears, somehow. My two and a half months were at an end and Africa had left me in awe.

My health had improved thanks to the climate. The dry heat was a god send for my limbs and I just knew I'd spend most of my life chasing the sun. I had a couple of vertigo attacks and the first one devastated Grahame and Jane as they watched on in total disbelief. After the first attack Grahame would just instinctively take control of the situation and calm me down. We used to spend most nights in his bar while Jane caught up on her soaps. You're not even safe from Eastenders out here. This lifestyle was a million miles away from the one I led and I felt totally alive whilst I was in Africa, *I was living not existing*. A guy once said to me that once you've got African soil under your feet, it never leaves you. That is certainly true of me. I have an affinity with this continent now and it's as strong as ever. I knew I'd be back someday soon.

Chapter 16

China

The first time I saw Andy after I got back, he walked through the door after getting back from work at eight thirty that same evening.

"Hey, you owe me seven hundred and thirty quid". Was the first thing out of his mouth, accompanied with a broad grin.

"Hi Ant, did you have a nice time?" I replied.

"Sorry mate did you have a nice time?"

The ensuing conversation brought about yet another realisation that a dream was about to be fulfilled, for Andy had booked us to go to Australia with Thomas Kelly-Fox and his dad. I was ecstatic. Then not five minutes later I turned to Andy,

"What do mean Tommy's dad's coming?

"No its right he's one of the lads, we'll have a ball".

"OK if you say so".

I now had two months before we went to Australia; I'd got the travelling bug. Within this time I managed to go to the 'Oktoberfest' in Belgium, back to France, a couple of trips to the Cotswolds and a trip to Scotland.

11th December1997, the date synonymous with one of the best holidays I've ever had but still second best to Africa. I awoke early with the memory of Andy leaning over the banister telling me that he and Thomas were off to Australia for Christmas was as fresh as the day it happened. I never gave my answer a second thought; after all I didn't need to as I was fortunate to have the money and I couldn't think of anything I'd much rather do with it. I turned over and made love to Joanne (a girl I'd been seeing casually) before taking her home. On the way there I told her to do what she wanted while I was away, I simply couldn't have her waiting around for me as the spirit of Christmas would undoubtedly bring temptation. That was it, no bullshit just straight talking, no pretence and definitely no lies. As strange as she thought this was, I'm sure she looks back on that with an air of relief because there's no point trying to pretend things are not what they are in life. When I got back to Andy's, Thomas Fox Senior was patiently waiting to meet 'the wee man'. I walked through the door and a bloke with long hair and a bull horned moustache was sat on the sofa,

"Awreet sun, I'm Thomas" I didn't know he was Scottish.

With the introductions over, a car's horn signalled that our taxi had arrived. We headed for a car rental in Oldham via Thomas junior's house. The boot swallowed four rucksacks and it dawned on me that we were actually on our way to the other side of the planet. Andy likes to be the one who is the organiser and so took the wheel; I sat in the back talking to my new friend like an excited schoolchild on a school trip. When Andy and Thomas originally booked the flights with China Airways they were offered the chance to have a stopover in Beijing in a four star hotel for £23 a night.

Once we'd landed and collected our luggage we changed some money and started a haggling war between half a dozen taxi drivers. The exchange rate at the time was 13 Yuan to the pound; the price of the taxi started at 180 Yuan but Tommy senior got him down to 130 Yuan. All we had was a conformation slip for reservations at the Peace Hotel which we flashed at the driver, a smile and we were on our way.

My first impression of China was a dirty collection of concrete buildings half finished whilst the other half was hidden from view due to scaffolding. It was smoggy, dusty and dirty. One thing that struck me was the amount of bicycles, everywhere you turned these black bikes were in your face each looking the same as the next. Traffic was horrendous; it was a relief not to drive. We arrived outside a 22 storey tower block, the gold leaf lettering complete with four gold stars beneath announced that we had reached our first destination to our total astonishment. I'd never stayed in such luxurious surroundings and it seemed somehow strange to be doing so in a country where the majority of the population live in poverty. The taxi pulled up outside the reception where we were greeted by a white gloved doorman wearing a red jacket, black trousers and a fez type hat with two gold bands but without the tassels complemented by a huge smile. He opened the door of the taxi and ushered us through the revolving doors whilst a porter removed our luggage from the boot.

As I entered the building the sheer scale and grandeur of the reception area took me by surprise; the Christmas decorations adorned every wall and a twenty foot Christmas tree stood proud in the middle of the foyer. The extravagance mindless but pleasing. There was a mix up with the reservation so we had to fax the travel agent back home and get them to fax the confirmation through; meanwhile Andy had to give his credit card details until the fax came through. Our rooms were adjacent on the tenth floor. The lift doors opened and a made to measure rug with Friday embroidered into it just added that little finishing touch, and this was changed on a daily basis. A very welcomed shower saw mid afternoon arrive, we decided to explore the hotel before venturing out. I was amazed by the size of the place it was rather like a self contained village than a hotel. It had 3 restaurants, a post office, half a dozen shops selling mostly tacky souvenirs, a gymnasium, a swimming pool and a beauty salon.

Walking down the road outside the hotel we witnessed organised chaos as cars and pedestrians intermingled with one another without any form of contact. Piled up snow lay in the gutters and ice glistened in the winter afternoon glow. A patch of ice teased us into re-enacting childhood playground winter sports much to the amusement of the Chinese. As the main roads crossed paths the busier of the two had a tramline, the trams edged their way along continually sounding their horns to clear its route.

Everyone seemed so blasé when crossing the road or tram track as though the trams and cars would wait for them. We however were a little more apprehensive when we had to cross the road to get to a department store. Every hundred yards or so were what can only be described as bike parks, there were thousands of them, same colour (black), same frames etc, the only distinguishing feature was a small (yes you've guessed it, black) registration plate with white lettering just under the back of the seat. The department store was as cheap as you can imagine and just as impressive. The entrance was only accessible by scaling a set of stone steps leading to a grand doorway dominated by the carved stone columns supporting the name of the store (in English, come in foreigner and spend your money).

It was my kind of store because as soon as you got through the door you were facing the elevators; the menu on the wall directed you to your desired department complemented by gold leaf lettering in Chinese and English. When you wanted to make a purchase the assistant gave you piece of paper with the item and price and you paid for the goods at a central till, then you gave the receipt to the assistant and in return your purchases were gifted wrapped if required and you were on your way.

We returned to the hotel and decide to go for a swim. When we got there the pool attendant motioned to us that we weren't allowed in the pool without skull caps and we all looked at each other and thought he was taking the piss. We all adopted an 'I'm not wearing that thing on my head' expression but we made light of it and put them on. When we got into the changing room all these Chinese men were parading around in the buff, I thought shit I'm in a gay club. It was hilarious watching Thomas senior trying to tuck his long hair in the back of his skull cap. We all jumped into the pool which was that cold that my manhood resembled a short stack of buttons, none of us lasted more than a couple of minutes in the water.

Later that night we walked across the car park of the hotel toward the club; the entrance was bustling with dainty women and kung-fu type doormen. Once at the bar we were surrounded by women wanting us to buy them drinks, their meal tickets had just arrived. To get a bit of peace and check things out we made our way to the balcony for a bird's eye view of the cabaret act. A Chinese pop star and his dancing troupe came on stage; everyone was going mad as we sat drinking our bottles of Budweiser. A steady stream of girls came to introduce themselves before asking for a drink. Andy and Thomas snr sat at one table having the crack with two girls whilst me and Thomas jnr sat at another table being amused by their antics until yet another girl approached with the 'will you buy me a drink line'. We got that pissed off with it that we held hands and told the girls we were an item but that didn't deter them as they just sent a lad over.

This guy introduced himself and asked if we wanted a drink but Thomas refused point blank but minutes later he was back with five cans of Bud (which was equal to an average week's wage). He offered them to us but still Thomas would not indulge this stranger. The guy then opened his can, drank the contents in one go before shouting obscenities at us, which was cool because we didn't understand any of it. His persona became more aggressive and two girls dragged him away; we could see him talking to three or four other blokes who then looked over in our direction. We told the other's what had happened and decided to go back to the hotel for a drink in their bar.

We made our way to the staircase and in the confusion of being followed around by a small group of men we lost Thomas snr. We started searching around for him to no avail and as I searched the numerous nooks and crannies I stumbled across the rooms the girls (or boys, which ever floated your boat) took you to, I shouted 'Tommy!' down the corridor but he was nowhere to be seen. I met up with the others at the entrance and volunteered to go back to the hotel to see if he was there. The gloved door porter opened the door but before I could acknowledge him Thomas shouted across from the bar, there he was larger than life wearing a smile with a pint in front of him. I went back to the club collected Andy and Thomas and returned to a table of drinks. As we took the tops off our pints there was a commotion at the doorway; the two girls that had been talking to Andy and Thomas were arguing with the door staff that they owed them money for the pleasure of their company and the time they had spent at the table with them. Luckily the door staff sent them packing and that was our introduction to China.

The following morning we were up early ready to hire a taxi to take us to the Great Wall. Three taxi drivers bartered with us and we eventually decided to go with a guy called Wylee who'd offered to take us for £10 each. Driving through Beijing was an experience as we were all amazed at the way the trams never stopped no matter what was in its path. The buses pulled out with no indicators blinking and pedestrians seemed to play the game 'Frogger' standing in the middle of the road darting in and out of traffic, we were amazed not to have witnessed an accident. As we passed the high rise buildings, KFC and McDonalds signs adorned the windowless sides signifying that globalisation had irradiated communist ideals.

The countryside opened up and the roads deteriorated to pot holed routes leading to Badaling. Our driver taught us some Chinese on the way to kill a bit of time in between taking in the distant mountain range. Badaling is located at Yanqing County, more than 70 kilometres northwest from the centre of Beijing City. It is a mountain pass of the Jundu Mountain. Badaling is at the highest point of the north end of the Guan'gou Gorge, in which the Juyongguan Pass lies. Badaling means "giving access to every direction" the name itself suggests its strategic importance. In history, the function of Badaling was to protect the Juyongguan Pass along with the Guan'gou gorge.

The wall of Badaling has a total length of 3, 741 meters with an average height of 8 meters the highest part being 15 meters. The top of the wall is wide enough to allow five horses to be ridden side by side. Badaling was the earliest section to be open to tourists among all the parts of the whole Great Wall and 130 million tourists from China and abroad have visited Badaling since it opened to the public.

This section of the wall is made up of huge bar stones; some being as much as two metres in height and the floor of the wall is paved with square bricks which makes the surface smooth enough to walk along comfortably. At the highest point of each ridge were signal fire platforms; one fire and the smoke signalled that the enemy were about 100 men strong, two fires indicated 500 men and three fires 1000 men.

As we began to climb high into the mountain region anticipation started to rise and our first glimpse of the wall came as we rounded the hillside. It's difficult to describe something that from one quick glimpse leaves you completely and utterly dumbstruck. Your mind just can't comprehend how anyone could of even contemplated starting construction on such a scale. The sheer grandeur and size leaves so many unanswerable questions because it's not as though you can ask the emperor or the labourers how they overcame the obvious difficulties. As the taxi pulled into the car park the now familiar ornate Chinese arch bridged the road, the carvings were exquisite.

I looked at how steep the wall was and the height we'd have to climb. I was completely unfazed and determined to walk on this construction that has bewildered man since its erection. Eagerly we bought tickets and made our way up the side of the wall to a steel staircase that allows access to the walkway on top of the wall. The platform elevates over the battlements which allow spectacular views of the surrounding mountains. My eyes followed the contours of the wall disappearing over a ridge and reappearing hundreds of metres into the distance.

The first segment of the Badaling section takes you to the top of a peak that has eight turrets on the way to the summit, each wall section snakes its way along the rim. I looked at the last turret and thought to myself 'that's my goal', I was determined that I was going to get there no matter what. It was a surreal moment that took me back to when I was stood in the Chinese Embassy in Manchester looking at the mural in the reception and now I was actually stood on the wall. It was bitterly cold, the wind biting to the bone reiterated by flecks of snow dotted around the hillside and in parts drifted against the wall.

There were hundreds of people, some making the accent, others making the decent but in a very orderly fashion. Bright clothing glistened in the sun light and brought a strange kind of warmth to an otherwise grey place. Hawkers followed each of us trying to sell us their wears ranging from snacks to calendars and jewellery to clothing,

"Harrow, how are you?"

"Where you fom?"

"Sherrl you much chipper!"

The hawkers seemed to allow you space the higher you climbed as if not worth pursuing or was it the thought of having to climb those stairs day in day out? More like I'll get the bastard on the way down. Luckily for me the stairs had one vital tourist friendly addition, a handrail. I wonder what the emperor would have made of that? The first set of steps were totally undaunting and I refused to use the handrail but by the time I'd reached the first turret I was breathing heavy and my legs were burning. I certainly wasn't going to stop now and continued regardless. The view down to the now distant car park and the rest of the valley was truly breathtaking and I savoured the moment. Two arches allow access to the turrets and the soldier's quarters along with the rest of the wall. A staircase takes you up to the first floor where the soldiers could attack the enemy from four small window openings and above that was the signal fire platform. It wasn't difficult to imagine life as a soldier on the wall especially with it being so cold. Once through the first tower the valley drops off and a downhill stretch was fantastic until I realised that we had to climb up the other side but at least it had a handrail.

The next tower was extremely hard to reach up a forty-five degree set of steps and I was soon lagging behind pulling my tiring body up each step with the aid of the rail and a tug of war technique. I was physically drained, my legs were burning and my lower back felt as if it had a red hot needle stuck in my spine. Thomas senior stood at the tower videoing me struggling to get to the top, I didn't mind because I now have that video for prosperity; it does bring back all the aches and pains it took to get there but what an awesome memory. The view just got better and better the higher you climbed and that was ample reward for the physical effort involved. I continued through the second tower and Andy and Thomas Junior were patiently waiting for me to arrive.

I had to take a breather for a couple of minutes before attempting the final stretch of the section and reaching the summit of this particular mountain. My legs were shaking uncontrollably, I hardly had the strength in them to stand but it didn't matter I was on the Great Wall overlooking an awesome mountain region warmed by physical exertion and wearing the biggest 'fuck you' smile.

On the middle stretch the stairs wasn't as steep but they were twice as long, a good fifty metres. I just looked at it and thought 'how the hell I'm I going to get up there'. I wasn't prepared to stop now and then Thomas Junior turned to me and said

"Do you want a donkey ride?"

I accepted but I didn't accept defeat. A good friend offered to help and I accepted his gesture with the same decorum of good intentions. With that I was on his back and he set off running up the stairs much to the amusement of the Chinese. Thomas is a really fit bloke and initially found my weight not to be a problem, until that is about two-thirds of the way up; he stopped running and broke into a fast walk he simply couldn't stop now because some Chinese people were at the top of the stairs taking photos of us. About half a dozen steps from the top the camera that I'd bought the day before fell out of my pocket and bounced down a couple of steps. The Chinese were shaking his hand and revelled at the spectacle insisting he had his picture taken with them. I retrieved my camera that now sounded like a set of maracas every time I tried to capture this spectacular scenery on film and I feared the photos I'd already taken were ruined.

We were almost at the top; the adrenalin was rushing through my body as much as through Thomas's legs. I looked around in a three hundred and sixty degree rotation mustering inspiration, it worked. With each tower passed the thought of the view kept my legs going and the encouragement of my friends who gave me the inspiration for this physically frustrating challenge. Just before the two hour mark I'd arrived at the summit and for a moment I felt like Sir Edmund Hillary reaching the summit of Everest; I wondered whether or not I was the first man with MS to reach the summit of the Badaling section of the Great Wall.

I sat on the top step staring at the wall disappearing into the abyss of the valley and revelled in sheer unadulterated pleasure. The decent was going to be a lot easier but still a stress on my legs, luckily for me the handrail came in very handy for sliding my arse along it. As we passed each tower on the way down the sheer scale of the angle was immense and the height that we'd climbed even astonished me. It is without doubt the most amazing man-made structure I'd ever seen and it was a surrealistic moment as I resurrected the adventurous spirit that had been suppressed by the onset of illness. It all seemed so distant like a dream only the pain made it a reality. My friends and tenacity got me to this point and I savoured every millisecond of it. China is a must for the adventurous type with an abundance of rewards for being a little different from the Spanish package special.

That night we decided to go to an English pub we'd been told about called 'The Red Lion'. When we walked in we were the only customers in there; after we'd finished our very expensive imported Budweiser's we were informed by the waiter who spoke very good English that the pub was closing. We asked him where we could get another beer. He told us that he was going to a bar that was open all night and we were welcome to join him so we jumped into a taxi not knowing where the hell we were going. The taxi went through all these little dodgy alleyways and back streets that had no street lighting. We ended up at a really dingy looking place but the waiter assured us that we would be made welcome which wasn't too unsettling because we'd found the Chinese people extremely friendly.

For me it was a privilege to drink with the Chinese on their turf away from the demands of tourism; for we were accepted as guests and made to feel very welcome. Once we'd got the whole Manchester United team list out of the way everyone in the bar found it highly amusing listening to us try to repeat our earlier Chinese lesson. We didn't buy another drink all night. With around four beers each stacked up on the table and more wind than a cowboy camp Tommy junior decided we should shotgun the beer. Thomas put four bendy straws in the bottles and challenged us to a shotgun race, when the Chinese saw this they joined in and the remainder of the night is a total blur.

We were all suffering hangovers but the Forbidden City and Tian'anmen Square was just down the road. Thomas junior was still in bed and when we told him we were going he just pulled the sheets back over his head and said

"Video it and I'll watch it later".

Armed with a map of the city we headed off in search of the Forbidden City. At a set of traffic lights we met a couple from England with a kiddie in a pram who was also looking for the square so we said they could tag along with us. This bloke informed us that he'd seen us the day before on the wall and sure enough later when we watched the video there they were kiddie in a back sling. The guy bought paper from China and exported it back home and he'd taken his wife for a break, they were staying with Chinese customers and gave us tips in Chinese customs which came in handy when we went to a restaurant that night.

It was freezing but the warmth of the suns glow made the long walk more enjoyable even though we were choking on the car fumes. The moat around the Forbidden City was frozen and right in the middle was an old Chinese man sat on a canvas stool fishing over a hole he'd made in the ice. Around the streets surrounding the high walls of the city hairdressers applied their trade at the side of the road.

The Forbidden City is called Gu Gong in Chinese and was the Imperial Palace during the Ming and Qing dynasties which is now known as the Palace Museum. It's the largest palace in the world and covers 74 hectares and is surrounded by a six metre deep moat. The wall is ten metres high and encloses 9,999 buildings. The Forbidden

City is divided into two parts, the southern section (or the Outer Court), was where the emperor exercised his supreme power over the nation and the northern section (or the Inner Court), is where he lived with his family until 1924 when the last emperor of China was driven from the Inner Court. Fourteen emperors of the Ming dynasty and ten emperors of the Qing dynasty had reigned there. Having been the Imperial Palace for some five centuries it houses numerous rare treasures and curiosities. Listed by UNESCO as a World Cultural Heritage Site in 1987, the Palace Museum is now one of the most popular tourist attractions worldwide.

Construction of the palace complex began in 1407, the 5th year of the Yongle reign of the third emperor of the Ming dynasty. It was completed fourteen years later in 1420. It was said that a million workers including one hundred thousand artisans were driven into long-term hard labour. Stone needed was quarried from Fang Shan, a suburb of Beijing. It was said a well was dug every fifty meters along the road in order to pour water onto the road in winter to slide huge stones on ice into the city. Huge amounts of timber and other materials were freighted from faraway provinces. The wall surrounding the city has an 8.6 meters wide base reducing to 6.66 meters wide at the top; the angular shape of the wall totally frustrates attempts to climb it. The bricks were made from white lime and glutinous rice while the cement is made from glutinous rice and egg whites. These incredible materials made the wall extraordinarily strong.

Yellow was the symbol of the royal family and therefore is the dominant colour in the city including the roof tiles and the decorations down to the bricks on the ground that was done by a special process. However, there is one exception and that's Wenyuange, (the royal library) which has a black roof, that's because it was believed that black represented water and could extinguish fire. The palace itself is adorned by gold leaf dragon decorations on every wall and ceiling supported by red columns, the throne was flanked by two gold Storks. Although the walls enclose the city with a secure apparition you don't feel closed in.

After an hour or so we made our way towards Tian'anmen Square. Built in 1417, the square is 880 meters south to north and 500 meters east to west, making it the largest square in the world. This gives it an area of 440,000 square meters. During the Ming and Qing eras, there was no public square at Tian'anmen, and instead the area was filled with offices for imperial ministries. These were badly damaged during the Boxer Rebellion and the area was cleared to produce the beginning of Tian'anmen Square. Enlarged in 1949 to the current size, its flatness is broken only by the 38 meter high Monument to the People's Heroes and the Mausoleum of Mao Zedong.

The square lies between two ancient massive gates; the Tian'anmen to the north and the Qiánmén (which literally means "Front Gate"), to the south. Along the west side of the Square is the Great Hall of the People, and along the east side is the National Museum of Chinese History. Trees line the east and west edges of the Square but the square itself is open with neither trees nor benches. The square is lit with huge lampposts which also support video cameras. It's heavily monitored by uniformed and plainclothes policemen.

Every visitor to Beijing gravitates to this square which has become the pulse of this exciting city of contrasts. It has been said that it can accommodate over one million people in its 122 acres. This area has attracted Beijing citizens and visitors since the mid 17th Century but only in the late 1950's was it formally laid out. Since then many changes have been made to the original concept. In late 1998 and for nearly half of 1999, the square was closed for a complete refurbishment because the 1st October 1999 was the 50th anniversary celebration of the founding of the People's Republic of China. The square has been the site of many momentous events such as the declaration of the People's Republic of China in 1949, the rallies launching the Cultural Revolution in 1966, the deaths of Mao Zedong and Zhou Enlai in 1976 when millions of mourners packed the square, and 1989 when student protestors occupied the square for nearly two months while the world watched the events unfold on TV screens in their living rooms.

In June 1989, government troops and tanks brought the event to a violent end. On each 5th year anniversary the government hosts huge military parades highlighting their military might and capabilities. Each day at sunrise the national flag is raised and at sunset lowered in a grand ceremony.

Our time in Beijing was short yet we'd packed so much into it. The Chinese were amazing making the trip even more enjoyable and after a fourteen hour flight we'd be able to enjoy the Australian sun.

Chapter 17
Australia

16th December 1997; flying over Australia was truly awesome from 37,000 feet, the desert roads are amazingly straight and the Tanami Desert took an age to cross. As we approached Sydney airport, the Sydney Opera House and the bridge came into view, the white of the angled roof dazzled in the sunlight. This was it I was finally here at a place I'd never in my wildest dreams thought I would end up but it just goes to show that you never know what the future may bring. The closer we got the more excited I became and I relished in the thought that I was about to spend Christmas and New Year at the other side of the world.

Once you're through customs you're greeted by helpdesks advertising backpackers accommodation all over Australia but our immediate thoughts turned to a couple of days in Sydney first. We quickly found somewhere to stay in Coogee Beach which is situated south-east of Sydney city centre and south of Bondi Beach. It was a bit of a feat with four beds to find in the same place. The assistants' on the helpdesks were amazingly accommodating given the fact that a couple of plane loads of tourists are trying to compete for reservations within a five minute period of passing through customs. Most of the backpacker places have their own mini buses to collect guests from the airport but we opted for a taxi, we'd well and truly had enough of airports. The moment we left the airport building the heat forced us to strip down to our t-shirts.

The taxi journey was one of the most exciting ones I'd had for the sights on route to Coogee held me spellbound and my mates' conversation fell on deaf ears. The house was at the top of a hill and the white-washed walls reflected the full glare of the sun making it virtually impossible to walk toward the entrance without squinting. The corridor walls leading to the reception was littered with tourist attractions and other accommodation all over Australia. I was bemused with the abundance of facilities available to backpackers and wondered whether or not the psyche of this industry has contributed to Aussies travelling all over the world.

The reception was a ground floor room that had been divided by a counter split two-thirds in favour of the receptionist. We were greeted by a middle aged bloke cockily treating the whole check-in process as though he was doing us the favour by letting us stay there; we were soon to discover that being in Australia in December wasn't such a unique decision after all.

The bloke explained the rules and took our passports as well as the money for two night stay. He gave us all a key and led us up a flight of stairs to the first floor and a door marked 'B wing'. The door opened and to my surprise instead of a corridor we found ourselves in someone's bedroom (which was occupied), with two additional doors, one to the left and one straight ahead. We were led through the one straight ahead in which we found ourselves in yet another bedroom (again occupied); this room had a set of bunk beds in it, a solid door which was the bathroom, a balcony and a

Georgian style glass door leading to another bedroom. This room had two sets of bunk beds and a door leading to the same bathroom, this was to be our room. It was a crazy set up having to go through two bedrooms to get to our room but I guess this is the unglamorous side of backpacking that you must tolerate when paying bottom dollar. It was clean and that's all that matters to anyone travelling.

We just dumped our rucksacks changed from our tracksuits into our shorts and headed for the beach. The stroll down to the beach was effortless apart from the heat of the Aussie summer which sapped my strength but the site of the Coogee Beach Hotel and the thought of a few cold Toohey's beers kept me going.

The name 'Coogee' (pronounced as "could gee") is said to have been derived from an Aboriginal word which means "bad smell". This is due to the decaying seaweed which is washed up onto the beach even today. In July 1838, the village of Coogee was gazetted with many of the streets in the district named after sea creatures. As surf bathing became more popular, so did the area gain fame and in 1907 the 'Coogee Surf Lifesaving Club' was formed. In 1928 an amusement pier similar to those found at many English beach resorts was constructed. It commenced at the promenade and reached over 180 metres into the sea, however, heavy seas took their toll and the structure was demolished in 1934. This tourist activity has also resulted in the appearance of a large number of 'Backpacker' style establishments, as well as a wide variety of cafes and restaurants. The beach is a semi-circular cove flanked by headland with a paved promenade area and steps with an amphitheatre style leading to crisp white sands and lawned areas with manicured trees. It's truly beautiful.

Andy had lived in Sydney for almost two years and knew the area well. Over a few cold beers he suggested that we go to eat that night at the world famous Bondi Beach. As the days light began to fade we made our way back up the hill to the digs which was tedious and long for me but after all I was in Australia. We got to meet our neighbours and it was strange that four lads had an adjoining room with a glass door with two girls on the other side. I felt really embarrassed for the poor girls who hid in the bathroom or the balcony while we were in our room but what could we do about it at this late stage? (sweet FA). The owners didn't give a shit as long as the money was coming in. One of the girls was Brazilian but had been brought up in Switzerland and so spoke French, although her English was word perfect I preferred to speak to her in French thus being able to air my embarrassment at the situation (well on their part anyway, we however was loving it). We came to some arrangement with the girls and we were ready and out on the town in no time.

Coogee's nightlife was rocking but the lure of Bondi Beach was too much and so a short taxi ride took us to the heart of the town. Unfortunately it was undergoing a major facelift and the sea front was reminiscent of the half completed buildings of Beijing, only without the dust. Bondi was all you'd expect from such a famous place that precedes its reputation; despite the chaos of the facelift it was the place to be and the place to be seen in for all the young Australians. A gentle stroll down the sea front amidst the array of people reminded me of the numbers strolling around Blackpool but it was a million miles away from the litter strewed Golden Mile. Each of the bars had an outdoor seating area and that was really refreshing at night with a gentle breeze coming in from the sea. There was a vibe about the place that made you want to stay there especially when all around you was scantily clad women.

Next morning we caught the bus from the top of the hill straight into town and once again my persona was like that of a kid in a candy shop, not knowing where to look next. Sydney is the most exciting city I've ever experienced and the youth of this relatively new city is apparent no matter where you happen to be. The exhilaration as we reached the harbour bus terminal was immense, I was about to see these two tourist attractions up close and personal. The scale of the buildings from the ground was astonishing. As we walked under the flyover to the bridge towards the Opera House it was like living the experience via someone else's eyes for it was hard to believe that I'd had so many dream-like experiences coming true. After all the shit, heartache and toil I'd been through over the last several years, this was my time; I deserved it and no one or anything was going to spoil the moment. I was totally uninterested in the future; I was living for the here and now and I was going to savour every second of this possibly unrepeatable holiday of a lifetime.

As soon as we set foot from the shadows of the flyover the sun's rays literally burned like a magnifying glass and Thomas junior was quick to get the sun cream out and protect my delicate fair skin (I only have to look at the sun and I'm red raw like a lobster). The Opera House was far more impressive from the air but nevertheless I was stood under this iconic building looking at the towering bridge and most importantly in a t-shirt feeling fan (fucking) tastic. I found the bridge far more architecturally appealing.

Our plans for our time in Australia was to drive up to Cairns at the northern end of the Great Barrier Reef where our friend Dean Kelly's step-brother Alan lived; Dean and his girlfriend Joanne were on a three month holiday around Australia and Indonesia and would be there the same time as us so it would have been rude not to. The added bonus was that it would be Dean and Alan's birthdays on the 22nd and the 23rd December so we wanted to go for a party. Thomas junior had been to Australia in the April and had seen the sights of Sydney so Thomas senior and I decided to do the usual ferry trip around the harbour to get a feel for the place; we opted for the two hour trip giving Andy and Thomas time to go and find a camper van to hire for a couple of weeks.

We climbed on board a boat at Circular Quay in-between the Opera House and the bridge and waved the others off from the top deck. We watched them disappear into the distance while the captain manoeuvred the boat from its couplings. First of all the trip took us back on ourselves under the bridge and into the inner harbour to see the delights of Darling Harbour. From on board the skyscrapers encircled the harbour. From the greeny-turquoise sea the Opera House can be appreciated for its uniquely shaped roof and the dark steel girders from the bridge fail in its attempts to block out the rays of the sun. Once under the bridge the Sydney Tower nestles in-between the skyscrapers of the central business district in the heart of the city standing at 305m (1001ft), the tallest building in Sydney. In the heart of Darling Harbour was a Christmas tree towering above the quayside warehouses along with its decorations, it seemed surreal as the sun scorched my back.

Sydney Harbour is commonly referred to as the most beautiful natural harbour in the world. The 150 miles of shoreline include approximately 34 square miles of water. Although there are exclusive homes dotted around the water's edge there are large tracts of parklands, reserves and gardens that help to balance the harbour environmentally. As we again passed under the harbour bridge the commentary on the load speaker gave out mind blowing facts such as, it's the world's largest but not the longest steel arch bridge with the top of the bridge standing 134 metres above the harbour and is fondly known to locals as the 'coat hanger'. Construction of the bridge started in 1924 and took 1400 men eight years to build at a cost of £4.2 million; sixteen lives were lost during the construction (it officially opened on 19th March 1932). Six million hand driven rivets (made just two miles from my home) and 53,000 tonnes of steel was used in its construction. It now carries eight traffic lanes and two rail lanes (one in each direction) but at the time of its construction the two eastern lanes were tram tracks but they were converted to road traffic when Sydney closed its tramlines in the 1950's.

At the time that we were there the now infamous bridge climb did not exist; that only started in 1998 but you can bet your life if I ever got the opportunity to go back, that would definitely be the top of my list of things to do. When the bridge first opened the average annual daily traffic was around 11,000 whereas, nowadays that number has reached an average of 160,000 vehicles a day.

The ferry made its way across the harbour to offload passengers at the zoo. We now made our way toward the opposite side of the harbour cutting across its middle giving spectacular views of the Sydney skyline and the flotilla from the round the world yacht race that just happened to be stopping off here at the same time as me. The convicts brought here in the early days must have thought 'I wish I'd killed the wife sooner'. We passed within a hundred metres of the replica ship 'the Bounty' (used in the film 'Mutiny on the Bounty' starring Sir Anthony Hopkins and Mel Gibson), at half mast drifting along as dignified as the original. An old American steam boat paddled past; it just looked so out of place. We were shown various tourist attractions including the old prison island, the prime ministers house and some of the more luxurious properties dotted along the shoreline before making our way back to Circular Quay. On the journey back we passed nearer to the Opera House and its quirkiness seemed somehow to be representative of the Australians I'd met. As we docked Junior and Andy stood by the quayside, their faces signalled that they'd been successful in their attempts to hire a camper van.

"Ant, what's a thousand and eighty dollars divided by four?" Said Andy.

"Two hundred and seventy dollars. Why?"

"That's how much you owe us two. We've just hired a camper van with a two man tent for two weeks it's being delivered at twelve-thirty tomorrow at the backpackers".

It was now the 18th and the guys bringing the van were half an hour late but stood on the balcony watching girls passing on their way to the beach was enough of a distraction to make it not matter, even though we'd end up at our first destination (Byron Bay) after dark. The camper van was a trusty Volkswagen that slept three; one on either side of the back and one space created by pulling a board out of the top were someone could sleep in the roof area. When we'd sorted all the paper work out and had our instructions on how to use the gas bottle and how to connect the electric cable it was time to go. Andrew decided that he was going to drive first because 'he knew the way'. I told him that I didn't care who drove just as long as we could drive over the bridge. He told me that we had to go that way anyway and to enjoy the scenery; I didn't need telling twice my nose was glued to the window taking everything in and I had to pinch myself as we were suspended over the harbour forty-nine metres above the water.

We headed north towards Brisbane stopping to fill the fridge with beer and buy a deck of cards. Andy and Senior were up front while me and Junior were in the back with our feet up on the seats playing cards in-between enjoying the scenery on route. The heat was stifling, so much so that we were all in our shorts with the air con on full blast. The back of the van was like a greenhouse so me and Thomas decided that a cold beer would go down a treat. Andy heard the clink of bottles and kicked off with us because he couldn't join in sneering at us all the while through the rear view mirror. But the fun really started when we opened another bottle,

"Hey, don't get drunk you've got to have your turn driving soon"

"What happened to I'll drive cos I know the way". I said taking the piss.

It was decided between us to share the driving, Andy and Senior would drive one day and Junior and I would drive the next giving us all a rest. This just gave me and Junior the excuse to open even more bottles helping to overcome the boredom of looking at a highway. We reached Coffs Harbour just as the sun retired for the evening; we still had a couple of hours driving before we would reach Byron Bay.

The radio station was playing tracks from the 80's and I sang along to almost every song, the beer was turning me into a crooner. We eventually arrived at the town around eight o' clock and made our way to a backpackers place called the 'Arts Factory' where Junior had stayed when he was there the previous April but it was full. It was the summer holidays and every camp site and backpackers was rammed to the rafters. It seemed for a while that we weren't going to find anywhere but we came across a place on the beach front but the office had closed for the night. We drove round the campsite twice trying to find a space and eventually found one. We connected the electric lead to the mains on a post and put the full beam of the headlights on so we could erect the tent. The wind had picked up and made the tent flap around like a flag in a gust of wind. There we were the four of us stood in the beam of the headlights trying to secure the ground sheet with bent tent pegs and hard ground. We were making a right dogs dinner of it until the guy from the next tent came over and said,

"Gudday guys, looks like your avin a liddle bit o trouble there"

We had the instructions unfolded; they were flapping in the wind more than the tent. This Australian introduced himself as 'Russ' and just took control of tent erection much to our appreciation. We offered Russ a beer before we went into town for something to eat. We didn't have a key for the shower blocks so we waited at the exit door waiting for someone to come out so that we could blag our way in there. After we'd all showered Russ came over to the van for a beer and we ended up staying at the camp site all night.

 The following morning bleary eyed and extremely hung over we sent Senior to pay for the pitch and packed up the tent; it was a dam site easier to dismantle than the night before but then again it was daylight, there was no wind and me and Junior wasn't pissed. We stood at the back of the van talking to Russ when his wife sheepishly appeared and offered us all a coffee. A bit of Manc banter and she was soon smiling and inviting us round to their place if we were passing through Brisbane anytime. It was time to hit the road and make our way to a small village situated a short drive inland from the coast called Nimbin. Both Andy and Junior had been there before and told us of the delights it had to offer.

 The landscape changed as dramatically as the humidity; vegetation was rich green and oversized with health. The roads became more precarious as they twisted their way round and through the valleys. Waterfalls and streams cut through the vegetation as effectively as the lain tarmac. A clearing at the top of a hill gave spectacular views of the forest plantation; it lay across the landscape like a rippled silk sheet. It took little more than an hour to come to the dilapidated wooden bridge that spans the stream outside Nimbin. We crossed the bridge listening to every creak but it held the weight and the Nimbin limits sign smiled at us with its psychedelic colours behind bold blue lettering. Once again we climbed a hillside before reaching level ground and a small stretch of tarmac flanked by a row of shops on either side.

 The roadside was strewn with hippie regalia and Aboriginal art. As we pulled up beside a war memorial a woman led a sheepish looking lad into the middle of the gardens; a plastic bag was exchanged for folded dollars, a drug deal conducted so blasé that no one batted an eyelid. I couldn't wait to explore this strange yet intriguing time warped village. The humidity was ferocious at this stage and all we were wearing was a pair of shorts, a cap and a gob-smacked expression. As we got to the road a four-wheel drive pick-up passed with a high-sided trailer with an unimpressed looking cow in the back. All the TV clips I'd seen over the years of 'flower power' at Woodstock were a living reality somewhere deep inside the New South Wales Mountains untouched by progress and how refreshing the experience was.

 We set off for Surfers Paradise and soon found ourselves on the coastal highway heading for the Gold Coast; Australians answer to Miami. Within a short couple of hours we'd reached the seafront with its huge expanse of sun obstructing row of skyscraper hotels and apartment blocks overlooking the ocean. Although it's a relatively short distance between Nimbin and Surfers these two places are worlds apart with simplicity on the one hand and overindulgent opulence on the other.

 From the camp site to the harbour was quite a walk and I found it really difficult because the concrete was stiffening my legs, the only slight relief that I got was by walking on the grass where possible; that acted much like cushioned flooring. My lower back and thighs were burning and it was nothing to do with the sun. The pain was intense but I really couldn't care less, after all I was in Surfers Paradise. I began to trail behind the others, "come on slow coach" was all I got sympathy wise, I just smiled at them and extracted a spliff from my bum bag and lit it up walking with added vigour. Junior stood and waited for me or was he waiting for a toot? I think the latter but they've all made exceptions for me which was a great comfort on a road trip of this kind. As I came level with him I handed him the joint,

"So are you going to do the Bungee jump?"

"You bet your arse Thomas, I did one in Africa and I'm determined to do this one even if you have to carry me there".

As we got to the harbour the tourists' mingled around the attractions and the many bars huddled around the shoreline. We sat at a table on a wooden slatted terrace over the water and drank a Toohey's whilst watching a couple of adrenaline junkies bungee jumping (the majority being dipped into the sea). Jelly fish swam lazily in the warmth of the sea right underneath our feet. All the lads were asking me if I was really going to do it. I told them it was a piece of cake and it wasn't that high. They should have seen the one at Vic Falls; now that's high. At the end of the jetty that was adjacent to the bar was the canopied motor boat that took jumpers over to the platform. The engine on the motor boat was working overtime as it ferried seven of us over to the platform in the middle of the bay where the bungee jump was positioned. The owner made small talk on the way across and jokingly told me to look down into the water before jumping so that I wouldn't end up with a jelly fish wrapped around my face. I paid the $60 dollars and signed the disclaimer form, got weighed and then had my legs strapped up ready for the ascent in the cage.

The cage was lowered onto the platform signalling my inevitable jump. As the cage left the deck the breeze filtered through the mesh cooling my sticky skin, even with the sun concealed behind ever greying clouds the heat generated made everyone lackadaisical. The attendant asked if I'd like to be dipped into the sea, he then jokingly added that if I returned with a fish I could jump for free.

At one hundred and fifty feet the view of Surfers was amazing, the safety bar was removed and I jumped forward and held on to the two bars placing my feet on the small jumpers platform ready to jump; firstly looking down at the water to make sure there were no jelly fish swimming where I would land and secondly at my friends patiently waiting to see if I had the balls to jump.

With Senior armed with a rolling camcorder I looked down once more, it took me fondly back to my childhood memories of the time I first dived off the top diving board at Oldham swimming pool. Although this was some five times the height, I had no fear whatsoever as I raised my right arm to punch the air to the countdown. The attendant said,

"Just look forward mate towards the horizon, that way it won't be so bad. O.K. are you ready"

"Ye"

"Right, 5, 4,3,2,1 bungee".

Right on queue my knees bent poised to thrust my body through the air with all the energy I could muster. I dived from the platform trying to distance myself as much as possible from my starting position emulating my childhood hero Tarzan. The wind rushed past my ears and the water rushed towards me like a speeding train but fractionally before impact the bungee cord (along with the attendance experience) slowed my progress down; I entered the water gently the salty luke-warm water cooled me down. The cord pulls you skywards again but the second bounce earth bound is disappointingly weak compared to the first. The remaining half a dozen bounces are a gentle floating sensation that ends far too quickly and is an anti-climax. We tried to talk Senior into having a go but he refused point blank.

That night we decided to go into town and see what the night life in Surfers had to offer. The main street where all the action happened was about a mile away so we made our way to the bus stop opposite the campsite; I approached a family that was waiting for the bus and asked what time the bus was due. The bloke replied,

"9 o'clock"

I looked at my watch and with a cheeky smile said,

"You've missed it, its twenty to ten".

"No mate its twenty to nine, where have you just come from?"

"Byron Bay"

"Well we're an hour behind here".

I started laughing; we'd crossed a time zone without the slightest inkling of doing so. We decided that we'd start walking and before too long I was trailing behind again and due to my leisurely pace the bus passed us in mid stop; the family staring out of the window at us trying desperately not to laugh in our faces. We now had no choice but to walk, there wasn't a cab in sight.

Australia's answer to Miami was full of bars, clubs and restaurants and an atmosphere to go with it. The street outside the club we'd just come out of was bustling with burger bars and rickshaws. We asked a puny looking lad to take us to the camp on his rickshaw. He said that he only took two people at a time and that he would try to get one of his friends to take the other two of us. The club was emptying and so was the rickshaw rank so we offered him double to take us, he agreed. Well this poor bugger set off trying desperately to turn the peddles and get some momentum going and eventually he got a slow pace going, it was a good job that we were on the flat or he would have been knackered. The only trouble was that people walking along the pavement was making faster progress than us so we just jumped out give him his normal rate for the two hundred yards he'd taken us and walked the rest of the way. I suppose I could have gone back to camp on the rickshaw and saved my legs but I was on holiday with the lads and I've never really been one for the easy option out when it comes to my MS.

Next day we went back to the harbour, only this time we decided to drive there. I think the lads were trying to save some strength in my legs. Whilst we were having brunch a guy overheard our accents and told us that Prince Naseem Hamed's world title fight against the American Kevin Kelly was on at the sports bar. We said we'd see him there when we finished our meal. By the time we found this sports bar the fight was over, Naseem had knocked him out in four rounds. So with our tails between our legs, I went with Senior to have a flight on 'The Red Baron' a 'two passenger' open cockpit bi-seaplane made by Brumman and was the plane appeared in the film 'The Phantom'. We were given 'Biggles' type helmets made of leather complete with ear cones. It was authentically old with the paint peeling from its pot riveted panels. We made our way slowly through the muse of activity around the harbour shoreline to open sea where the speed was picked up for take-off.

The feeling when we left the water was extremely gently and we were soon flying over the inlet to this amazing harbour. The noise from the propeller was deafening and we had to shout at each other to be heard but the view was spectacular. The pilot flew us out of the harbour entrance and down the coast line giving us the opportunity to see the whole of Surfers in a new light. The ocean on one side appeared flat except for the white froth from breaking waves racing towards the golden strip of beach separating the skyscrapers from the ocean. We turned and headed back to the harbour entrance and a helicopter flew passed us maybe only a hundred metres away and only about fifty meters higher. The pilot banked the plane half a dozen times before setting it down slap bang in the middle of the harbour only occupied by speed boats. The flight was an awesome experience and thoroughly recommended.

It was now approaching 4 o'clock and we all decided that instead of staying another night we would drive through the night each taking a turn at the wheel to get to Airlie Beach by morning.

I was awoken to an idealistic beach and the faintest of ripples washing the sand. The palm trees indicated that we'd arrived in paradise, it was a little before seven. The café adjacent to the car park opened at eight so I got on one of the bench beds in the back while Senior and Andy took a stroll along the sleepy high street. I was roused by the side door sliding open and Andrew's beaming smile.

"Hey Ant, you owe me $45, we're going snorkelling on the Barrier Reef on Christmas day".

Over breakfast we all decided that we'd just carry on driving and get to Cairns so that we could have an extra night with Dean and Jo Kelly.

As we left Airlie Beach behind us and joined the highway northwards the trees hung devilishly over the road, heavy with the weight from the rainfall; all the while the windscreen wipers struggled to expel the water long enough to see clearly. The road twisted and turned carving its way through thick rain forest and skirting the shore from time to time. I was still exhausted from the night before and spent most of the day curled up in the back. Cairns is a garden city between the sea and the rainforest mountains, it was founded in 1876 as a port for inland gold fields, its small but cosmopolitan and a stopping off point for many yachts, liners and tour boats. We had Alan's address and asked for directions once we were in the town centre. Alan's four bedroomed house was a wooden building on stilts with the lower section being partitioned off with wooden slats concealing a couple of rooms. The wooden staircase at the front of the house led to the balcony complete with hammock and the entrance door. The back of the house also had the same staircase and balcony. The front garden had plants that were as tall as the house. Dean appeared at the top of the stairs, Jo peering over his shoulder,

"Welcome to sunny Australia" he shouted down at us; it was pissing down.

We were introduced to Amanda (Alan's wife), who's hospitality was as though we'd known her as long as she'd known Alan. That night we just caught up with Dean and Jo and their adventure so far and we told them the tales of what we'd been up to and fighting over whose turn it was to chill out on the hammock.

As dusk fell I could see strange shapes in the sky. When the shapes got closer I could make out that they were bats but these things were huge. Dean explained that these were fruit bats and before too long the sky was littered with hundreds of bats.

At some stage during the night a parachute jump was mentioned and Amanda played a video of Alan doing a parachute jump over Cairns. Junior turned to me and asked if I was up for doing it, it was a stupid question in hindsight. Andy said that he'd be up for it as well.

The next morning Amanda left for work waking me from a deep sleep on the hammock, she asked if I was going to do the parachute jump that day and I told her that by the time she got home that evening I would have come back from heaven. After yet another brunch which was really the order of each day because we were never up early enough to have breakfast, we all jumped into the camper van and drove to the sea front.

The tourist office was open for business only there weren't many tourists about in-between the showers. Junior and I inquired about the price of the parachute jump and for a tandem jump from 10,000 feet and a video was $350. Andy asked the bloke on the other side of the counter whether or not we could do the jump the following day and he said,

"I'll just phone through to ask".

He phoned Paul's Parachuting Company and they said that they could come to collect us there and then; I said,

"Tell them to come for us we're having a bit of that".

Andy went grey and the guy from the tourist office ended up giving him a glass of whiskey to calm his nerves.

A short guy with a goatee beard and shades pulled up in a mini bus decked out with Paul's Parachuting plastered all over the side and that was it, we were off to the airfield. We followed this guy out of town and headed for the airfield all the while the excitement and exhilaration mounting. Before too long we were inside the office filling out disclaimer forms and handing over the $350, Dean was green with envy but he was on a budget.

In the office the board on the wall marked out the details of the jump; flight 10, Antony, instructor Ross, video jumper to accompany us Del. This was it we were actually going to do it and while we watched the promotional video of the numerous people that had done the jump before us, my instructor and the one assigned to Andy were casually playing table football so blasé that it put me at ease. We were then kitted out with jumpsuits; mine was a yellow and blue number. We were given a safety briefing before having a harness fitted, the instructors told us that when we exited the plane we were to keep our arms folded until they tapped us on the shoulder and then we could spread them out; they joked with us by saying that if the parachute failed we could flap our arms and promptly gave us a demonstration. We walked out to a waiting twin-engine plane with the rear door removed. Thomas was told to go in first because he was jumping last, then me, then Andy last because he was going first.

Once in place the pilot asked the control tower for permission to take off and we taxied down the runway. As we left the ground my stomach had butterflies in it and as we flew over the town of Cairns at around five hundred feet I became a little apprehensive. But that however faded as we flew over the harbour with its edges littered with industrial units and jetty's sitting at the bottom of the hills covered with tropical rain forest; that was a magical site. We steadily gained altitude to 10,000 feet all the while the town and the hills becoming smaller. The cloud base was now well below us and once above the clouds the intermittent patches of cloud revealed glimpses of the tropical rainforest below. It was now time and Andy was ushered to the exit door. The camera man leaned out of the door as Andy's feet were placed outside the door. He placed his hands at either side of the door pushing back against the instructor, but he just pulled them into Andy's body and then the camera man exited fractionally before Andy and his instructor. They disappeared, it was now my turn.

I hitched my way to the door but the instructor pulled me back fastening me to him; I was by now getting rather giddy. With the cameraman leaning out of the plane and my legs dangling from the doorway, I crossed my arms. Ross said in my ear "OK, 3, 2, 1 lets go", whilst he held the side of the doors in a rocking motion in time with the countdown.

We fell from the plane and the ground could be briefly seen through the cloud and the first initial feeling was a tickle in the pit of my stomach as we travelled through the air at 120 mph. Within seconds Ross tapped my shoulder and I splayed my arms out, the sensation of falling through the air was heightened. The adrenalin pumped through every sinew and I can honestly say that I have never felt so alive, fear had evaporated into shear unadulterated excitement. The camera man drew level and for the camera Ross took us into a spin, each time we rotated 360 degrees I caught sight of the cameraman and shouted "this is awesome" at the camera.

After half a dozen spins we faced the camera for the final time, for Ross pulled the cord and the cameraman fell to earth as our speed rapidly decelerated into a gentle glide. Freefall was over far too quickly, the thirty-five seconds gone forever only to be replayed on video and extracted from my memory. Ross began to pull on each side handle swinging us from side to side as we drifted effortlessly down to the ground. Ross told me to hold the handles and pull on each side but as I tried this, my attempts at swinging the canapé were feeble compared to the six foot plus frame of Ross.

We went through the cloud base and the moisture left droplets of water on my goggles. The clouds faded and the ground appeared in wondrous shades of green hues. We were now over cleared fields and Ross pointed out our landing area. I could clearly see the two mini buses parked side by side. The decent to earth was much quicker than I imagined it to be and Ross reminded me to lift up my legs ready for landing.

I could make out Thomas landing in-between the cameraman's canapés laying on the ground. I lifted my legs and we landed on our feet but this was particularly easy because of Ross's large frame. He unclipped me and the cameraman rushed over to record my immediate reaction to the jump; I was overwhelmed. Thomas stood behind me his face told the whole story. Senior came over with Dean and Jo with an opened bottle of beer.

We all stood around clinking the bottles of beer together with the instructors and the cameramen, us celebrating our first jump and the others just being who they are; men who fall from the sky for a living. The guys told us to follow them to a bottle store so they could buy us some beer before going back to the office to have our videos done. It was the most awesome adrenaline rush ever and I couldn't have wished to have shared this experience with better friends. That night was Dean's birthday and we celebrated with a Party at Alan's while we watched our videos with Amanda. Alan was working away from home and wouldn't be back until the following day which just happened to be his birthday; so we had to do it all over again.

24th December, it was close to nine before we said our goodbyes and hit the road south for the first time on this road trip. The weather hadn't improved much but the further south we travelled the more intermittent the showers became. We reached Airlie Beach (Gateway to the Whitsundays) in time to get a camp site just north of the main street and make a much needed trip to the supermarket for supplies. As we pitched the tent nearing dusk, the trees behind us began to fill with Fruit Bats and this gave us the opportunity to see these huge yet cute bats up close and personal. I just sat on my chair beer in hand mesmerised by the gradually growing colony all the while their screeches tried to drown out the radio.

Christmas morning we drove down to the quayside and were greeted by a guy in a Santa outfit; somehow in blistering heat the illusion of Christmas was as wasted as the giant Christmas tree in Sydney harbour. We boarded a two story ferry and sat on the top deck, it seemed as if all the passengers were vying for a place up there but we managed a seat. Before long we set sail for the platform on the Barrier Reef but first stop was Fraser Island to pick up some passengers from there. The Island is idyllic and I was glad we stopped there.

The staff of Reefworld with their white motif golf shirts and blue shorts mingled with the passengers, explaining the rules and the marine life we could expect to see. We approached the reef platform with caution and once disembarked were told of the few activities on offer. The first was snorkelling which was included in the price as well as a buffet style lunch. Some of the other activities included scuba diving and helicopter rides to outlying islands for a secluded picnic.

Me and Junior went to book ourselves on the scuba diving but when we got there all the places had been pre-booked, so we opted for the helicopter ride over the reef. Again not a chance, all the flights had been pre-booked by all the Japanese that were on Christmas holidays. There wasn't a cloud in the sky which was in contrast to Cairns and the sun was so hot that when I went snorkelling I wore a t-shirt. Senior remained on the platform armed with his video camera while the rest of us got straight into the water which was teeming with fish of all description and size.

One fish was the size of a man and gently floated around the platform oblivious to the many visitors it now found itself with. Large parts of the reef were cordoned off due to the level of water over the top of the coral so we swam as far from the platform as we were allowed. The coral glistened in the dabbled sunlight and an energy of colour came from the shoals of fish using it as a safety haven.

Air bubbles rose to the surface as scuba divers swam underneath us; we watched them with great envy as they pulled themselves along a pre-laid rope whilst following the instructor.

After a while we returned to the platform to see Senior who couldn't swim and had been on the submarine type vessel to view the reef and its inhabitants. The buffet lunch was a poor excuse for the Christmas dinner it was trying to portray but with roast lamb and beef on the menu it was more than ample for the after swim hunger. After dinner and a couple of beers we all decided that we'd try to get Senior into the water with the help of the very friendly staff by covering him head to foot in buoyancy aids. We didn't rush him and he nervously entered the water but as soon as he dipped his head under water and saw the delights of the coral through the mask, there was no stopping him. He asked us to swim with him a little further from the platform. Once he'd had enough excitement for the day he returned to filming us while we ventured as far as we could, then all of a sudden Junior came up to me and Andy,

"Jesus, I've just seen a huge Barracuda and you could see its teeth"

"Where?" I said.

"Over there I'm not going back"

So me and Andy set off in search of this huge fish. Then from the distant shadows this silvery reflection appeared from nowhere and swam passed us only about five meters away; its face was best described as ugly with its protruding rows of teeth. Luckily it was more scared of us and disappeared as quickly as it appeared. Swimming in the sea was really peaceful and being in water eased all the aches and pains. That is, until I got out and then my legs turned to jelly. My legs felt as if I was wearing concrete shoes and all I could do was to sit and watch the world go by until it was time to go. What an experience and worth all the pain in the aftermath of a tantalising glimpse of the largest living organism in the world.

We'd picked a leaflet up from the local tourist office of possible places of interest to visit while we were on our way back to Sydney and we found a place called 1770 so we decided to go there. We turned off the highway just south of Barmundu and headed for the coast. We turned onto a dirt track road leaving the comfort of tarmac behind and finding ourselves in the middle of nowhere. The track went on for miles and we found ourselves alone apart from the occasional vehicle headed in the opposite direction.

The Town Of 1770 is a picturesque seaside village surrounded on three sides by the Coral Sea and Bustard Bay. Historically this is the second landing site of Lieutenant

James Cook and the crew of the Endeavour in May 1770. This is a very sleepy town with only natural beauty and the ocean in its favour. A short stroll along the beach was all that was on offer to four party animals and we soon bored of it and decided to push on south. I was overwhelmed to have stood looking out to sea day dreaming of what it must've been like to come ashore over two hundred years ago. How things have changed in that time.

We were a lot more relaxed due to the last few days being less frantic and this just reinvigorated me. As night fall approached we found ourselves just outside Noosa Heads and decided to stay there for the night. We sat on the edge of the inlet watching the fishing and pleasure boats returning to the safety of the harbour.

That night we didn't even venture into town, opting instead to chill out on the shore and watch the sun go down. This is a beautiful part of Australia and the affluence was plain to see. There seemed to be a weary reluctance to our journey back to Sydney but we decided to go back to Byron Bay for a couple of nights and re-visit Nimbin.

I was really looking forward to returning to Byron Bay because we hadn't really seen much the last time. We decided to go inside a steak house and chill at the back where it was much quieter. In the restaurant was a guide advertising a tandem hang-gliding session so Senior called the guy and asked for an appointment the next day. The guy said he was booked up but after a little persuasion he agreed to take me and Senior early the next morning.

We were so tired that after only a few beers in a couple of the bars along the front we decided to go back to camp and chill with a game of cards. I revelled in the delights to come as I re-lived my experience flying in the Peak District some few years earlier to Thomas who couldn't contain his excitement.

We sat outside the office of the gliding school for over twenty minutes after the time stated before some lanky scraggly haired guy turned up with a glider tied to the top of his pick-up with a square steel frame. As he opened the door we more or less barged our way in.

"Struth, you guys are keen, ain't ya?"

As he tried to compose himself, it was clear to see that this guy was well and truly hung over and Thomas ushered me forward to fill in the form, which I eagerly signed. We followed him to a lay-by and then Andy and Junior carried the glider up the hill to the launch site. The view was breathtaking as the ocean opened up before us. To our left sat the peninsula and the light house sitting reassuringly on top surveying everything in sight. I looked to the right and the beach curved into the haze of the morning and disappeared from view. The wind gently gathered pace as it swept its way up the hill until it was strong enough to create that annoying blowing sound in the eardrum.

An Eleanor's Eagle played in the thermal and the instructor turned to me and pointed out its significance. We were about to have a good wind for flying. Soon we were kitted out with a red plastic 'piss pot' helmet and a wind proof suit wrapped around the torso with your legs hanging out. We were ready to go. The instructor had enlisted the help of a couple of locals to hold the edges of the glider before we took off from the platform. The green wooden platform lifted you seductively above the bushes some ten feet below and the contour of the hill fell away into the ocean.

I was given instructions before being ushered towards the end of the platform, all the while the wind attempted to lift the glider into the air. As the other lads held on to the edges of the glider the wind picked up and the glider rose almost lifting my legs. The instructor gave the go ahead and before I knew it I was taking three very short steps and the wind did the rest with the experience of this birdman.

I was told that under no circumstances must I touch the bar which he was manoeuvring like a conductor's baton. The birdman swung the glider to the right and flew majestically over the hillside with the beach to our left. We started to make small talk and I told him of my gliding experience some years earlier. It was then that he told me that he was the current Australian three-time hang-gliding champion. As corny and uncanny as this may sound just as he told me that, his phone rang and he retrieved it from a pocket in the breast of his suit and answered it. I was bewildered as he nonchalantly asked the person on the other end very politely could he phone them back because he was in the air at the moment. His left arm pulled and pushed at the bar and I was dumbstruck. He answered that phone three times before he decided to switch it off.

I began to take in the scenery and really enjoy my flight; I knew I was in safe hands. He manoeuvred the glider along the edge of the hillside and circled in figure of eights whilst allowing me to catch sight of the winged gliders as well as the other hang-gliders that had joined us to frolic in the thermals. Then he sharply turned to fly past the launch site, descending in altitude and building up speed. As we flew past my friends I waved ecstatically. I looked forward and the white lighthouse stood proud as the white contrasted against the green, turquoise and navy blue of the sea. We gently gained height until we were over a thousand feet above sea level but even from this dizzy height we could wave back at the many tourists strolling along the cliff edge pathways.

The water was crystal clear and we were extremely fortunate to catch sight of a reef shark. It was truly amazing to be flying a couple of hundred feet above the lighthouse and to this day I still have the same excitement as I did back then when I watch the video. The twenty minute flight was over far too quickly and the beach was soon fast approaching our feet. I could see the lads on the beach patiently waiting to see the expression on my face. The landing was as perfect as the parachute jump as my puny weight once again made light work for the instructor. I was elated yet disappointed at the same time, for I wanted to stay up in the thermals, literally as free as a bird.

I watched with excitement as Thomas left the safety of terra firma and floated as effortlessly as I had done.

Next morning we toured the harbour, getting a parking ticket in the process. By mid-afternoon we'd reached Coffs Harbour which is known for its Cedar trees, gold mines and a huge Banana plantation. This is yet another beautiful part of Australia and we were fortunate enough to get a place along the shore adjacent to the river outlet. By now we were used to seeing white sands and crystal clear waters but it was still a sight to behold. A huge rock rises from the sea almost obstructing the entrance to the river known locally as Little Mutton Bird Island. Once again the scenery and the relaxed atmosphere along the shoreline was far more alluring than a pub crawl, and we walked bare foot allowing the waves to wash our feet. We had to return the campervan before closing time on New Year's Eve, so we decided to get to Sydney a day earlier and relax; I was suffering from exhaustion. Our final evening on the road trip was something to savour. The sunset that night was particularly poignant as it set on our Gold Coast adventure but we were about to embark on a week of exploring the delights of Sydney.

We were on the road before eight; that gave us plenty of time to reach Sydney before returning the van to its rightful owners.

By mid-afternoon we'd reached Palm Beach the northernmost suburb of Sydney and the home of the popular Aussie soap opera Home and Away. This is only an hours' drive from the centre of Sydney so we decided it would be rude not to make a small diversion. This is yet another peninsula embracing a river outlet but this is lushly coated with evergreen bushes hemmed in from the Pacific Ocean by golden sands. The road weaved its way around the headland giving spectacular views of the harbour littered with yachts and then the open ocean on the other side. As the bay opened up before us it was surrealistic as I remembered the opening titles on the Home and Away show but I was now here in the flesh. The beach front houses were palatial, the gardens secluded by palm trees. We walked along the beach and stood at the side of the rock pool that has been featured in the programme many times. A woman walking her dog along the beach informed us that the outdoor filming was done on Tuesdays and Thursdays; it was Wednesday, just my luck.

The drive across the bridge still held the very same sense of childhood excitement and the sight of towering skyscrapers meant that the road trip was over. I was glad that we didn't have to spend hours driving and looking forward to exploring the city. The office for the campervan was in the King's Cross area of town so we decided to find digs and see what the backpacking scene had to offer us. There were no vacancies anywhere because of the amount of people converging on the city for the New Year's Eve firework display (said to be the most expensive in the world at that time), with Sydney council spending two million dollars on the event. After roaming around King's Cross for a while we found a bit of a dive but the room had four single beds and they definitely looked more appealing than the pavement. King's Cross is a vibrant part of town with an array of different bars and nightclubs and we had to run the gauntlet of people trying to get you into their establishments.

New Years Eve and Sydney became electric as the anticipation of the forthcoming event was hot on everybody's' lips. Evening fell upon the city signalling the end of 1997. We slowly made our way towards Circular Quay, home of the Opera House stopping off at an off-licence to buy a crate of beer. The light was beginning to fade as tens of thousands of people descended upon this exceptional vantage point. It was bewildering as the scene resembled an army of ants but with far less organisation. The steps to the Opera House began to fill like a football terrace so we retreated to the comfort of a grassed area and sat patiently waiting for the stroke of midnight.

The sky was clear and stars twinkled unaware of the chaos going on all around us. The countdown to midnight was shouted out simultaneously with collected enthusiasm. Then the first of the fireworks raced into the sky from the tops of the skyscrapers followed by an appreciative cheer from the crowd. The colours of the fireworks were iridescent and I stood transfixed totally engrossed in the moment. Within minutes the whole of the harbour was awash with rockets being fired from platforms in the harbour and the bridge (which was central to the display).

Music played from loudspeakers situated on every lamppost in perfect synchronicity to the display. The noise from the fireworks sounded like a battle zone and comfortably drowned out the cheers from the crowd. The display was brought to a close by rockets being fired from one side of the arch to the other, slowly building up speed until the whole arch was alight with colour. A huge smiley face appeared in the centre of the bridge before a crescendo of white sparks fell like a waterfall into the harbour below. It left everyone wanting more and a hush fell upon the harbour side. Sydney now holds the reputation for the best firework display in the world and it is richly deserved.

We moved out of the hovel and into what has to be said is the best backpacker accommodation in Australia, the youth hostel next to the central railway station. The hostel has every amenity you could wish for including a roof top pool. This place had a vibrancy of its own and this extended to the people staying there. Although we were in one room with twin bunk beds it was more than comfortable except for the snoring and farting. Each day we visited a different beach and while Andy and Junior spent the daylight hours topping up their tans (to show off when they got back home), Senior and I explored every nook and cranny of the beachside attractions.

The evenings would always start in the Scubar, which is situated at the side of the hostel, where we would meet up with fellow backpackers and explore different nightspots around the city. This became like a small community and just finished off the holiday nicely. I loved Sydney with its fresh mixture of culture and contemporary lifestyle. Those last few days were a blur as the return flight to China came around far too quickly but we made the most of being 'Down Under'.

Chapter 18

What next for Mr. K?

On returning from the trip of a lifetime to a dreary overcast Failsworth, reality gave me a good kicking like a school yard bully and I contemplated my next move.

Since leaving the bungalow, in six short months I'd travelled to the other side of the world, to four different continents and to seven different countries. I'd seen the largest natural waterfall in the world at Victoria Falls, walked on the Great Wall of China (the largest man made structure in the world) and swam on the Great Barrier Reef (the largest natural living organism in the world) and it was all thanks to Multiple Sclerosis; I'd finally taken something back from it.

I took great solace in aimlessly driving around in my Porsche but because of the long trip to the other side of the world and the damp Manchester atmosphere, getting in and out of the car was difficult; I just wasn't supple enough. I remember once while I was at the art studio, a policeman came in to ask who owned the red Porsche outside and when I went outside with him he looked at me as if I had someone else's badge. I'd set the time on my orange disability badge at the time I was leaving instead of arriving but when I explained to him that I had MS he told me that his friend had it and he understood. That was one of the funniest things about the orange badge; I deserved one because I couldn't walk very far and I had to use a stick but when I used to pull up in a Porsche and stick the badge in the window, I used to get some odd looks. This is one of the most difficult aspects of this illness because people can't see a cast or a scar or even a missing limb; it's invisible until you try to walk or hold a cup to your mouth and your hands shake uncontrollably. On occasions it does really get to me but I've no choice in the matter so you either put up or shut up; if you don't mentally conquer the pain barrier then you're basically fucked.

It was now a little over four years since this thing inside me had forced me to finish work and with it steal my identity. I was a completely different person to the happy go lucky person I once was; although I still portrayed that demeanour, inside I was crying out for some relief from this relentless assassin and some form of normality.

I threw myself into my art and found solace in re-directing all the frustrations and fears each attack brought. I'd been going to an art studio in Hyde called KT studios where the people were varied but all shared a commonality, a simple love of art and creativity. Kenneth Miles the proprietor had been in the Church Street studio for years and the upstairs had been converted to accommodate a dozen artists working alongside each other in a totally relaxed atmosphere. Kenneth worked downstairs in his studio and would come upstairs from time to time to give tips and encouragement on how to use different mediums and techniques; he would often show you how to create an image. All the people that attended the studio became acquaintances of mine and I would often make the effort to attend on certain days when I knew certain people would be there. We had a collective exhibition each year and that was the highlight of all our pain staking work and a pat on the back for Kenneth. A few months went by with nothing really unusual happening and as a result my body began to regain some of its strength and I became mentally stronger with my outlook on life being far more positive. I was having less attacks and I was able to leave my walking stick at home.

A couple of months into the year and Andy started to have a certain glow about him; he'd fallen for a girl who was the receptionist at one of his suppliers and a little bit of harmless flirting and banter had stirred them both into a frenzy. She soon started to visit and within a few short months she was coming up for the weekend on a regular basis; the house was transformed into a card shop with all the cards and letters she was sending on a daily basis. Love had blossomed. As June approached he announced that she was moving in with him so I put my name on the council housing list and enlisted the aid of my doctor to draw up a letter to help with getting suitable accommodation and to speed the process up.

Within no time I was offered two flats, one just outside the town centre and the other one just around the corner from my mother's (it was directly across the road from the junior school I used to attend). I'd arranged to view each of the properties with my mother and my social worker Liz. Firstly, we went to the flat which was a ten minute walk from the town centre; it was a first floor flat. Liz rang the doorbell and a man's voice on the intercom invited us in. The buzzer sounded and Liz pushed the door open to reveal a stair lift. I looked sheepishly at my mother; she gave me a reluctant reassuring smile. Liz urged me to try the chairlift reiterated by the guy at the top of the stairs. The motor started up and the chair was sent down the staircase and I was ushered onto the chair by Liz. I was gently being raised up the staircase. When I eventually got to the top of the stairs I didn't even want to look around and this poor guy tried his damnedest to sell his flat to me. His efforts were futile and wasted on me there was no way on this planet that I was going to allow myself to admit defeat and end up in a situation there was no return from. My viewing was half hearted, I just wanted out of there. I wouldn't even accept his kind offer of a cup of tea I just wanted to go.

It was now time to go and meet a guy from the council and view the flat near my mother's that I'd always known as the 'Old Folks Flats'. With a sunken heart and a despondent demeanour I went through the motions for the sake of my mum and Liz (who was in my opinion going above and beyond her job description to try and get me some sort of independence for myself which I really did appreciate). We met the man from the council and straight away he was an arrogant arsehole with a 'take it or leave it but don't waste my time attitude'. Instead of being accommodating towards him I just wanted to punch his lights out and I'm far from a violent man, in fact I couldn't fight my way out of a wet paper bag but this guy just got right under my skin.

We walked into the flat and the first thing that hit me was the woodchip wall paper in every room including the bathroom. The bath was about a foot deep due to the disabled woman who previously lived there; if you'd have filled it to the brim it would have only covered the nick of your arse. I didn't like it one bit but my mother was smitten with it encouraging me to take it and pointing out its potential. When we walked into the bedroom there was a cross hanging on the wall, my mum said that it was an omen and that I should leave it where it was; 'fuck off' I thought but didn't dare tell her that. I didn't like this place either but Liz told me that she would see to it that I had a nice shower fitted and that it would look totally different. I needed to be out of Andy's and in my own place (not because of Andy and his new love Louise who both said that I could stay as long as I wanted) but because three's a crowd especially when love is young and all you want to do is christen every room in the house.

I accepted the flat and the ball was set in motion. Although I had my reservations everyone was near to this flat and it was central to everything that was going on in my life whereas, Andy's was away from where I grew up and all the mates that I'd grown up with and that was the factor that I needed at this particular time. I met some great people in Failsworth and still see many of them but I needed to return to Waterloo just so that I could have the security I was craving at the time.

It didn't take long to get the keys and I set about decorating the flat getting rid of all the woodchip wall paper and adding my touch to the place. My mum was there one day with me and we were doing a bit of painting; I was feeling really disillusioned and told her that I was going to emigrate to South Africa. I just couldn't see a future here for myself and bless her in true parent-child style she convinced me to give it a go. Once I'd given the place a lick of paint and had a few friends round it didn't seem all that bad after all and once people got used to me being around again the bell never stopped ringing; in fact that is still the case to this day the flat is never empty.

Well it was two years since I sold the business to our kid and the money was starting to run dry but I'd had an absolute ball on it and lived like a king for those couple of years doing exactly what I wanted to do exactly when I wanted to do it; so there were definitely no complaints from me. In fact, I wouldn't leave the house unless a had a couple of hundred quid in my pocket; I lived as if there was no tomorrow and I still live my life like that now. I really don't give a shit and that's what keeps me one step ahead of the illness. Stress is a killer no matter whether you are ill or not. By the August I'd sold my pride and joy but I'd enjoyed it for two years. I bought a Cavalier SRI and decided to drive to France in it.

Christmas came and went and in the March 1999 I received a phone call from Grahame asking if I could go to Huddersfield to collect some chalk that he used in the gym and take it to Birmingham where David one of his gymnasts was visiting his missionary parents who were there on a five year sabbatical. It was a great opportunity to visit my godson Sebastian and the gang down in Evesham. When I did eventually get to Birmingham and in the company of the Pallas's their phone rang and it was my cousin from sunny South Africa. He thanked me for taking the chalk down for David to take back and said that in return he'd send me a plane ticket to go over for a couple of months. I took that with a pinch of salt but sure enough six weeks later I got a call from him to say that my ticket was at the Lufthansa desk at Manchester airport and I was flying out in a couple of days; that at the time was like a date with Kylie Minogue.

If anyone ever needed a boost this was it.

Grahame's had changed, this was evident when Grahame pressed the key fob and the electric gates slowly opened. The place had a bar, swimming pool and of course the bungalow had been finished. I arrived on Thursday morning two days before the F.A. Cup and Grahame said that we were going to watch it at the football club (where he had started to help the coach Wilson Hepplewhite who used to play for Arsenal to do the warm up), just behind Johannesburg Zoo aptly called Zoo Lake. I wasted no time phoning Griff who'd returned from Zambia because things didn't work out for him. He agreed to meet me at Zoo Lake on the Saturday to watch the match with me and the lads and have a few beers. United were on for a historic treble after clinching the Premiership against Tottenham 2-1 and the atmosphere in the club house was electric because of all the ex-pats in there.

The Reds beat Newcastle United 2-0 and set us up nicely to take the treble if we beat Bayern Munich on Wednesday night in the Champions League final at the Nou Camp Stadium in Barcelona. Wednesday night arrived and we went to a German pub a ten minute drive from Grahame's place. When we walked in, there were three German's (the owner, his son and his brother-in-law) and about ninety United fans. That night has gone down in history but this is what happened on that night. Before the match had started a sweepstake went around the pub 'which team was going to score first and in what minute'. I said that Bayern would score in the forth minute, which was at the time indicative of the way United were playing in the champions league going down to a silly goal in the opening minutes before coming back into the game. Everyone was giving me some grief but it was a ten Rand stake (equal to a quid at the time) so there was nothing to lose. Sure enough after the sixth minute Bayern scored and I won 360 Rand; I was quickly indoctrinated into the South African culture of buying a crate of beer for the lads.

The German's were smug even though outnumbered and then the famous dying moments unfolded. I was dying to go for a pee but didn't dare just in case I missed something and then United equalised, the place went crazy. I was dancing half from the goal and half from wanting to go. Moments later the referee blew his whistle and I thought that he'd blown for full time meaning that the match had gone into extra time. I rushed to the toilet and almost pissed in my pants trying to undo my fly, I stood there with absolute relief, the flood gates had opened and there was no turning back. Halfway through there was an almighty cheer from the pub and I didn't know what had happened and I couldn't do anything because I was still emptying my bladder. After what seemed like an eternity I rushed back to the bar to see what the fuss was; everyone was dancing around and I was just in time to see the replay of Ole Gunner Solskjaer's goal. That was it we'd done the treble, what an awesome start to three months in Africa.

Griff phoned me and asked if I wanted to go to Kruger Park for a couple of days with him and his friend Radley, who was inspecting all the petrol stations in the park. We headed north toward the north-western area of the park and through thousands of acres of orange and banana plantations. The Punda Maria gate (the most northerly entry gate) was quite like going through customs with cars' registrations being meticulously double checked for safety reasons. I was now in the largest game park in South Africa with a surface area of 7,580 miles or the equivalent of 2.2 million hectares (which equates to the size of Wales). First camp we came to shared the same name as the gate and as we drove into the petrol station, Radley barked out orders of what we had to inspect; I had the job of toilet inspector (I always seem to get the best jobs). After a braai and a couple of beers we made our way south to tick another camp from our list and by late afternoon we'd reached Mopani camp.

After inspecting the petrol station we went to the reception to camp for the night. With only a few spaces reserved for cars the car park was full, so Radley just parked on the grass next to them. The reception was busy and we had to wait for a good ten minutes before being seen to. Griff told the receptionist that we wanted to camp and we were promptly told that this camp site didn't have an area for tents, this camp only had chalets and the prices started at 700 Rand. Griff told the woman that we were not going to pay that price because we could do our whole trip for that and so we got back into the car and made for the exit. As we drove to the gate the guard refused point blank to let us out saying that it was too late. In Kruger Park there is a speed limit of 30km per hour and the guard said that we could not get to the next camp within the speed limit and so we had to stay. We went back to the reception and Radley parked in the same spot. We all went into the reception and Griff told the receptionist that the guard wouldn't let us out and we were going to camp on the grass outside the petrol station; to which we were told under no circumstances were we to pitch a tent in this camp site. Radley argued the toss saying that we were not paying the price they wanted because we could have got to the next camp, so it was their fault and not ours.

Next minute we heard this irate voice from behind us coming from the reception door,

"Who's parked on my grass?"

We looked round and this ranger in a pristine khaki uniform walked up to us with steam coming out of his ears.

"I have" said Radley.

The receptionist explained what was going on and the ranger said,

"Follow me".

With that he led us to the car and started going off his head at us and he was being really rude.

"Speak to me like that again China and I'll knock your fucking head off" Said Griff, squaring up to him nose to nose.

He thought for a minute before putting his view across that he didn't believe that we could be travelling around Africa with no money. Griff told him we were all students at Jo'burg University and if we paid the 700 Rand we would have to cut our trip short and that's why we were camping adding that it was the guard's fault that we were still there.

The ranger then disappeared into the reception area and as soon as he was out of sight I doubled over, laughing like a giddy school girl. I was stopped dead in my tracks when a reception window flung open and the ranger shouted over at me to go to him with 50 Rand, which I did. The next thing he come out all apologetic saying that he'd been to a meeting and it didn't go well because his job was quickly changing from a park conservationist to a tourist minder. He wasn't happy but he said that we could stay in one of the chalets for the price of camping on another site. He gave us this map of where our chalet was and hoped that we enjoyed ourselves.

The lodge was luxurious but I preferred it when we camped, it just seemed that we were closer to nature and there's nothing like a camp fire. Radley told me to let my eyes become accustom to the dark whilst I stared at the stars. After a few minutes he asked me to join him away from the lights of the lodge. Again I stood transfixed as I allowed my eyes to scan the night sky, all the while stars started to appear. He then took me over to the electric fence at the boundary of the camp and completely away from any light pollution caused by the lodges. It was pitch black on the ground; however, the sky came to life. There were so many stars in the sky that night that there was no darkness just a sea of pin-prick holes. I was completely blown away by the Milky Way. I'd experienced night skies before on my travels but this was completely different, with only twelve camps in the park there was absolutely no light pollution. Radley pointed out all the star formations and the different constellations and I was like a child at a Punch and Judy show.

I could hear the gentle roar of Lions in the near distance and then Rad shone a torch through the fence; eyes reflected back at us and I was glad I was on the opposite side of the electric fence. When we got back to the lodge he told me to look at the brightest star in the sky and then point my telescope at it. As I looked through the eye piece I could see just as many stars in that small viewpoint as I could with the naked eye looking at the whole sky. It made me feel small and completely insignificant yet grounded and absolutely in love with life and all the wonders it can bring.

Rad woke me at five-thirty with a coffee, I was knackered. By a quarter to six we were sat at the gate waiting for it to open. Six came and went. Radley started to get agitated and banged on the guard's door shouting for him to open the gate. The guard told Radley that the gate wasn't allowed to be opened until six-thirty and with that Griff and I saw the Tasmanian Devil. Expletives poured from Radley's mouth but he soon subdued to a wasp in a bottle. The guard opened the gate and off we went to the camp of Letaba. On the approach road to the camp we spotted our first Lions but the view was brief. Time was against us and Radley hardly drove under the speed limit in his quest to visit twelve camps in three days. The only time we had to get a feel for a camp was at meal times or when we slept there. The next camp offered this opportunity to us with open arms. Radley took us to the Olifants camp which overlooks the Mozambique border where he played mum and cooked us sausage butties.

"Hey Ant, before we go we godda take a look at the view bru and you bedda bring that telescope thingy with you". I followed laden down with optics and a beer in each hand.

We walked through a small wooded area before coming upon a couple of wooden cabins. As I walked around the corner of a viewing platform the whole countryside opened up before me. We were at the top of a valley looking down on a river where an abundance of wildlife went about their daily routine. I was mesmerized as the telescope picked out different species quicker than David Attenborough; even time conscious task master was hard pushed to leave but we stayed for 20 minutes.

We really started to see a lot of wildlife and it seemed for a while to be as well orchestrated as Knowsley Safari Park. The light was beginning to fade on another day so we made for the Skukuza camp at the bottom end of the park. A traffic jam on the approach road to the camp seemed surreal as we'd only seen half a dozen cars in between camps. This could only mean one thing, one of the big five. Inching forward we got a glimpse of a lioness lying in the middle of the road and cars we trying to drive around her. The closer we got the greater her arrogance became and the thrill of lions strolling nonchalantly around the car, feet away from a steel cocoon was a moment that still brings Goosebumps.

This camp was superb as we camped under a tree and had a double area to ourselves. It was great to just sit under the stars next to a roaring fire.

We were to do a loop around the south-east side of the park and then out through the Paul Kruger gate. Giraffe was our first encounter and it just got better from there. We parked at the side of the road to photograph a Jackal suckling her young when I spotted a Chameleon (we'd almost run over). On our way to Lower Sabie we saw a herd of Elephants across the other side of a valley, making their way east. A huge bull Elephant indiscriminately forged a pathway through the dense undergrowth and ripped bushes from the ground like pulling Daises. Females herded the young with their trunks like a nomad and his goats. We had no option other than to sit and wait for the twenty-three strong herd to clear the track and for once time stood still, even for Radley.

As part of the survey we had to ask the staff questions about the wildlife around the camp. Radley had sent me to the bogs again but when I got back to the car he said he had a little surprise in store for me. Off we went once again following the farty little signs where tracks met, when we came across a couple of cars in a lay-by. We got out of the car to find a ranger and five people down the banking crossing the trickle that used to be a river. The guard told us to join them. Once with the group (four adults and a girl of around eleven), the guard went thought the safety procedures for approaching Hippo's. The ranger had a rifle that was straight out of the Boar War (one of them bolt action rifles), the strap was a piece of frayed string. He then proudly showed us a bullet in the chamber and four spares attached to his belt. Radley had said nothing and I felt a hot flush of adrenaline pump life into my legs; I was ready to go.

He led us across the dried up river bed and into some reedbeds, slowly edging forward until we were at the edge of a sand bank. At the other side of the river, not twenty metres away sat a herd of Hippo's with their young. The noise from the autowind on my camera temporarily disturbed the dominant male but they knew we weren't a threat and carried on allowing the sun to warm them up.

We had one last stop before leaving the park and heading back to Jo'burg; Berg-en-Dal. Because of the distractions Radley drove like a lunatic, until that is he almost hit a Rhino. It came from nowhere appearing from the bush but it ran off as quickly as it appeared, just giving me enough time to take a couple of photo's. Berg-en-Dal's notice board said that there was Leopards around the area and even had colour coded pins on a map to help you find it. I pleaded with Rad to take us but time wouldn't allow it; I was gutted. Before we left the park a Cheetah walked across a track just in front of us and more than made up for missing the leopard but that's just another excuse to go back and find one.

The three months pasted far too quickly and I once again found myself sat in my flat trying to deal with day-to-day functioning and desperately trying to hold depression at bay. Life was just passing me by and there seemed no end to the frustration of trying to keep warm. Weeks merged into months and time wasn't going to stand still, I had to do something but what? The Millennium came and went and this just added to the weight of self doubt and I began to lose interest in everything around me including chasing women. Now that's not like me, I had to do something to keep my sanity and I wasn't looking forward to another harsh winter and all the problems the cold weather brings.

Chapter 19

Florida

Almost a year after I'd got back from Africa I received a job offer from a bloke I'd met at Zoo Lake. He had a window cleaning company and wanted me to be a manager, driving around Jo'burg checking on the guys working from him. I really wanted to come off 'the sick', so I decided to give it a go and maybe have the chance to emigrate to a warmer climate. I had an extensive art collection and I knew it was worth thousands so I set about selling it to fund the trip and take a chance in life.

I wasn't due to go back to Africa until early November so I decided to visit one of my mates who'd emigrated to Florida.

Approaching Orlando I could see lakes and ponds everywhere and it reminded me of a wet bank holiday in Manchester. As I exited the air-conditioned terminal building the humidity broke me out into a sweat. An hour or so later we were met at Geoff's place by some of his friends for a welcoming bar-b-que. I met Ray and Eileen, an English couple that had made Florida their home and owned a flying school where Geoff had learnt to fly. They'd asked Geoff to collect a radio from Merritt Island a short flight away and I was invited to go along for the ride, I couldn't wait.

The next afternoon I found myself at Titusville's main air strip surrounded by private jets and people with money oozing from every orifice; it was a world away from Ashton. Before long I was introduced to the two-tone blue and white two-seater Cessna that was going to take me into the skies of Florida. My friend suddenly changed from the happy-go-lucky joker I knew and loved, to a very serious and conscientious pilot. He went through the safety checks with me and then the excitement grew as we boarded the plane and donned the headsets. He radioed the control tower asking for permission to take off and we were given the go ahead to taxi to the runway and wait until a private jet landed. The flying jargon rolled off his tongue as he communicated his intentions to the tower. I was living in a dream like state as I watched the jet approach from our left, a brief puff of smoke appeared as the tyres gripped the hot tarmac.

"You are clear for take-off" came over the radio and I was as excited as a bloke entering a brothel after a large stretch inside.

Before I knew it we were at the end of the runway with the engine working overtime. The tarmac underneath became more and more blurred as we picked up speed and the hangers we'd taken the plane from faded into the background. I was transfixed as the light aircraft left terra firma and danced in the air as it climbed higher and higher giving us with spectacular views of the surrounding area and the landmark sight of the NASA building as well as the shuttle which was due to launch a couple of days later. I was taking everything in, absorbing every second of my first experience of flying in a gravity defying coffin.

We were heading for a small air strip at the south end of Merritt Island which was only a very short ten minute flight but we had to fly over Indian River. From 1500 feet the boats looked like aircraft leaving vapour trails in the water. The Atlantic stretched into the distance, the horizon disappearing into the haze of the midday sun. As Merritt Island air strip came into view the runway dipped its toe into the river and landing meant descending over the water. It was incredible as the water came to almost meet us but once over the tarmac the trees on our right created turbulence and made the landing more difficult to control as the planes right hand wing lifted making Geoff fight with the joy stick until he'd levelled it off. The landing was quite hard but I was completely unfazed by the near fatal landing; I had complete faith in my friend's ability (after all my life was totally in his hands, it would have been a good way to die though). The return flight was just as exciting and the view of the shuttle just wetted my appetite for the launch two days later.

The morning of the launch Geoff woke me at 6.30am and we made our way to one of his friends who lived in a huge house overlooking the river in-between Titusville and Merritt Island. It was a typical wooden mansion as depicted in the television series North and South complete with its Georgian windows. The circular pebbled driveway added to the mystique and the grandeur of this three story building. The noise of rubber on gravel made the door bell redundant as Geoff's friend opened the large green door and greeted me as if she'd known me as long as my mate. As she ushered us through the hallway I was blown away by the size of the staircase. I hardly had chance to take it in before she took us through to the veranda at the back of the house overlooking the river and the launch site. The rear garden was some fifty metres long and fell away into the river where a jetty stood as proud and almost as long as a seaside pier.

A TV in the room had live coverage of the countdown and as I organised my camera I could hear the reporter preparing to astonish her viewers. The time was now fast approaching and the countdown had already started when I placed my eye to the viewfinder patiently waiting for lift off. "We have lift off" was clearly heard from the TV and my finger was poised to depress the shutter as the shuttle climbed into the sky but there was nothing; I moved the camera from my face and I could clearly see a huge plumb of smoke in the distance, I'd been looking at the wrong launch pad. I quickly recomposed myself before snapping away like the intro to 'Girls on film' by Duran Duran.

I was fortunate enough not to miss the shuttle climbing above the smoke and the sight of the burning fuel spewing from the bottom of the shuttle was truly breathtaking. The shuttle had climbed high before the noise of the engines met us but when it did the sound and the resonance vibrated through my body like a bass at a rave. As the shuttle effortlessly gained altitude the reflection in the river made this sight all the more alluring.

The shuttle seemed to twist in the air and arc to the left as if the earth's rotation could be seen. As it reached the height you would normally associate with a passenger plane just visible from its vapour trail the side fuel tanks were jettisoned peeling away to either side. I watched intently as the huge orange tanks gave way to gravity and made their way earth bound. Seconds' later three parachutes on each tank opened and it reminded me of the toy soldier and attached parachute we had as kids. The shuttle continued to climb until eventually it disappeared into the abyss of the atmosphere while the tanks disappeared into the haze of the horizon. I had to pinch myself for once again this was no dream I was well and truly living in it.

Geoff worked as a handyman and was given the job of refitting two bathrooms and tiling the ground floors of two holiday apartments; I had chosen to go along with him not only to spend time with my friend but to help out and learn some new skill. It worked out wonderfully as two pairs of hands made light work and left the afternoons free to go fishing.

One afternoon Geoff decided to take me to the nature reserve adjacent to NASA, at the northern end of Merritt Island. The 140,000 acres hosts more than 22 threatened or endangered species including the 2,000-pound Florida Manatee (Geoff took me to a place where I was lucky enough to see three), Eastern Indigo Snake, Gopher Tortoise and Peregrine Falcon, more than any other refuge in the United States. There are up to 400 Manatees making the North Banana River home in the spring. The area teems with more than 31 species of mammals, 331 types of birds and 113 species of fish - over 500 species of wildlife in all and also home to 1045 species of flora.

Just before you reach the beach there's a huge lake that overlooks the Shuttle launch site and a couple of blokes were fishing there. We stopped and asked about permits and they said that you only had to be a member of the reserve, which Geoff was. The very next day we returned armed with our fishing rods and shrimp as bait. Geoff parked the Station Wagon in the lay-by and removed the back seat placing it no more than ten feet from the water's edge to use as a bench on which I could sit rest my legs and fish from. We'd seen a huge Alligator the previous day but didn't think any more about it as we cast out into the water.

Before too long we were catching fish called Black Drum which are edible. In fact, we were so successful that I became so blaze about it that I lay on the bench seat in a semi-sleep enjoying the sun on my face with my bait patiently awaiting a passing fish. I barely raised an eyebrow as Geoff once again caught a five pound plus fish. As he reeled in the fish to the bank the fish fought with all its worth causing the surface of the water to clap with frantic action. Just as Geoff got the fish near the edge, I got a bite and still lying down just lifted my arm so the lines wouldn't tangled. My friend was by now only a few feet from the water's edge when all of a sudden an Alligator came from under the water with the fish that Geoff had caught in its mouth; it marched up the banking tossing the fish to the back of its snout. Geoff jumped out of the way and I had no other choice but to follow suit because the Alligator came for me.

We'd got as close to that Alligator as Steve Irwin used to (god bless his soul). Geoff had to cut the line and the Alligator sat ridged for a couple of minutes before returning to the safety of the pool. It was for me a unique and exciting experience made even more exciting due to the fact of where and who I was with. Although this was a close call we continued to fish there for the rest of my stay. We once saw the Alligator on the other side of the road and one of the locals told us that it was affectionately known as old Alfie; it was about 15 feet long. It was amazing to be able to fish for our dinner and be about 800 metres from the Shuttle launch site.

About half-way through my holiday Geoff was asked to fly a Cessna back to Titusville from Kissimmee, an air strip just down the road from the Disneyworld Park. Ray drove us to the air strip and upon arriving quickly tended to the safety checks before Geoff and I took to the air. Once again, as soon as Geoff donned the headset his persona changed and Mr. Serious the pilot was back. With permission for take-off granted I got really excited and looking forward to seeing Florida from a bird's eye view.

As the little two-seater Cessna 152 climbed into the sky Geoff introduced me to the controls giving me a free lesson in flying. I took in the information with added interest for as he said, 'the plane was foreign to him and we could only hope that all the mechanics were in full working order', for it would take us around an hour to get back to Titusville.

As we gained height the highways stretched into the distance and I was told that if the navigational instruments failed then we could always follow the road. Within ten minutes we were at our altitude of 2100 feet.

"Do you want a go" came over the headset; I didn't need asking twice.

I was told to keep the revs at 2300 rpm, the altitude at 2100 feet, the wing indicators level with the horizon and whilst doing all this, "keep an eye out for an appropriate landing site in case of engine failure". I took the joystick and tried to concentrate on what I had to do, with little success at first. I kept drifting to the right dipping the right hand wing and dropping in altitude. The horizon indicator danced around on the line and Geoff had to tentatively take control until I'd got used to the delicate and sensitive controls.

Although I found it very difficult at first, once I'd relaxed leaving anxiety a few minutes behind me, I began to enjoy this unforeseen opportunity. I began to look around at the scenery but only briefly just enough to get my bearings but not long enough to distract me from the instrument readings. In the distance we could make out two huge antenna's about half a kilometre apart towering into the sky; Geoff told me that they were 2000 feet high and that it was now my job to fly in-between them but first I had to increase our altitude to 2300 feet.

Nerves were non-existent as I had an auto-pilot sat at my side who'd been correcting my mistakes. Before I knew it we'd passed through them and now we could clearly see the NASA building some thirty miles away, which just exaggerated the sheer size of the place. At the same time it gave us another reference point to where we needed to go. As if the antenna wasn't enough of a distraction, a call came over the radio to be careful of a group of parachutists' up ahead but we never saw any. The final approach was upon us and I had to hand over without the temptation to grab at the controls. My forty minutes were over far too quickly and I just want to fly. It was without doubt one of the most adrenaline filled forty minutes of my life and if it wasn't for the illness I may never have been sat in that seat.

I only got the chance to fly one more time and that was in a four-seater Cessna when Ray flew us to Winter Haven. I was sat in the back with Ray and Geoff taking up the controls. This gave me the opportunity to snap away with my camera and really enjoy the sights and landscape. We were told to circle the airfield and land on the southern runway due to cross-winds. Ray prepared to land, a cross-wind hit us and the plane swung to the left; we were only about twenty feet from the ground. Ray fought with the controls. He quickly gained some height before levelling out the wings and then landing with not much spare tarmac. They fell silent in the front while I laughed at their frantic actions; they weren't impressed with me but I had complete faith in their ability and wasn't fazed by the near miss. It just added to the excitement of life, especially after the incident with the Alligator. The return flight was uneventful but just as exciting for me and it's a memory that I cherish.

I'd deliberately missed my flight back because quite frankly I was having a ball and had a good few weeks before I returned to Africa. I wanted to visit NASA, the only touristy shit that appealed to me (apart from the fairground rides, which wasn't that appealing when you had to queue like sheep at a sheep dip). It was while I was there that an astronaut demonstrated the amazing heat resistance of the tiles covering the Shuttle. He heated one of the tiles up with a blow torch and then just ten seconds later placed his hand on it; I was blown away by it. During his demonstration and subsequent talk he told us that the next launch was going to be at night and that it would be the 100th launch. That was it, I simply had to stay and witness this milestone and at the same time give me the opportunity to experience a day and night launch.

There were still a few days to go until the launch and when Geoff, Rachel and I fished the lake overlooking the launch pad, a DC10 could be seen climbing high into the sky and descending steeply before going back up. This helped prepare the astronauts for zero gravity in what's commonly known as the 'Vomit Commit'.

We went to the same house for the night launch, the moon reflected in the river and a small light at the end of the jetty swayed in a light breeze. There was no mistaking the launch pad this time around, for it was lit up like a Christmas tree and I couldn't wait. Once again the TV commentary in the background prepared us for what was to come.

"We have ignition...10, 9, 8...3, 2, 1, we have lift off".

At that moment the plumb of smoke from the engine had an orange glow as the flames illuminated the night sky. Slowly the Shuttle left the platform and as it emerged from the smoke it was only visible due to the flames spewing from the engine. As the Shuttle gained altitude the reflection of the engine flames glistened across the river like a sunset and the silhouette of a boat added to the atmosphere.

The noise from the thrusters crept up on us gradually but fiercely when it arrived. The night sky was cloudy and as the Shuttle momentarily disappeared behind the clouds they were temporarily illuminated orange, the vapour trail could clearly be seen. The ejecting of the fuel tanks took my breath away and they soon fell into obscurity as there was nothing to illuminate them. I watched intently as the flames of the engine vanished into the atmosphere like the dot at the end of a cartoon's credits. The Floridians seemed rather blaze about the whole affair as they were rather bemused by my reaction. Each one of the launches were amazing, it was sheer luck that I'd witnessed the 99th and 100th launches.

I'd ended up spending six weeks in Florida and was reluctant to leave but I had to sort myself out for Africa.

Chapter 20

Moving to Africa

Friday 10th November 2000 and already this Millennium year was nearing a close. The birth of Khloe (daughter of Thomas junior), my forth god child couldn't have been orchestrated better, the day before I left. Holding her in my arms gave me pangs of mixed emotions, firstly I wouldn't lay eyes on her again for some six months and secondly, that wasn't going to spoil my trip for my love for her would transcend any distance I put between us. It also meant that there would be two absentees from my party that evening.

I recalled the New Year party at Brian and Val Derbyshire's and how Brian had hoped that I made it back to Africa this year. The day I told him I was going back for six months, he nearly choked on his pint.

"Fuckin ell Ant, you don't do things in half's do you?"

I'd invited half of Ashton for a few beers as a bit of a send off and that just spelt disaster with a 12.30 p.m. flight. Nevertheless nearly everyone turned up and I subsequently didn't go to bed until around five. I woke stark upright at eleven thinking I'd miss my flight; a pile of bodies laid all over the living room but most importantly my chauffeur to the airport. I made a brew and swept a pair of feet to one side as I perched at the end of the sofa, a body slowly pulled the coat from over its head and looked at me; it was Dean. I had to be at the airport for no later than 11.30 so hung over he drove me to the airport. I didn't get there until 11.55 and I was literally frog marched to the plane.

As I daydreamed looking out of the window the most noticeable feature of the landscape was its transformation to a lush green carpet interrupted with sporadic concrete. The sky was cloudless and as we flew over Johannesburg the skyscrapers seemed to reach up in a vain attempt to touch us. Grahame and Jane throw a braai that afternoon and all the old crowd turned up to see me. The bar got some use that day and I was starting yet another bizarre twist in my life; I'd never felt better.

I got up at seven feeling remarkably fresh and energized at the prospect of making a new life in the sun. I rang Wilksie (who's dad had offered me the job) that afternoon but he had bad news for me, his granddad had passed away and his dad had gone back to the UK for the funeral and so I would have to wait to see his father. My heart went out to them all but I'd soon see my friend at football practice.

That first week was a whirlwind of catching up with old mates and doing my best to impersonate an alcoholic and culminated in a fancy dress party where Jane went as the Mast and me and Grahame went as Laurel and Hardy. I was settling in to life here but then again I'd already spent six months here over the last two trips.

My health was improving by the day but I had to be careful in the midday sun because the heat made me tired. During the hottest hours I would stay indoors painting. Grahame had come up with an idea for me to sell my art at the side of the road while I waited for the job to start. I was excited at the prospect because I'd already had numerous exhibitions both individually and collectively through Kenny at the studio. But first of all Grahame was going to Vienna as head coach of the youth team and would be away for a week giving me ample opportunity to produce half a dozen pictures.

While Grahame was away it gave me the chance to catch up with Griff and Nikki and to see their new house they'd just bought at an auction. The bungalow was the end property of a leafy suburb in a quiet part of Ferndale which boasted four bedrooms and a large garden with a swimming pool; I ended up helping him to re-concrete the rockery surrounding the pool. I could never have dreamt of doing this back home but because of the weather I could manage to do a lot more due to the dry heat and the altitude giving me the same results as a top athlete. The rest of the house and garden needed a lot of renovation but that's the beauty of an auction property you get a blank canvas to work with. While we worked on the patio we discussed the dramatic lifestyle changes compared with back home and Griff told me he was never going back to the UK; I expressed my desires to leave all the stress behind and to start living instead of just existing. Becoming an artist was at this point just a romantic notion but one that had to be explored and embraced; I was looking forward to my cousin returning from the competition and selling my creations.

Grahame and some of the ex-pats had set up a business buying run down properties and renovating them. Chris, one of the members was a builder and so the idea in principle was a sound one. They'd bought a house near the university and set about adding an extension and off road parking; an absolute must in the crime capital of Africa. As soon as my cousin had returned from his very successful trip where the team won, he took me to see the house and the progress made. Whilst we were there Chris's son Tim was fabricating a wrought iron fence around the driveway. Grahame asked him if he could make a stand to display my framed paintings and that was the start of my new career as an artist. Everything was coming together but not in the way I'd anticipated. I was used to setbacks due to the years I'd spent building up my business but that just made life more interesting. With the display stand being the next job on Tim's list I set about buying frames.

The beginning of December was ticked off on the calendar and I saw Wilksie at football. He told me that his dad still wanted me to work for them but I would have to wait until the New Year because everything shuts down for the summer holiday which in Africa falls over the festive period. He wanted to see me over the Christmas holidays to discuss it, so I looked forward to meeting him for the first time. So I busied myself indulging myself in my paintings. This wasn't such a blow as my family was going to their time share at Sun City for five days. I'd been to Sun City a couple of times before but only seen around a quarter of the place so I wanted to see it all this time.

The resort has two golf courses and it just so happened that the main course had just hosted the Nedbank golf open won by South African Ernie Els. The stands around the eighteenth hole were still in place and I simply couldn't resist having my photo taken sat in the middle all alone. Later that day we hit the casino and I managed to double my money which helped to pay for all the beer that night.

One morning I got up at five to go on a game drive in Pilanesberg reserve which is next to Sun City and is the fourth largest in South Africa. It was amazing to watch the sun coming over the hill tops and eventually dispelling the morning mist. We didn't see a great deal of animals but the highlight was White Rhino. Luckily for me the guide was a keen birdwatcher and introduced me to the birds in the park. It was quite amusing when in the middle of answering questions asked by some Americans, he would stop mid-sentence and point out a bird to me. The tour was over far too quickly but I'd been, seen and was still keen. Grahame's an eager golfer and I always drive the buggy when he goes to a course so that I can get really close to the wildlife. This was no exception on the smaller of the two courses which is called the Lost City. On the thirteenth hole between the tee and the green is a Crocodile pit, so if your ball lands in there you can kiss it goodbye. I was more interested in the colony of Egrets nesting in the trees precariously above the water all the while the Crocs lay in wait just in case a chick fell from its nest. The rest of the week we lazed around the man made beach, the Valley of the Waves. I really enjoyed my time here but it's just pure indulgence and a million miles away from the surrounding shanty towns but that's Africa for you.

On my return to Jo'burg Tim had finished my stand for the stall and I went to a wholesaler to buy more frames. I'd got together over twenty pictures to sell and it was all systems go. Just down the road from our kids was a dual carriageway and every weekend people used to set up stalls along the middle and sides selling allsorts, with no licences needed I decided to set up there. I got there at around eight and set up my stall under a gazebo. During the day I got increasingly excited as every car pulled up near me but everyone kept going to the stalls near me. In fact, the only cars that pulled up at my stall were my friends bringing me drinks and food and allowing me to go to the loo. After two days sat for around eight hours I hadn't sold a thing; I was disappointed but not put off by the experience. I decided to try to sell at the indoor market which is always busy at the weekends but first my product had to be approved by the market manager; needless to say they were impressed and gave me the go ahead. I was to start the following week which was the weekend before Christmas so if I couldn't sell any on this weekend then I never would; my optimism was at a premium.

I didn't sleep too well on the Friday night because I was a bit anxious about how my stuff would sell in the market but I still got out of bed at six and drove to the market to place my name on the casual traders list; it was a case of first come first served and the number of casuals changed with the absence of the regular traders. I went back at nine and stood in the queue not really knowing what to do. Grahame and Jane came along to help me to set up the stall. The market managers opened the office and then started to work their way through the list. Eventually they got round to my name and told me to set up in the corridor which was fantastic because that's where everyone walked through to all the other stalls. Once the stall was set up they left me to it and I sat there for half an hour crapping myself but found comfort in watching all the women walking past.

With absolutely no attention at all I decided to do a pencil drawing in the hope that it would create some interest; it worked a treat because people stopped and asked questions. The day passed really slowly and it wasn't until a friend of mine turned up to see how I was doing that I got the chance to go to the loo and grab a bite to eat. As four approached Grahame came to collect me as most of the stalls had already gone. I managed to sell four prints that day which covered the costs for the day but didn't really make a dent into the investment but then again you can't expect to do that over night.

When I got back to the house there was a party going on because Jane's brother and his family had come over from their place in Hong Kong where he was an English teacher along with his wife. Some of my cousin's friends were there for a braai and once they'd found out where I'd been they wanted to see my artwork. I subsequently sold three more paintings there and then. I was a little dismayed that I'd had to endure sitting all day in a market and sold almost as many on my own doorstep but that's the way my life has always gone. I was really knackered that night and consequently the day after I couldn't get out of bed; the MS had grabbed a day off me but I stuck two fingers up at it that night and got out of bed and joined in the Christmas party. Christmas and New Year in Africa was awesome, just as hot as Australia but a bar-b-que almost every day.

The beginning of the year was quiet, I hadn't heard a thing about the job but I was commissioned to paint a mural at Glenn's gym, which I really enjoyed doing. I busied myself preparing for the market but instead of sitting there all day I employed one of our Grahame's lads to stand in for me. The wages in Africa are so low that it wasn't worth me going through all the pain. At the end of the day I didn't sell a thing but it was just after the festive spending spree and the lack of expendable income in January is globally equivalent. Despite all this I continued to produce as many different pieces of art as I could, the sun revitalised me and my brother Darren and my mate Dave (Diddy) Butler were coming over in February for a couple of weeks holiday.

It was mid January and I bumped into Wilksie at the football. He explained to me that his sister had had a baby girl the week before and it was a shock to all the family because she'd hidden it from them. With this revelation I knew that I'd have to bide my time and wait until things were on an even keel again before I could contemplate my future here. I really do think the world of these two but in life you have to love a lot, trust a few and always paddle your own canoe. Within a couple of days of this conversation I was invited to a braai to discuss my future as a window-cleaner in Africa. I went along with a really open mind due to the fact that I'd been here for just over two months and this was the first time I'd set eyes on Tony (Wilksie's dad). We got on like a house on fire right from the start and I knew that despite the delays he was genuine in his offer. He offered to sell me and Wilksie a house round that was getting in the way of the industrial round. He showed me the figures and they added up nicely; I just knew from that moment that if everything did come to fruition I could make a real go of it. I was invited to go to work with them the following Wednesday, I couldn't wait.

Their offices were in down town Jo'burg which is worse than the Bronx but this factor alone gave me an adrenaline buzz due to the constant threat of danger; this was exaggerated by a guard in uniform making sure no one wandered uninvited through the electric shutters and into the basement car park. We got the lift to the fourth floor and as the doors opened I thought we'd got the wrong block of offices because the whole place looked due for demolition. Their company rented a few rooms which comprised of a reception area, a stock cupboard and two further rooms which were Tony and his partner's offices. Tony made a cup of tea whilst Wilksie organised the workforce into groups. Tony's partner Dave was also from the UK and was always late, we were introduced briefly before the three of us set off to drop the lads off at the different jobs they had for that day. Tony took ten lads in his pick-up and me and Wilksie took eight in ours.

We followed each other around the corner to a take away where the lads bought a typical African dish called Pap and Stew, the Pap being similar to dumplings. I got out of the pick-up and walked round to the back soaking up the atmosphere only to be told in no uncertain terms to get out of a car in this black area. I smiled to myself that the shoe was now on the other foot and the white supremacy that once dominated this part of the world was fast fading. When all the lads returned to the pick-ups we went our separate ways, heading in opposite directions. We headed north along the highway and to Westcliffe where we dropped off three of the lads at an office block before dropping the rest off at another office block.

I loved driving around Jo'burg taking it all in. At one point the road up in front became backed up due to four black guys trying to take a burnt out shell of a car to trade it in for scrap on a supermarket trolley with a broken wheel. They were desperately trying to balance the car to the side with the two wheels on. We couldn't help ourselves but laugh, yet it's a stark reality of this part of the world. We had five estimates to do and this gave me an awesome opportunity to get my bearings around this huge expanse of urban sprawl. It was like I'd never been away from it and by the time we'd got to the last estimate I'd got it but I'd always had the ability to price myself in a realistic market.

We got back to the office around midday and I talked Wilksie into taking me across the road for a KFC just so I could experience being an intimidated minority; I thought that this would be the perfect place to experience the atmosphere but everyone just smiled at me and was really friendly. We went back to the office and played a game of darts while we ate our dinner. I thought ye I could handle a job like this. It was time to collect the lads because they weren't allowed to work after three-thirty without getting overtime. By the time we'd finished driving around the different jobs we'd covered almost three hundred kilometres, I was told that was usual. 'Nice one' I thought I'm gonna be a driver not a window-cleaner.

I was invited to sit in on a disciplinary hearing and it turned out to be a real eye opener. This guy was being given a written warning for asking for Christmas tips from customers and his representative who was translating from one of the many languages used in South Africa was telling Tony and Dave that he denied all the charges. Tony read out a list of disgruntled customers, the dates and most importantly what was said. It seemed that his English improved every time he asked for money; it was a complete farce but because of the new laws employees have to be given three written warnings before you can fire them and it has to be for the same reason; so if this fellow stuck to one crime it would take three years to sack him. It suddenly dawned on me just what a difference working here would be but I really wanted to do it. We didn't get back to Grahame's until half four so we sat at the bench table outside the bar and had a sun-downer and discussed the future. I went with my friend for the rest of the week and enjoyed every changing minute of it.

My shattered life was full of Africa's wonders, my soul was healing and my illness was nothing more than just a part of who I am. But with the weekend came my chance to show just what I could do and I really wanted to see if Wilksie was all mouth. The Pom Projects house was finished and ready to be cleaned. I got stuck in and showed my friend where seventeen years of practice gets you. He's a fit lad playing football three times a week but he found it hard to keep up with the master. He told me that he was going to organise a race between me and one of his employees that just happened to be the quickest window-cleaner in Jo'burg. I volunteered to clean the patio doors because they were full of dried on concrete and plaster from where the lads had been mixing on the veranda. Ten minutes after I'd finished cleaning it, Jane walked into the glass; a compliment if I ever needed one which was reaffirmed when she placed stickers on the glass. I'd now cleaned windows on two continents and if you'd have told me that some ten years earlier I'd have never in my wildest dreams have believed it but there it was for the taking; I had arrived at a place in my conscience that can only be described as euphoria.

It was now the end of January and I found myself with three of the lads on the domestic side of the business and the part that was up for sale. This gave me a great opportunity to assess whether or not it was a viable business proposition and worthy of taking over. As we exited the van on the first job I grabbed a set of pockets and a small V-ladder and started to clean the bottom windows; one of the lads joined me but I asked him to do the top windows with the other two and then join me on the bottoms. I almost finished in sync with them and they were blown away with the speed in which I cleaned the windows. I explained to them about the life I once had some six thousand miles away and that just seemed to catapult me to their affections as they called me Mr. Antony. I was a little bemused by this old colonial requirement and instructed them to drop the Mr and just treat me as one of them. That was never going to happen and their insistence made me feel uncomfortably superior, a feeling of white domination that left a bad taste in my mouth. They had a little difficulty in finding the next job and I ended up showing them how to map read which was made even trickier due to the fact they couldn't read properly but I got through to them by showing them how to use the index by matching up the street names and landmarks.

Subsequently we arrived at the next job an hour early much to the dismay of the customer who pretended to have just finished a tennis lesson from her lover. She was completely thrown by me and retreated to the security of her kitchen followed by the sheep dog tennis stud.

At this point the lads sat semi-circled on the lawn and started to eat the stew they'd bought earlier. I didn't have anything to eat as we Brits didn't dare touch the stew with a barge pole but the lads insisted on me joining them. I wasn't their boss so I had to go along with their daily ritual. I was humbled as they shared their food with me and it actually turned out that the stew was really tasty although you could tell that the meat was cheap. We exchanged life experiences which made me feel as though they'd accepted me with less suspicion and not as a mole put there by the management. They were slow to take to the job again but I got up and started to work telling them that I was getting out of the sun which was fierce by this time.

This house was huge with Georgian windows at every vantage point. It took just less than an hour to finish and yet again the lads exclaimed,

"Eeesh, you are very quick Mr. Antony".

There was just one more house to clean before we went back to the office and the boys wanted me to take my time so they wouldn't have to do anymore work before they went home but I ended up showing them how to reach windows that had never been cleaned before. I got the house owner to open the two windows and I climbed the ladder with all the lads watching my every move. They were impressed but yet I'd just given them more work the next time they called here so things were a bit strained on the drive back to the office. Wilksie asked how things had gone and before I knew it I was then challenged to a race with the firm's quickest window-cleaner.

A couple of days later I found myself at a large industrial park to clean the windows at a telecommunications head office. The building stood out amongst its counterparts largely due to the glass pyramid reception and the impressive fountain. The entrance to the office block had an angled glass roof that was being cleaned by two blokes with rock climbing equipment. I was told that we were sub-contracting to the guys on the ropes and so we had the task of cleaning the two ends of this huge office complex. All together we left thirteen guys there with specific instructions to finish cleaning the four storey buildings by the end of the week. When we returned to the site later that day to take the lads back to the office, the job wasn't finished due to some problems over health and safety so I volunteered myself to be left there the next day and help iron out the problems.

I was really looking forward to being the ambassador for Tony's company and proving to him above anything else that I could be a problem solver. The next morning we were left at the site as usual and I busied myself organising the lads into their particular roles. I however, had an appointment with the managing director of the rope access company for breakfast and an ear bashing about finishing the job on time. When I returned to the lads they were all sat on a wall waiting to tell me they'd been stopped from cleaning the windows. Just at that moment an Afrikaans woman came up to me and said that she was in charge of health and safety on the site and she had stopped us working because we had no safety equipment and she was nervous about one of the lads falling from the ladder. I tried to convince her that the lads knew what they were doing but she was having none of it, eventually I asked the rope access lads if they had a spare harness I could use. I quickly organised two of the workers on to the roof to attach the safety rope at each point and one of the lads to wear the harness and run up and down the ladder with purpose. I also showed them all how to clean two floors with the ladder in the same position by moving it closer to the wall and leaning forward. I had six men working on the top two floors whilst the rest of them finished the lower two floors and the inside.

With things back on track the inevitable race was mentioned along with a one-sided bet. If I was to win I got nothing but if Rufus (the company's fastest window-cleaner) won then I would have to give him 100 rand (£10). I accepted the challenge and put my money where my mouth was. Along the ground floor of the office was a glass wall with each pane measuring around eight feet high and six feet wide, this looked like the perfect place for a race and so I told Rufus that we had to clean two panes each to win. He was cocky especially as the other lads taunted me about the expected pay out. Off we went going at full speed and I ended up not only winning but helping him to finish the final half of the second pane much to the dismay of them all. I had by now won them over and I could do no wrong. This was a fantastic experience and gave me a real boost in the confidence department.

Over the next few weeks I divided my time between going to work with Wilksie and Grahame. I became a lot stronger and the dry heat of the African summer.

It was now the end of February and Darren and Diddy arrived for a two week holiday. I was taking them to Cape Town which was a first for all of us but the first few days were spent taking them around the sights of Jo'burg and inviting Griff and the rest of the ex-pats round for drinks and a braai. It seemed that before we even had time to catch our breath we were at the car hire office in Cape Town for a four day break. Our hotel was opposite the lighthouse at Mouille Point just a few minutes' drive from the famous waterfront.

As soon as we found the hotel, checked-in and unpacked, we all met downstairs at the bar and I called Dave Botha to tell him that we'd arrived (he'd moved to Cape Town with his job). I was anxious to hear how his family was settling into their new lives down on the Cape and the differences between here and Jo'burg. The boys sat in disbelief as Dave told them that his wife Julie was born in Stockport, only a few miles from our birthplace. As we caught up with each other he suggested things to do and places to go.

That afternoon was bright and clear, Dave advised us to go for sundowners on the mountain because of the clear weather and wait until dark to capture the essence of the town and harbour by artificial light. As Dave left to return home we made our way to the waterfront for lunch and explored some of its attractions and atmosphere before making our way to the foot of the mountain and the cable car station. From here the concrete stretches from the foot of the mountain to the sea, the skyscrapers indicated where the financial district lay and also where Dave worked as an insurance underwriter.

The ride in the cable car was an experience in itself for as it rises up the steep metal cable it slowly rotates giving everyone ample opportunity to view Cape Town and how incredibly close you are to the mountain side. At the top of the mountain a path winds its way to various viewing points which on a clear day gives spectacular views over the Cape peninsular. Small animals that look remarkably like overgrown hamsters called Rock Hyrax graze on the foliage totally complacent of the ever replenishing crowds, whilst birds flit from shrub to shrub. Each vantage point renders you speechless especially the couple of triangular platforms that hang precariously over the rock face with a 1500 foot drop. As the sun dipped over the horizon we sat outside the bar and waited for darkness to descend. The hustle and bustle gave way to a more relaxed atmosphere as many of the tourists left the mountain top with the fading light leaving the best viewing platforms uncluttered. The transformation of this vibrant city under the cloak of darkness is truly remarkable as the clear sky gave way to many emerging stars twinkling in unison with the neon signs and street lights. I literally had to be dragged off the mountain and would have slept there if I could.

Day two of the trip and we headed off to explore the Cape peninsular passing through St. James with its beachfront changing huts painted in prominent primary colours contrasting against a stark landscape. This side of the peninsula overlooks False Bay with its beautiful villages along the way including Kalk Bay, Clovelly, Fish Hoek and Simon's Town before you get to the scintillating Boulders Beach where a colony of Jackass Penguins swim alongside tourists. This small nature reserve is like nothing I've ever come across before for you are allowed to swim with the penguins as long as you don't disturb their breeding areas. This place has a surrealistic atmosphere with its white boulders scattered along the shoreline dotted with penguins sitting under the sun. The wardens watch for disturbance from a distance just making their presence felt.

Darren stripped to his shorts, got into the sea and swam in a small bay whilst penguins approached him inquisitively. I stood transfixed as my brother's smile said it all. He sat on a rock and posed for photos with his new found friends. As you enter Cape Peninsula National Park a road cuts its way through the landscape and up and over the hills to Cape Point and the home of the famous lighthouse sat precariously on the ridge of the rocks that has doubtlessly saved thousands of mariners since its construction. There are two lighthouses on Cape Point due to the fact that the first one was built too high up on the ridge at 283 metres; for in thick fog the cloud base would be lower than the lighthouse thus the ships could not see it. It was decommissioned in 1933 when a tanker ran aground. We were at the viewing point just under the highest lighthouse looking out over a vastness of greeny-blue water cloaked under a cloudless turquoise sky. A small pathway alone the cliff tops gave spectacular views of the rocks and an insight into the power of the currents in the swirling sea. A tramway up to the lighthouse was a god send when I saw the steep stone steps. From the lighthouse the whole of False Bay opened up and the South Atlantic Ocean was still.

A short drive and we were standing on the beach on the opposite peninsular the Cape of Good Hope, the south-westernmost point of the African continent and from this vantage point the full force of the Atlantic could be appreciated as the seemingly calm sea crashed deafeningly against the rocky shoreline. We made our way north through Chapman's Peak to Hout Bay where we enjoyed freshly caught fish and watched the sunset cast an orange glow that illuminated the mountain side.

Our time here was passing quickly and I simply couldn't resist a trip to Robben Island where Nelson Mandela was imprisoned. We had dinner at the waterfront before the catamaran left for the island. The trip was shrouded by low cloud which spoilt the view of Table Mountain from the island but that was secondary to the whole purpose of the trip. Apartheid activists were incarcerated here and the prison is now a tourist attraction, attracting thousands of visitors each year. At the harbour a guide ushers you onto a tour bus and over the intercom the history of the island is unfolded. I hung on to her every word only looking out of the window when she told us to do so and when she paused. The first stop on the trip is the quarry where the prisoners were forced to do hard labour. The quarry was quiet apart from the chitter chatter from the tourists, lifeless in many ways. On a ledge within a cave was a birds nest containing two chicks, I thought that this was rather poignant because the rebirth in the quarry is like the rebirth of the modern South Africa. Both the chicks and South Africa have a long struggle ahead but there is hope and as long as there is hope there's a future.

Driving around the island gives you the opportunity to see for yourself the different purpose's the island has been used for. In its 400 year history it's been used as a supply station for the Dutch East India Company, an asylum, a leper colony and then a maximum security prison. There are even large artillery guns from the Second World War but they were never fired in anger or defence. The bus stopped briefly by the beach for an opportunity to photograph the view of Table Mountain but unfortunately the mist was so dense that we couldn't see it or 200 yards in any direction. The five minutes or so that we strolled along the shingle and rocks listening to the sea birds calls hid the underlying feeling of the last couple of decades the island now stands for in the eyes of the world. From the beauty of the sea shore the next to last stop is the maximum security prison and the home of many political prisoners during the days of apartheid. The coach stops at the steel gates of the prison where an ex-inmate gives you a guided tour and an insight into how life was like under the previous regime.

Groups of tourists filter through the huge steel doors and as they are closed behind you with that distinctive slammed thud the feeling of incarceration and claustrophobia hits you immediately (but in the back of your mind you know full well that this is only a tour). The tour takes you through to the exercise yard where the inmates were forced to smash rocks with a lump hammer whilst sitting on the ground no matter what the weather was like. In the yard is a picture of Mandela doing just that and another one of him with Walter Sisulu.

From the exercise yard Eugene (the ex-inmate) points to the small windows of the cells overlooking the yard, the forth one along from the left hand side is the cell that Nelson Mandela occupied for a number of years. That's the queue for the next (and probably the most important) part of the tour, the walk along the corridor of the prison and a look into the cell of the great man himself. The inmates had to live in conditions that most of us wouldn't let our dogs live in. The cell is about two meters by one meter with just a shelf and two blankets to sleep on. It's hard to get your head around being forced to live in such a confined space. The guide gives you an indication of what daily life was like in the prison but in all honesty there's no way on this planet that you will ever be able to justify your imagination. This is the most solemn part of the tour and the prison.

The significance of what the inside of these walls represented is most felt as you stand outside this cell. I'm sure that every inmate had his own story of oppression to tell but this man came through the adversity and walked to freedom to become one of the most influential leaders in the modern world. From the cells your led to the hospital ward with its exhibition of political leaders that influenced the rest of the world as well as the spirits of fellow inmates.

The final part of the tour is a look around the dormitories where the inmates lived in close proximity to each other. On display were copies of inmates release papers that had no release date on them as well as food rations that states that the blacks were only allowed half rations of any other Caucasian inmates. As you filter out of the gates the guide shakes your hand; it's one of the most humbling experiences of my life and the struggles of those brave men just wanting to be seen as fellow South Africans left me feeling ashamed to be a white man. Although it was not my country and not my fight, the fight against racism will go on as long as there remains ignorance in the world. The tour finishes with enough time to stroll up the harbour to see the Penguin colony that breaths life back into this island. On the return journey to the mainland there was a distinct serenity amongst the tourists.

On day four after all the running about we needed to chill out a little and enjoy the relaxed atmosphere of the Cape so we decided to return to Hout Bay for a horse riding trek in the sand dunes. When we set off from the stables the weather was bright but the higher we climbed the more the mist scuppered our view of the bay but it didn't matter. Our last afternoon started to tick away and we found ourselves at the end of the waterfront chartering a six-seater aquatic plane for a pleasure flight over the Cape peninsular. It took just forty minutes to fly to Cape Point and back giving excellent views of the peninsular especially as the cloud base hung seductively in-between the peaks of the twelve apostles.

I was really glad that I'd managed to see this amazing place with my brother and be able to regurgitate these memories at will. That is the only thing that the Multiple Sclerosis can't take from me. My memories are as precious as gold to me and each time I enjoy a new and exciting experience I'm simply replenishing my soul, the body is merely a vessel, knackered or not.

The second week had come quickly and day trips filled the calendar trying to let the lads see as much of this place as humanly possible; the obligatory visits to Sun City, the Lion Park and the world famous Sterkfontein Caves, the most famous of 13 excavated fossil sites in the broader 47,000-hectare Cradle of Humankind site. Three million years of human activity have taken place in and around the Cradle, including man's earliest-known mastery of fire. Forty percent of all human ancestor fossil finds have been made here, including several of the world's most famous and important fossils - among them Mrs Ples (now believed to be Master Ples), dating back 2.5-million years, and Little Foot, an almost complete ape-man skeleton between 3 and

3.5-million years old (though a recent study puts it at just over 4-million years old). The holiday was over for my brother but he'd seen more than most and more importantly seen the real side of South Africa where tourists don't dare to tread.

I had barely two months left of my trip and I had to do something soon if I was to eventually live here. Tim had been doing some welding at the gym and I helped out by holding the steel in place. I simply couldn't resist trying my hand at welding and within no time at all I was welding half decent joins and so I'd found a new vocation in life. He told me that he'd been researching the cost of building bike trailers for the off road market and that he could make a healthy profit. I was desperate to stay in Africa and with the window-cleaning job on the back burner I jumped at the chance to do something different in my life. I agreed to put up the cash to get us started and hoped that things would work out. Before we started to build trailers willy nilly, I wanted to research the potential to sell them and in doing so came into contact with a guy called Haydon who said that he would be willing to buy at least ten a week from us if indeed they were to his specification. With that we bought the necessary materials and set to work.

Tim was a very ingenious problem solver and within five short hours we'd not only got the skeleton of a trailer built but he'd made a couple of jigs to speed up the process next time. When we took it to Haydon he moved the goal posts by demanding that we get the road worthy certificate and this ended up making the venture a non starter due to all the legalities. We ended up taking the finished trailer to a bike shop for them to sell on our behalf for a percentage, where it sat long after I returned home. Not to be disheartened we wasted no time making wrought iron furniture which was quick and easy to make and the profit was realistic. I was becoming proficient at welding and although my hands continually shook from MS it didn't matter.

Weeks were passing very quickly by now and my visa expiry date ticked away like a date with the vasectomy clinic. All I wanted to do was to make something positive happen and all I got in return was a lazy bastard for a business partner and a load of debt around my scrawny little neck. In fact, my final two months was a continuous string of frustrating events culminating in being shafted by Tim. I should have known better because his dad is the same, like father like son; in fact there's more work in my sick note than these two put together but despite this I can't help but like them.

My time here was over and I'd done, seen and experienced so much. I didn't know what the future had in store for me but who does? I had to leave this lifestyle behind and face the realities of England and the fact that the MS would get continually worse over the coming months due in part by the change in climate. All I could do now was to face the music, dust myself down and enjoy the fact that despite everything I wasn't in a wheelchair and reliant upon others. I had a lot to reflect upon and had absolutely no regrets at all.

Chapter 21

College

After returning from Africa I became very disillusioned about life in general because I'd just spent the last six months living life how it should be lived. Waking every morning to the ever replenishing sun made me feel totally and utterly alive, especially when bird song is all you can hear.

Although it was now September and I'd been back for the whole of the summer, it certainly didn't feel like it. The realities of England's existential lifestyle were simply too much for me to bear; I soon became depressed. I went for a few beers with Ronnie one night and I'd just finished writing the first part of this book, which he'd just read. During the evening the conversation inevitably came round to the subject of the story I'd just written. Ronnie commented that he didn't realise just how articulate I was and that in his opinion I could do a degree. We talked a while longer over more beers and he asked what subject I'd be interested in studying. I said that an art degree would be the most obvious to take due to the experience and my love of the subject but I soon added that for me to do a degree in art wouldn't be that much of a challenge. If I was to do one then it would have to be more of a challenge. I've always been fascinated with people and I'm an avid people watcher, especially in social settings such as pubs and restaurants. Therefore a degree in Psychology would be more beneficial in terms of a challenge and for future prospects if indeed my health improved in the future.

That was it, the seed was sown. Shortly after this conversation I was invited to a party to celebrate Nick (Ronnie's son), passing his degree in Geography at Sheffield University. The very same conversation came up that evening with his uni mates and they advised me to go to college to enquire about an Access Course in which people returning to higher education can do so without any previous qualifications. It just so happened that the following week was enrolment week. I saw this as an omen.

When I got to the local college the staff explained everything from enrolling to applying to university. The first stage was to enrol in college; they explained that to apply for a degree course you had to achieve sixteen credits, three of which were compulsory. I signed up there and then and because I was on Incapacity Benefit I wouldn't have to pay any fees. I was to start the following Monday.

When Monday morning finally arrived it actually felt good to be up with a purpose. The class started at nine-thirty so I decided to walk up to the college from town which is only half a mile, this gave me the opportunity to clear my head and mentally prepare for a new and exciting experience. Finding the classroom was child's play due to the provided site map. As I got to the door a dozen or so faces stared intently toward me,

"Is this the psychology class?" I said.

Everyone in the room answered at the same time, I knew it was a stupid question but it was one of them ice breakers. I sat in the nearest seat next to a guy called Sam. We made small talk until the teacher arrived and introduced herself and the course. We all had that first day self intro to the others with a touch of trepidation but we all soon relaxed a little with one another. The course was to run on Monday's and Wednesday's from 9.30am through till 3.30pm taking Psychology in the mornings and Sociology in the afternoons. It was explained from the outset just exactly what was required to obtain a place at university and that we should maybe have a think as to which uni we wanted to attend because we would have to apply in January for a place. This was a little daunting to say the least as we'd not even started the course never mind even had some feedback from an assignment.

The first introduction to the psychology realms was done by members of the class reading chapters from a handout. That first lesson went quick and we were handed homework even quicker. I sat in the classroom looking around the room wondering how on earth I ended up there; but that was soon quelled by three or four girls that caught my eye and my trepidation went out of the window (in fact so did my attention span). That afternoon was the sociology class and with it a new bunch of people joined from social services, so there was a good mix. The teacher explained in detail what we had to do to reach our goal of a place at university. The sixteen credits would be spaced between the two courses with three credits being compulsory for presentation and communication skills. It was a great feeling to be doing something constructive and giving me something to aim towards. I found the work relatively easy, all you needed to do was read up on the given subject and write about it in a constructive and precise manner.

It took a couple of weeks for the class to get comfortable with each other and I really looked forward to going; I now had a sense of purpose in life and I relished the thought of hopefully going to university. In fact on the days that I couldn't attend due to illness I really missed my classmates. It wasn't long before we were all in a routine of attending class in the morning and then going to the pub at dinner. As Christmas approached and a couple of assignments were under our belts the thought of uni seemed not so daunting after all.

January 2002 and the application forms for a place at uni were filled in on the assumption that the required sixteen credits would be gained within the following months. We were told categorically that Manchester University were refusing to take any access students at all and this was explained by the fact that they had over 2000 applicants for 240 places. My choices included Manchester Metropolitan, Bolton, Salford and Huddersfield; the latter being a bit ironic due to the fact that that's where the Fidlers' lived for years. It was around March and April that the invitations for open days at the universities came through the post. I'd met some great people at the college and two in particular (Shaun and Sam), they had chosen similar choices to me. We were soon on the open day circuit deciding which uni we were going to attend and they were all vying for your signature.

I went to all the open days with Shaun while Sam couldn't make his mind up exactly where he wanted to go. The first was at Salford, I liked the uni but I didn't relish the journey there; it was the same score with Manchester Met. We went to Bolton University and the journey took a little over an hour and then when we finally got there the uni was a shithole; I told Shaun that I thought the uni should be condemned. Then finally we visited Huddersfield, the difference was decisive. The staff was falling over themselves to help with the process.

The psychology department was in a listed building packed with character. The staff answered all of our questions and gave us a guided tour of the main areas of the campus that we would be using; this included the impressive five story library boasting some 400,000 books and the students' union bar. When the staff explained that the entire course was available to us via the internet I just knew instantly that this was going to be the place for me as I instinctively knew that my attendance would be at the mercy of the MS. It just felt so comfortable and that was due to the staff's attitude towards the prospective students.

One of the staff who'd been one of the main speakers in the introduction spent some considerable time with me explaining the course with both vigour and enthusiasm; but the most important part of the university experience was that of the aid available to disabled students. He explained in detail how my disability would be incorporated into the university process without too much disruption to all parties involved. He even explained in length the situation of an extension on assignment deadlines and that was all I really needed to hear to convince me that this was the place for me to study. When eventually we left the campus I turned to Shaun and told him that I was definitely going to Huddersfield if I could get in. This mild mannered gentlemen that I'd become very fond of reiterated my enthusiasm for the uni and we commended the staff on their attitude toward us. I was so excited that that evening I went straight to my mother's to let her know which uni I'd decided to go to. All I had to do now was to obtain the required sixteen credits and I would be commuting across the Pennines for the next three years. In fact at this point I'd already achieved eleven credits so I could almost taste it.

Nevertheless the goal hadn't been scored yet and we had to concentrate on getting the magic sixteen credits to allow this dream to flourish. My sixteenth credit was to be a presentation in front of all the psychology class and maybe because I was the classroom joker I was made to go first. Not a problem I thought, get it out of the way and in the bag. The teacher gave us all a subject we'd have to discuss and told us that the presentation would last for ten minutes. I was given the top-down theory as my presentation. We were all instructed to use visual aids to help with the presentation and told to do the preparations there and then. I had from the Wednesday's class to the Monday to prepare an example for my attempt at gaining the magic ticket to university and finding myself in yet another surrealistic situation.

I busied myself over the weekend trying to come up with different ideas that would first of all be fun and secondly get the message across within the allocated ten minute slot. I drew a one way sign with the words 'go straight ahead' and a no entry sign with 'strictly no entry' on the reverse side. It seemed as if I'd not had the luxury of enjoying the weekend before Monday morning woke me like a kick in the balls but I was revved up for it and unreservedly excited at hopefully gaining the magic sixteenth credit.

As Maggie our psychology teacher walked through the door and wished us all a good morning, my nerves were non-existent. I was used to everyone in the classroom and they all knew just what a joker I tried to be. Well Maggie stepped down and sat at the back of the classroom and I was given the floor. I stood on a chair facing the class. I placed the one way sign level with my knees and grabbed my crotch and said "Good morning girls", then I turned around and placed the no entry sign just under my bottom and added "Good morning boys". The class was in uproar because they got the meaning straight away making the actual presentation child's play and thus the ten minutes went with the blink of an eye and sixteen credits in the bag.

Although I'd achieved the magic number of credits for entry to uni I didn't have the three compulsory ones and so I had to do another presentation in the sociology class. We could choose our own topic this time as long as it had a bearing on a social aspect; I chose depression, a subject I was personally familiar with. This was totally different to the psychology class because the atmosphere was less relaxed. Unlike the psychology class I was going last and the pressure was on to emulate the successful presentations of my classmates. The actual presentation went well except I felt uneasy because there was a girl in the class that was absolute model material and she was sat at the front of the classroom staring intently whilst resting her chin on her clenched hand. It was difficult to concentrate on exactly what I'd rehearsed but I blundered my way through it delivering the presentation slightly short of the ten minute target but the teacher enjoyed the content and gave me seventy-nine per cent.

Weeks and months merged with one another until finally we received the acceptance letters from the relevant universities. I was accepted at both Bolton and Huddersfield and I couldn't contain my excitement as I phoned everyone who'd listen to my ramblings. I promptly filled in the 'thanks but no thanks' part of the return slip for Bolton and signed on the dotted line for a three-year stretch at Huddersfield.

When the letter of acceptance came through the door we had to go for an interview at Huddersfield University and convince them to allow us on the course. Shaun was to be interviewed at the same time as me so we went to the uni together. My interview was with a guy who originally came from South Africa so we had some ground in common but that wouldn't hold any weight if I couldn't convince him I was the right material for the uni. The interview lasted about an hour purely because this guy was so intellectual that he wanted to knew a few things about me and my past life as well as full explanation to his questions, which included "If I was in government how would I go about solving the immigration problem?" I won't go into detail of my answer but it struck a cord with him and by the look on his face and his mannerism toward me I was very confident of the outcome. I left his office to find Shaun patiently waiting for me; he'd been there over twenty minutes.

"How did you get on?" he enquired.

"I'm in, I just know I am. What about you?"

Shaun's a quiet guy and a little shy and he thought he'd done ok in the interview but he was a bit reserved about it. I explained to him what had happened in my interview and told him that I was more than confident that we were both going to get a place there. It wasn't long before our acceptance letters arrived in the post and now with the sixteen credits in the bag we were definitely going to Huddersfield to do our degree. We still had a couple of months to go before the summer holidays and more assignments and exams to go but these were done in a blaze fashion.

The world cup had started and we had an exam to do for sociology on the very day that England met Brazil. Once again we had to choose a subject with a social aspect from a media source and write about it for an hour with as much explanation as possible. The more detailed the explanation the more points we'd accrue. I chose to write about a documentary that I'd seen about a London based hostel for recovering alcoholics and their daily challenges to overcome their addictions and re-integrate with the community.

On the morning of the exam all the lads made their way to a pub that was opening its doors at seven and laying on full English breakfasts ready for the match. It was packed to the rafters and the makeshift staff ran around like headless chickens pulling pints and serving breakfasts. It felt really unusual to be having a pint with your breakfast but this was a special occasion for us football fans. As the match unfolded the crowd became more and more rowdy with each pint consumed. The atmosphere was electric as peoples' anticipation had grown to support the national team in their endeavours to deliver the world cup to the whole nation. It was 1-1 with moments to go when Ronaldinho scored from a free-kick that was in hindsight a miss-kicked cross but that was it we were out of the knockout stages.

Everyone had taken the day off work and was determined not to let the result sour any form of celebrations. The party continued in the town centre quite like a wake, everyone sad but yet still smiling. I was half cut as the exam time approached and I sloped off to attend leaving my friends contemplating how we would fare in four years time.

When I turned up for the exam the faces on my fellow classmates said it all; I think my glazed eyes, slurred speech and unsteady feet gave the game away. Luckily for me I was well prepared for the exam and tackled it as though it was second nature scoring a remarkable eighty-six per cent. After the exam was over I invited some of my fellow classmates to join me and my friends to console the disappointment felt at yet another failing of an English team.

By the middle of July and the end of college I'd obtained twenty-three credits, a reserved place at Huddersfield University and a large pat on the back from my mother and Ronnie who'd followed my progress with avid interest. The friendships that we'd made during the time at college made the approach of uni all the more intimidating. We had a party to celebrate new friends met and the beginning of something new and exciting, the summer holiday would soon be over and three years of hard work would be one of the most difficult challenges I'd ever faced but I was relishing the thought of starting a new and exciting part of my life.

Chapter 22

University

After an action packed summer in which I travelled to France and Portugal I was ready for the challenges ahead. I remember being sceptical about being able to keep up with the intense workload that is expected of you at a university level but I was more than willing to give it my best shot; but then again if I'd have adopted a negative attitude I wouldn't have got to this position in the first place. The curriculum year had already started three weeks previously to the start date of uni which just brought it home to me that I'd soon be back into a routine and trying to juggle my personal life with that of the inconveniences of an indiscriminate illness.

The morning of the twenty-eighth of September 2002 was a crisp autumn morning; the sun was desperately trying to rise above the morning mist and leaves floated in the breeze. Ian (Tiggy) Turner had lent me a car to use and it was an absolute joy to be driving over the Pennines' at a time of day that I'd usually be wrapped in a duvet. I met Shaun and Sam and we sheepishly walked into one of the old converted churches, which was a lecture hall; the other being the students' union bar. A sea of faces greeted my gaze as I looked up at the auditorium, the ratio of women to men was about six to one; I was in my element. We took our seats but whilst all the introductions were being made I found myself glancing around the room checking out all the girls.

It all seemed a bit beyond me and I felt as if I didn't belong there but with added incentives I thought I'd take it all one step at a time. Once all the introductions were taken care of we were alphabetically placed into groups of seven with a personal tutor who would take care of our problems and make sure that we were all up to speed with university life. I was temporarily separated from my friends and when I met with my tutor I was delighted to discover that I was the only guy. The start of uni couldn't have got off to a better start. The assignments were explained in detail and I felt more at ease with what was expected of me as a student. One of the most positive aspects of being at uni was that when I introduced myself to new people I could now say with immense pride "I'm a student", instead of having to explain that for some years I'd been a drain on tax payers; it gave me a sense of purpose and a feeling of self worth.

Within that first week we found ourselves overwhelmed by the amount of information overload and the prospect of the second week being thrown in at the deep end; having been given the timetable and finding that we were to attend lectures every day of the week. As a disabled student, the help in place was for me in particular a relief, for it meant that I could work from home on my bad days. Everyone had a private meeting with their personal tutors to discuss any problems we may face and upon doing so I found that the uni had a complimentary strategy in place to allow disabled students equal opportunities to work alongside their peers. I was advised to speak to the pathway leader about my situation and when I entered her office and finished explaining my circumstances, the advice I received had such an effect on me that I literally skipped out of the building brimming with confidence. I knew that this would be no walk in the park; I would have to earn every credit in order for me to achieve my dream of obtaining a degree.

Right from the offset I knew I was in for a hell of a ride for the lecture halls seating was far from comfortable and after only a few minutes I was wriggling around in my chair like I had a bad case of piles. In fact, I couldn't concentrate properly and I couldn't wait for the break and especially the end of the lecture. In the break more often than not I would swallow three pain killers and hope that they'd have the desired affect but it wasn't to be. At times when the pain swayed me from my studies I would glance around the room imagining which girl I'd like to have sex with, it kept me sane. During that first year I'd have to leave home just after seven thirty and wouldn't return until just before five; it was an extremely long day for me and the first thing I did when I got back to the comfort of my sofa was make a cup of tea and roll myself a big fat spliff. I'd smoke it and then fall asleep often waking around seven. It was extremely difficult trying to juggle uni life and cope with the illness. During that first year I only managed to attend a full week once and on the days that I couldn't summon the energy to make the journey over the Pennines I caught up on sleep often working when my P.A. Sarah could come round to do my typing.

The first year's marks didn't count towards the final degree mark so that in itself relieved the pressure, all I had to do was pass each subject in order not to repeat the year, which I did by a narrow nine per cent. Being a disabled student gave me a little bit of a lea way where attendance was concerned and all my lecturers were more than happy to accommodate me by e-mailing me lecture notes and allowing me extensions on assignments. When the exams were due I was allowed an extra thirty minutes and a room to myself or maybe just one more person in the room and the opportunity to walk around the room if need be. All these little things made a huge difference to be able to get the work done. By the end of the academic year I was completely drained and looking forward to three months off before commencing with the difficulties the second year would entail. I'd passed the first year and now I was relishing the thought of starting the second year.

From the outset of the second year I knew that this would count towards my degree but in all honesty I continued in the same manner as the previous year; I just wanted to pass, after all who really gives a shit what mark you get? A degree's a degree at the end of the day and I had enough to contend with anyway. The timetable for the second year was kinder by far for we were only in uni four days a week and on Friday's we didn't start until 1.15 PM so we got to stay in bed longer. The workload was much tougher and the assignments were more detailed. I found it hard going as some of the compulsory subjects were, well lets' say boring. But despite this factor, I enjoyed the challenge immensely and I had far more motivation than in the previous year.

The second year was crucial to secure a base line for the third year project that would inevitably be the 'be all and end all' of the dissertation. We had to come up with a proposal that would in the first instance be a subject that would illicit the very best of our abilities and in the second instance be ethically accepted.

Christmas came and went and I spent it in France, all the while I was working on assignments much to the amusement of my friends.

January was particularly difficult as I was ill the whole time missing many of my lectures but I managed to complete the assignments albeit through the power of the extensions route and of course Sarah my P.A.

In February I went to Prague for a stag party and the chance to let my hair down was not only welcomed but very stimulating as I ventured out into the town becoming just another tourist and leaving my mates to drink themselves silly. I just couldn't understand why they'd gone all that way spending good money on flights and hotels and stay in the bars all day when they could have just stayed at home and got pissed; still each to their own.

The distraction was great because I didn't have to think about assignments for four days. It helped me to focus more and really think about how I was going to tackle my third year proposal. Everyone's dissertation centred on subject matter that was close to their heart and I was no exception choosing to write my dissertation on the subject of 'Men's experiences of living with Multiple Sclerosis'. A proposal is rather like a synopsis and mine was initially accepted; the ethical issues are always dealt with in the third year.

The academic year passes very quickly and this seemed to pass even quicker than the last but then again with less attendance combined with a thirty-five week duration it was hardly surprising that the summer holiday was just around the corner. However; my summer holidays were cut short by the fact that I had to repeat an exam. Griff 'The Spliff' was in town; once a year his company would send him to their headquarters in Germany for re-training giving him the opportunity to visit his family and catch up with a few of his friends. The only night that a few of the lads could get together was the night before one of my exams; you can guess the rest as I ended up inviting the lads back to my house for an extended session and thus doing so went to bed at five leaving just two hours of sleep before I had to set off for the exam. I was still pissed when I got to the students union bar; I was trying to sober up with a coffee when some of my university friends joined me. When I explained the circumstances to them of my previous night they were dismayed that I was actually sat there. Eventually it was time for our final exam of the year and we'd all arranged to meet up afterwards to have a celebratory drink; they all commented that I would just need topping up. I went to the exam but after only fifty minutes I excused myself opting for a re-sit. I went straight back to the union bar and awaited my friends return before joining in the party. It took me three days to recover but it was well worth it. I re-sat the exam and ended the year with a one per cent average improvement. Now one per cent isn't a substantial improvement but in uni terms it's the difference between a third and a two-two degree. The mark was still irrelevant to me because I'd passed and only had one more academic year to go; I knew this was going to be tough but I was really looking forward to it.

I was fast approaching my 40th birthday and I'd promised myself that I would go to an exotic location for it. I couldn't possibly go away for my actual birthday because it was the start of my final year and far too important to be voluntarily absent. During the summer holidays one of my friends Rob told me that he was going to Thailand to buy a house and I should go out there and join him. I didn't have the money to go but I had a very special piece of plastic that made my dream come true.

I met up with Rob in Chiang Mai in the north of Thailand and where his dad had lived for almost twenty years. The minute I left the airport I knew I'd made the right decision, it was paradise. Although I'd landed slap bang in the middle of a thriving city, on every corner was a permanent reminder of the past. Temples stood on virtually every street corner and monks in their distinctive orange robes strolled nonchalantly from one to the other. The old city wall ruin stood proud at the side of the one kilometre square moat. The mountain towers above the city cloaked in jungle and the golden dome of the Doi Suthep temple glistened in the sunlight like the beacon of a lighthouse.

Even before I'd left the airport building I realised just why they call this country 'The Kingdom of the smiles'. Every Thai that you meet place their hands together, place them below the chin and bow as they show you respect whilst saying hello.

The first couple of days were spent enjoying the sun, meeting ex-pats and all of Rob's Thai friends and learning my way around the town. The humidity was stifling yet all my aches and pains were at bay as I began to relax into the Thai laidback lifestyle.

Rob was married to a Thai girl and in order to buy the house he had to go to her parents just an hour and a half's drive north of Chiang Mai. I went on the trip with him and we stayed with Gung's parents. It was a very small village and the only concrete structures belonged to the Government and half a dozen shop owners. Rob's parents-in-law lived in a wooden house that sat on stilts with a menagerie of animals in the garden, from chickens running around the place to a cow tied to a tree at the bottom of the garden.

Because of the mortality rate on rural roads in Thailand the king had put street lighting on all the main roads throughout the country (which did reduce the death rate). This gave Rob the opportunity to bring his in-laws into the twenty-first century by introducing them to electricity. He did this by breaking into the nearest lamppost, connecting wires to the source and then he hid the wires under the soil to the house. In order for the authorities not to get wind of this he placed blackout blinds on the windows facing the road. He bought them a fridge, a microwave, a coffee maker, a TV, a stereo and even put in a couple of English plugs complete with an iron. I'd only been in the house for half an hour when a young girl from the next house came over to ask if she could iron her school uniform for the following day. I watched her as she struggled to get the creases right. Without thinking of the cultural differences, I got up and showed her how to do it correctly (yes I am a modern man, I can iron as good as any woman and I love it). Rob's mother-in-law was overwhelmed that a man was ironing and when she found out that not only was I single but didn't have any kids she disappeared with squeals of laughter. Next morning I was introduced to four women from the village that were single and asked which one I wanted to marry. If I was looking for a wife I'd have found her there. There's a particular charm to the Thai culture and life is about practicality rather than love.

It was a remarkable experience to be in the middle of a jungle with people who were prepared to give you their last breath whilst wearing a permanent smile. I was sad to leave; I could have stayed there for the whole month. I fell in love with the place and I felt really alive, Thailand had me in its spell, I knew I'd be back.

The first week of the final year was by far the most daunting of all for not only did we have a ten thousand word dissertation to write but we also had to bring together all we'd learnt and write every assignment to a professional standard. It was only the second week when I hit the milestone of becoming forty years young and the partying that subsequently followed for a couple of weeks distracted me temporarily but I came out fighting afterwards and I was more determined than ever to finish the course in the three year period. The degree was taking its toll on me but the third year brought about more time at home to work and I was only in uni for three days a week.

On Mondays my lecture started at 4.15 PM, so any cobwebs from the weekend could be dismissed with extra time in bed on Monday mornings. This was fantastic for on Monday nights I would stay with Jack and Paul Dickinson and roll into uni on Tuesday's for my lecture at 2.15 PM on Tuesdays. With Wednesdays free and only two lectures on Thursdays, it meant that I had a long weekend every week and plenty of opportunity to rest up for a very difficult and demanding year.

Our personal tutors changed in the final year for we were appointed a tutor to help with our dissertations. My tutor just happened to be the pathway leader and the woman that would cement the necessary attributes I needed to complete the degree to the best of my ability. Nancy Kelly certainly knew just how to get the best from me and her encouragement and constant challenges made sure I wasn't falling short of my true potential.

It was February before we got the ethical approval for our dissertations and by this time all the preparations could be put into place and the serious task of writing up our introductions could start in earnest.

For my final year project I intended to interview six male participants who'd been diagnosed with MS for over three years. I made this stipulation in order to illicit a real sense of how their lives have been affected by the illness and what it meant to them. It was particularly difficult as I had to try to be objective and not subjective, taking into consideration their feelings and thoughts about how they lived their lives. I couldn't influence the findings with my own experiences because that would have defeated the object and it wouldn't have given my paper any credibility whatsoever.

Some of my findings were what I was expecting but yet there were certain aspects of the interviews that surprised me. All in all, I was more than pleased with the final draft and although there were areas that could have been improved I was aware that within the time limitations I'd done my utmost and did a good job. This was reflected in the mark for I was awarded sixty-four per cent, which when you consider a first class degree starts at seventy per cent, I didn't do that bad.

I ended my university career by handing in two assignments on the same day and the feeling I had that day was a strange mixture of relief and sadness; relief that the finishing line had been crossed and yet sadness because the challenge was over. I got confirmation in the post a few weeks later along with my certificate for an Upper Second Class degree which was upgraded to a Lower Two-One due to a nine and a half per cent increase in my final year. Although the classification was of secondary importance for me, it was rewarding for me that I did so well and achieved more than my wildest dreams could have anticipated. The best part of the degree was simply the title on my certificate 'Antony Andrew Kelly Bsc (Hons). Job done, challenge met and it was all thanks to what some may call unfortunate circumstances. Unfortunate maybe but I don't think so it's made me stronger and more appreciative that I got MS and *not* cancer.

Chapter 23

Teaching English as a Foreign Language

There was now a void in my life that had to be filled. I once again threw paint at countless canvases and started to get creative. The Tinnitus was now a permanent fixture and insomnia was turning me into an owl. I would spend night after night painting large canvases in the living room dreaming of the places I would go with the proceeds of selling these artworks. I got more and more ambitious and as friends came to visit they would buy the artwork before they were finished. I was hoping to have another exhibition but I ended up with nothing to sell.

The insomnia gave me plenty of time to mull things over and I needed to, not only do something with the degree but something positive with my life. I had a conversation with Carmolina and she suggested that I do a TEFL teaching certificate because I loved travelling. TEFL is short for teaching English as a foreign language and this certificate enables the holder to teach abroad.

I did some research and quickly found out that it would cost over a thousand pounds to do. I didn't have that kind of money but I set about selling my artwork. Thomas senior was at my house one night and we had a look on the internet for courses because he said that he would help me to pay for the course. We soon found out that I could do the course in Thailand for half the price and he suggested that we go out there for an extended holiday and I could do the course. Jack Dickinson decided that he wanted to come along and do it and so the three of us set off at the end of October 2006.

The course was in Chiang Mai of all places and I found myself back in a place I love attempting to become a teacher. Rob had got us a three-bedroomed bungalow to rent on the same estate as him and the ex-pats that I'd met before and only a ten minute ride into town on a scooter. The bungalow was detached and had a small garden at the front where we would sit and watch the world go by.

The last few weeks before we left for Chiang Mai I started to have some vertigo attacks again. I was devastated and really nervous about them because I'd not had these attacks for some years and I had visions of all the chaos starting all over but I was off to the other side of the world and I did have my friends with me to make sure I was okay. Within the first few days of arriving I had a couple of attacks and Jack and Thomas had never seen this side of the MS before. Their faces said it all as once more I was rendered useless for a day. I was determined to overcome these attacks and set about getting on with my life.

The course started a couple of weeks after we arrived and I had to be at my best to start studying again. I had plenty of rest and looked forward to meeting new people and learning to become a teacher. We wasn't going to start teaching students until the second week so that first week was spent trying to get to grips with learning nouns, pronouns, verbs, adjectives and parts of speech as well as the theories behind teaching. It was a great way to ease ourselves into the course and get used to the others on the course.

The course started at twelve-thirty for four hours with a break in between. The classrooms were air-conditioned and it was a real pleasure to be inside studying away from the humidity. It also meant that we could ease into the course and I didn't burn myself out on the first week. Each night we would go back to the house and study for the next day and prepare for the assignments.

The second week got increasingly busy with the teaching classes starting. These classes were two hours long and by the time we'd given feedback to the teacher we weren't getting back home until half past eight. By mid week I was getting really tired and mentally exhausted and I was having trouble sleeping because the Tinnitus was driving me crazy. I'd have to get up after just a couple of hours of sleep and finish the last bits and pieces for my lessons. Thomas would have to go out with some of the other ex-pats because he didn't see me or Jack; we were always busy doing assignments and lesson plans. He ended up going to meet some of his mates from back home and chill out at the beach for a couple of weeks. I was gutted because I wanted to go on some adventures with him but we both knew I had to try and get this certificate if I was going to support myself while we were on sabbatical.

During the third week I was sat in class listening to our tutor when I felt a little strange like I was floating. I told the tutor I needed to go outside and Jack came downstairs with me. I had a vertigo attack. It was horrible, I felt sick. I then had to wait for a taxi because there was no way I was getting back on my scooter. I slept for fourteen hours.

I went back to class two days later feeling really refreshed. I got through the afternoon and was feeling great. We'd all go for something to eat together before we taught the students and I was still feeling well when we started the class. I wasn't teaching on this night but I was assisting which we all did when it wasn't our turn at the front of the classroom. Senior was back from his beach holiday and wanted to come and watch us teach, I bet he never expected this. The teacher started the warm up session and we all stood in a circle with the students. We would do little games so the students could engage with English and prepare them for learning some new words and sentences. This had barely started when I had another vertigo attack. All the students saw my distress and the university ended up having to call a taxi again.

This was horrendous because I ended up in bed for six days and missed teaching two of my lessons. There was now no way of making up for the lost lessons because of the other student teachers' having to do their supervised teaching.

I went in for the last week and did the exam but I couldn't be awarded the certificate until I'd done all the teaching hours. The university told me not to worry and that I could go back in the New Year and do the course again.

I stayed on in Thailand with Jack ready to redo the course but I had to return home to sort out some personal problems and try to save the cash together to hopefully go back and finish it. I was gutted especially as Jack stayed on and tried to get a job teaching. I've had to be patient over the years so I gritted my teeth and just got on with it, having to smile every time someone asked me how I'd done. Eh you can't win them all you know!

Jack came back a couple of months later because he only had an English Diploma and all the language schools required a degree. We were both back to square one but at least Jack had his TEFL certificate.

When Jack got back he told me that Manchester Metropolitan University were running a Master's Degree in TEFL that started that September. I went for an interview and got a place on the course. I was ecstatic.

My life was full of twist and turns and as September approached we were informed that the course had been put on hold for twelve months because they had a low number of interested students. So while I was waiting to start the course I decided to go and do some voluntary teaching at my local Adult Learning Centre.

I asked to do the Monday morning classes because of the fact that everyone hates Monday's and I knew that the teacher I'd be covering for would really appreciate it. It didn't matter to me what day it was they've always been the same for me since finishing work (except for when my beloved United play). In fact, one of my friends once asked me what I was doing for the Bank Holiday; when I told him that I wasn't doing anything special he said that you've got to do something on the holiday. I told him that every day is a Bank Holiday to me.

I only had a small class of five but we had great fun and I really enjoyed teaching them. I prepared lessons and lesson plans and it felt self gratifying to be putting something back. I prepared the students for their exam for English proficiency and was pleased when they all passed.

There were a couple of occasions where I couldn't go to teach because I was too ill but I did well and my confidence was beginning to grow as well as my stamina.

The start date for the course was looming so I had to leave to concentrate on the degree because I knew it was going to be a real challenge and I needed to give it my all if I was going to pass it. I couldn't get any funding at all and it looked as though this dream was over before it started. I didn't know what I was going to do and I was really deflated. I needed to go as far as I could because if I'm going to make a return to the workplace I need to hold my own when I go for a job with multiple applicants.

Thomas senior could see what this meant to me and he offered to pay for the course and I kissed him that day (no tongues). He has helped me out so much over the years and he's got the biggest heart.

First day at school again but this was now the big time, I walked into that University that morning with a pair of tits on my chest, that's how confident I was. I felt invincible.

Within no time at all I was back in the realms of academia and thinking 'opps', what have I let myself in for. We had three lectures a week Monday to Wednesday for three hours. Right from the offset the workload was astonishing. I spent all my spare time reading and making notes for assignments.

I'd only been there for a week when I had to go to Cyprus for a week because I was best man at Thomas junior and Kerry's wedding. All the family was there and it was a magical week with great weather and a fairytale wedding with my two beautiful god-daughter's Khloe and Gracie-Mae as bridesmaids. They've added a little boy Samuel since then and guess whose god-father to him. See mum I don't need any kids, got seven already.

Thomas senior smiled when I sat on the balcony during the day doing my assignments for uni and trying to get my head around all the new things I was learning. They dragged me away from work a couple of times and it was great to be away with the kids seeing the big smiles on their faces.

I had to get the train into town at peak-time and you could never get any empty seats (or standing room for that matter), and it always had to wait outside the station for a platform to become vacant. It was absolute torture on my legs and lower back, they would burn with pain. I was always desperate to sit down on the bus. I'd have to take pain killers as soon as I got to uni and get a coffee to take into the lecture. That wasn't a great start to the day and made the start of the lecture difficult to concentrate properly but I was there and that was the main thing. My toes would curl under without warning and it feels like I've been hit with a hammer on my toes. I have to get someone to stand on my toes so that they are flat again. When my toes are flat the pain goes away but sometimes it's really embarrassing.

By the time I'd been to the library to read a few chapters so that I didn't have to carry the books home, I always got stuck in the traffic on the bus and end up missing my train and then I'd have to wait another half an hour in the cold and rain. It was horrible because the pain made me feel like giving up but that's not Mr. Kelly's style.

I was really enjoying the course and I became a student representative (which was thrust upon me) but I enjoyed that experience and it gave me a sense of responsibility and belonging to the University with a sense of pride.

All that winter the weather was relentless with cold winds and typical Manchester rain. I got so run down that I collapsed and ended up having two weeks off. Trying to keep up with the work was becoming a real problem and I had to ask for extensions all the time; plus I would go into class having not read up on the given subject and then have to rely on my classmates to get me out of the shit. That wasn't nice for me or my classmates, they were doing their share of the work and they needed me to do my bit. The tutors were brilliant and supported me to the hilt and my classmates were patient. There were times when the Tinnitus was a real problem and I couldn't hear what the others were saying properly. I sometimes used to sit there wishing I was back in bed; then I just thought to myself that there are plenty of people in the graveyard who wish they could be where I was, so I just got a grip of myself and thrust myself into what we were doing. It helped and I gloated inside as I walked to the canteen looking like I'd pissed my pants.

Because I didn't get the funding I needed until the eleventh hour I hadn't been able to sort out the disabled students' allowance which was there to help with travel costs and getting a computer to do the work with. It was a couple of months before this was in place but when it was all in order it helped tremendously. I was able to get a taxi to and from university and that it itself was an absolute godsend, it meant that I could arrive at my lectures with a vibrancy I'd not had before and I started the lectures with more vigour and a fresh mind free of pain. It was help of this nature and the cooperation and understanding from the tutors that helped me to get through the process of ticking off each assignment and slowly but surely getting nearer to the dissertation.

Each assignment really tested our resolve and brought out the best in us as we had to interview foreign students' and interpret the findings in a professional manner. I even amazed myself with the wording and the way I fitted the pieces of the jigsaw together.

There were only fifteen students on the MA course, five English and ten foreigners' from all walks of life. It was a really good mix and each one of us made a real effort to integrate and respect each other's customs. I made some really good friends along the way and it added to the experience. In fact, it was quite humbling that students using English as their second language were able to cope with the language to such a degree; it puts English speakers to shame because we tend to have the attitude that everyone should speak English.

For my dissertation I decided to investigate how teachers could motivate students. First of all I had to decipher whether students responded to internal motivational factors which would be subjective to that person, or whether a student responded to external factors such as the learning environment in the classroom or a student wanted to learn English to work or travel. I also had to investigate strategies that could bring out the best in a person or students' collectively and how teachers' may go about implementing these in the classroom.

I set about designing a questionnaire and how I could make sense of the results. It was a long winded process and although it was difficult, I loved every minute of it. Once again I had to request an extension and I ended up taking fourteen months to complete the degree but I did finish it.

I waited with baited breath for the results, this was far more important than my degree in the sense that it was the next step up. That doesn't take anything away from my degree purely because I couldn't have been at this stage without it. With the Master's, it was a step that helped other's to see that I'd arrived at some form of normality, the degree's speak for themselves they aren't burdened with MS.

I got my results back fairly quickly, within three weeks due to the fact that everyone else had already been given their results. When the letter came in the post I ripped the envelope open, I was apprehensive and yet excited all at the same time; this was by far the most important letter I'd ever received.

I read the word in bold, **Pass**: I cried with delight and rang my mother immediately; she shrieked with joy and (I'm sure) pride.

The graduation was held in the Bridgewater Hall, Manchester; I briefly felt really important and special as I walked across the stage to receive my certificate as my mother, senior, junior and Kerry cheered me on from the gods of the concert hall. I looked a million dollars in my graduation gown and I was very grateful to Thomas, all the staff at MMU and of course the disability board at Tameside Council for all their help with assisting me to step upon another ladder; not the ladder I was used to but the academic ladder and self-worth and pride.

It was over; I'd done it, I'd pulled it off and let me tell you **Antony Andrew Kelly MA** has a certain ring to it.

Chapter 24

To Teach or not to Teach

There was only one direction I wanted to go now I had the 'golden Willy Wonker' ticket and that was to re-address the pain I felt at not finishing the TEFL course. I was determined to do the Cambridge University certificate with its global recognition because my head of department at MMU once told me that he would only employ someone with this certificate. This certificate is known as a CELTA (certificate in English language teaching to adults) and there are only a handful of places in the north-west that run the course.

It was now just over twelve months since I finished my degree and yet again I was bailed out by Thomas senior, as he helped me to pay for the course. I applied to do the course in Manchester city centre at the Manchester Language Academy. It had a good reputation, plus some of the students from the degree had done the course there. My friend Paul Ames who was on the degree course with me advised me to do the part-time course because the workload would be too much for me to do within the four week period of the full-time course.

I had to go for an interview and I had to teach for a ten minute slot to my fellow potential student teachers. Each course only has twelve students per course because of the teaching schedule and competition for places was rife. Although it was a case of first come first served, if you didn't meet their criteria you weren't getting on the course.

When I arrived at the language school there were three other's waiting to be interviewed for a place on the course. One guy was there for the full-time course and me and two girls were there for the part-time course. I was the first to be interviewed whilst the other's had to complete a short grammar test. I felt that the interview went well as I immediately struck up a rapport with the interviewer and convinced her that I was committed to completing the course and I was the right kind of person to teach in the future. This gave me the reassurance that this language academy was the right place to study because of the procedures they had in place. After I'd completed the short grammar test (and passed) and stood up in front of the other three and the teacher who interviewed us and gave a short lesson on using perspectives in art, I was offered a place on the course.

I had a little over a month to prepare for the start of the course and I spent that time trying to master the art of grammar. As English speakers we tend to forget the forms of language and how to describe various elements of English and I was no exception. I had to get to grips with it quickly because I would have to be teaching it soon.

The part-time course ran from Tuesday to Thursday from five-thirty until around eight-thirty. This wasn't so bad but it meant that I had to leave home at four to be there on time and I didn't get back home until gone ten. It was mid-February when we started and it was bitterly cold.

The first week was spent in the classroom learning the techniques of how to teach and getting to know our fellow students. Like any course I'd been on before you either connect with someone or you don't, either way you're there for a reason and you just have to get on with it.

Within the first week we were given our first assignment, which was a grammar test. I failed my first attempt but passed at the second attempt. However, as soon as we started to teach the different aspects of grammar we soon got into the swing of things and we could explain ourselves with conviction.

I didn't teach until the third week and it was for only thirty minutes but I was a nervous wreck. I'd watch some of my colleges teach and some of them were fantastic, it came so naturally to Sarah, Christine and Hayat and I watched those girls with awe.

The class was split into two groups of six and we had to teach elementary and intermediate English over the four month course. When it was your turn to teach you had twelve students, five of your fellow student teachers and of course our tutor who assessed your teaching techniques. You were told there and then if you'd passed the teaching session.

I really struggled with a lot of pain and I had to stretch my legs at the break and take a couple of pain killers. I also sweated a lot and I could smell myself which gave me a real complex, I was always nipping off to the toilet to spray deodorant under my arm pits.

After my very first lesson (which I was quite happy with), I got a spasm in my toes and it was really painful. I asked Sarah to stand on my toes; it was embarrassing as one of the students asked if he could help me. It made it difficult to concentrate at times but you've just got to push that to one side and get on with it. Nobody's going to give me anything I've got to earn it. Feeling sorry for yourself is futile.

A month into the course and one of my closest friends Gary Derbyshire (the Chinese firecracker starter) passed away from Cancer. It absolutely floored me and I had to have a week off because I just couldn't stop thinking about it and it brought home to me just how important things are in life. I was doing this course to make sure that I could move on with my life and not end up just being on benefits for the rest of it.

I returned and had to once again catch up with the others but I was used to it and didn't let it get me down. I knew I'd be there at the end of it and I'd have given it my all. If I failed then at least I tried to do it instead of giving up and that's more important in my book.

As the weeks merged into one another the assignments were being crossed off and the teaching sessions were beginning to reduce. We swapped levels half way through and with it the tutor. A new set of students smiled at us from the other side of the tables and a new challenge presented itself. I absolutely loved teaching, in fact after one particular lesson I didn't want to hand over the second part of the lesson I wanted to continue right to the end. It was amusing when the students repeated sentences in my broad Manc accent.

Once we were two-thirds of the way through the course I really started to feel the pressure and I couldn't wait for the course to be over but I still had a couple of lessons to teach.

On the next to last week we had a visit from a woman from Cambridge governing body to check all our work and assignments and to watch a couple of us teach. This was what this certificate was all about and why it's accepted worldwide. It all made sense when the examiner gave us all the green light and told us that we had shown a high level of work.

Because I was absent I had to do my last lesson with the other group and at a different level. Right from the word go I messed up big time and from that moment on my class was doomed. I made some fundamental mistakes at the beginning and I had to try and get it back on track. My tutor could see the distress I was in and she quietly pulled me to one side and gave me some encouragement and words of advice. The girls in the group sat at the back of the class giggling behind their hands at my expense. It was funny but not from where I was stood, I had to try to ignore them and get on with the lesson but they just sat there whispering to each other and pointing at me.

Dolores signed the magic pass and that was that, I'd passed the course and was now ready to face the world and teach.

Chapter 25

Reflection not Regret

It seems like a lifetime ago since those dark days of total despair when everything was crumbling around me and every direction I took was a dead end. I still to this day remember sitting in a chair in the living room of my castle, imprisoned within four walls and of course my body, from which there was no escape or reprieve. The business had already gone and the house was under offer awaiting the vital searches and the signatures of Jennifer and I. Very soon I would be free from the material ball and chain I'd self imposed upon myself. I sat in total contemplation wondering what the hell I was going to do now; but as I smoked a spliff and listened to some tunes on the stereo, I wondered about the future of the illness and not about what was in store for me as a person.

At this point I had more money than I'd ever had in my life and I thought long and hard about what I would do with it; should I invest it to help make my life without work more comfortable? Or should I squander it and enjoy myself? If I did invest it that would definitely mean that the interest would pay my bills and make life less stressful but I didn't work all those silly hours to pay bills; I did it to have a better standard of living. My thoughts soon fell upon the probability of whether or not I would end up in a wheelchair and at the time the possibility of this was more prevalent than me falling in love again. As I stubbed the roach into the ashtray with a wave of total relaxation I decided that if I did end up in a wheelchair, then I was going to sit in that chair with reflection, *not* regret.

I wanted to be able to tell people of my adventures and wear a smile instead of being able to pay a bill and then sit there with bitterness and venom. Thankfully I have never had to use a wheelchair but if I did, my reflections would be paramount.

Today as I write this I can honestly say with hand on heart that MS is the best thing that has ever happened to me. Yes it can be said without reservation that I would love to be cured of this nasty disease, for every day is a constant battle but unfortunately that isn't going to happen. When I use that phrase (which I do frequently), I use it in the sense that due to Multiple Sclerosis I have had the opportunity to travel the world and experience things I would never have if I'd still had my business. Have I any regrets? No not really, regrets are a negative entity that can eat away at a person from the inside out and it always manifests itself as jealousy and bitterness. I have achieved what I set out to do and that was to be able to reflect on a life I've lived and not just existed in, which in all honesty is what most of us ever achieve in life. Most of us go to work week in, week out, pay through the nose for the house that we've bought (and everything that comes along with it), tending our gardens and washing the car every Sunday. Then we save up all year for our annual holiday in Costa Del Package, kids go for next to nothing and then we come home and go straight to the travel agents and place a deposit for the same place, same time next year.

I certainly don't regret not getting married, I would never have done the things I've done if I had a woman in tow and equally not having kids; I've got three nephews' a niece, seven god children and countless adopted kids from close friends of mine, so in that aspect I don't miss the pleasurable side of children. In all honesty, to have kids of my own would be equal to a bird's wings being clipped. I can put up with the pain, vertigo, Tinnitus and the ability to function properly because it simply makes me appreciate life. I try to do as much as I can and fit as much in as possible and my illness has never stopped me from doing that because if I did let it, then I would be in that chair having done nothing but spew venom for having my quality of life taken from me.

It is true that I don't have the quality of life of most but when you compare me to other suffers of this condition, I am very fortunate. Some of my friends with MS have no choice in the matter; their nervous system has packed up. People's ignorance pisses me off no end for their words and attitude can be demoralising for others' with MS. The simplistic description of people's attitude is that they do judge a book by its cover; one can't see a plaster, scar or injury. As humans we're all guilty of that but it's not always possible to read the book so what's left? First impressions which can be deceptive.

My reflective thoughts are numerous and are just rewards for all the suffering I've had to endure throughout my twenty-two years trying to cope and live alongside this Invisible Stranger that is MS. I respect it immensely, one has to in order to gain the upper hand and move forward making sure that the prison door stays open. And now after all this time if it did get the upper hand I will be able to sit in that chair and smile while I relay my experiences to appreciative ears.

I now take in my stride the effects of MS; it is an inconvenience and **not** a hindrance.

Thank you very much Multiple Sclerosis for giving me a life of dreams and fulfilment. In short Antony Kelly no longer suffers from Multiple Sclerosis; Multiple Sclerosis suffers from Antony Kelly.

To be continued......

Printed in Great Britain
by Amazon